Behind the Backlash

Some Books from Social Science Press

Windows into a Revolution: Ethnographies of Maoism in India and Nepal (HB)
Edited by Alpa Shah and Judith Pettigrew

'When the war began we heard of several kings': Indian Prisoners in World War I Germanys
Edited by Franziska Roy, Heike Liebau and Ravi Ahuja

Unruly Hills: Nature and Nation in India's Northeast (HB)
Bengt G. Karlsson

Marriage, Love, Caste and Kinship Support: Lived Experiences of the Urban Poor in India (HB)
Shalini Grover

Telecommunications Industry in India: State, Business and Labour in a Global Economy (HB)
Dilip Subramanian

The Many Worlds of Sarala Devi: A Diary
Translated by Sukhendu Ray
and
The Tagores and Sartorial Styles: A Photo Essay (HB)
Malavika Karlekar

Reflections on Cambridge (HB)
Alan Macfarlane

The Everyday State and Society in Modern India (PB)
Edited by C.J. Fuller and Véronique Benei

The Sundarbans: Folk Deities, Monsters and Mortals (HB)
Sutapa Chatterjee Sarkar

India's Economic Future: Education, Technology, Energy and Environment (HB)
Edited by Manmohan Agarwal

'Good Women do not Inherit Land': Politics of Land and Gender in India (HB)
Nitya Rao

New Mansions for Music: Performance, Pedagogy and Criticism (HB)
Lakshmi Subramanian

Writing History in the Soviet Union: Making the Past Work (HB)
Arup Banerji

Political Theologies: Public Religions in a Post-secular World (HB)
Edited by Hent De Vries and Lawrence E. Sullivan

Regulation, Institutions and the Law (HB)
Edited by Jaivir Singh

Globalization and the Millennium Development Goals: Negotiating the Challenge (HB)
Edited by Manmohan Agarwal and Amit Shovon Ray

Cultural History of Medieval India (PB)
Edited by Meenakshi Khanna

Literature and Nationalist Ideology: Writing Histories of Modern Indian Languages (PB)
Edited by Hans Harder

Religious Division and Social Conflict: The Emergence of Hindu Nationalism in Rural India (PB)
Peggy Froerer

The Enigma of the Kerala Woman: A Failed Promise of Literacy (PB)
Edited by Swapna Mukhopadhyay

Cultural History of Modern India (PB)
Edited by Dilip M. Menon

Nature, Culture and Religion at the Crossroads of Asia (HB)
Edited by Marie Lecomte-tilouine

Delhi: Ancient History (PB)
Edited by Upinder Singh

Unbecoming Modern: Colonialism, Modernity and Colonial Modernities (HB)
Edited by Saurabh Dube and Ishita Banerjee-dube

Social and Economic Profile of India (HB)(In full colour)
Peeyush Bajpai, Laveesh Bhandari and Aali Sinha

India and China in the Colonial World (PB)
Edited by Madhavi Thampi

Everyday Politics of Labour: Working Lives in India's Informal Economy (HB)
Geert De Neve

Viramma: Life of a Dalit (PB)
Viramma, Josiane Racine and Jean-luc Racine

Lived Islam in South Asia: Adaptation, Accommodation and Conflict (PB)
Edited by Imtiaz Ahmad and Helmut Reifeld

Human Security in South Asia: Energy, Gender, Migration, and Globalisation (HB)
Edited by P.R. Chari and Sonika Gupta

Forthcoming

Behind the Backlash: Muslim Americans after 9/11
Lori Peek

The Telecommunications Revolution: Mobile Value Added Services in India
Mukesh Kumar and Ram Kumar Kakani

Behind the Backlash

Muslim Americans after 9/11

Lori Peek

SOCIAL
SCIENCE
PRESS

Published by
Esha Béteille
Social Science Press
69 Jor Bagh, New Delhi 110 003

Distributed by
Orient Blackswan Pvt. Ltd.
Bangalore Bhopal Bhubaneshwar Chandigarh
Chennai Ernakulam Guwahati Hyderabad Jaipur
Kolkata Lucknow Mumbai New Delhi Noida Patna
www.orientblackswan.com

ISBN: 978-81-87358-67-1

Set in Minion Pro
Typeset by Eleven Arts, Delhi 110 035
Printed by De-Unique, Delhi 110 018

For Justin

Contents

Acknowledgments

This book would not have been possible without the help of many people. The most important debt of gratitude I owe is to the Muslim women and men who participated in this study. Because I promised to keep their identities confidential, I am unable to thank each by name here. They should know, however, that the most compelling and insightful words in this volume belong to them. I am an outsider to their faith community, and I entered their lives during a time of intense sadness and uncertainty. Yet from my first encounter with each of these individuals, I was treated with a level of trust and respect that I had not yet earned. Over the years, their kindness and generosity never faltered. I am grateful beyond measure for their willingness to share their experiences with me.

I began this research during my years as a graduate student. My mentors and the members of my dissertation committee—Patti Adler, Dennis Mileti, Janet Jacobs, Joyce Nielsen, Peter Adler, and Frederick Denny—were always gentle but firm in offering critiques of my work. Their feedback ultimately helped shape many of the ideas that appear in print here.

As this project progressed, a number of friends and colleagues provided various forms of intellectual and emotional support. Sama Alshaibi, Elaine Enarson, Wendy Estes-Zumpf, Julie Gailus, Sandy Hills, Eric Klinenberg, Heidi Marshall, Michelle Scobie, Rachel Smith, Jeannette Sutton, Megan Underhill, and Sammy Zahran encouraged me and offered clear-headed advice regarding the publication process. When I was feeling stuck, I turned to Jeni Cross, Jessica Hamblen, Rachel Luft, David Neal, and Debra Schneck for suggestions. Their comments on particular sections of the book enabled me to find the right words at just the right time. The wise and wonderful Nancy Whichard kept me motivated and moving forward with the writing.

Norbert Baer helped me navigate New York City after 9/11. Without him, I would have been lost—literally and figuratively. Since our days in graduate school, Alice Fothergill has guided and reassured me at every turn. Alice is not only my most frequent scholarly collaborator; she is also a friend in the truest sense of the word. Kai Erikson has brought many gifts to my life, and his compassion for those who have endured unspeakable calamities continually moves me. I have lost count of the number of times that Kai paused from his own pressing work so that he could help me with this book. I hope he knows how truly grateful I am.

The faculty and staff in the Department of Sociology at Colorado State University gave me the time and space I needed to complete this book. The graduate students who participated in my Qualitative Methods seminar in the spring of 2008 showed a sincere interest in this project, and they helped me think through the conceptual organization of the chapters. Laura Ridenour, a student in that class who later worked as my research assistant, deserves a special word of thanks for her many helpful suggestions. Sandy Grabowski expertly transcribed thousands of pages of interview data, and Darshini Munasinghe and Clark Niemeyer-Thomas assisted with the management of the data. Sara Gill conducted literature searches and many other research errands on my behalf. My warm thanks go to Jennifer Tobin-Gurley, Michelle Lueck, and Andy Prelog, who carefully reviewed the chapters and checked all the endnotes. Their keen attention to detail is unsurpassed.

I am ever grateful for Huma Babak, Sahar Babak, Isra'a Belgasem, Samina Hamidi, Sayaros Mohamed, and Meena Oriakhel. Each one, in her own way, helped me consider broader trends and patterns affecting the day-to-day lives of Muslim Americans.

As I finished each chapter, I would send the pages off to Zaki Safar, a friend who now lives halfway around the world. Zaki read every word with an incredible level of care and precision. He also provided an insider's perspective, and his knowledge allowed me to clarify several key details in the book.

Once I had assembled a full draft of the manuscript, I mailed it to Jen Lois. Jen is an amazing sociologist, and her methodological and theoretical insights pushed me to sharpen my core arguments. Larry Palinkas, mentor extraordinaire, helped me start writing this book. He also offered valuable suggestions on a second draft of the manuscript. A third draft landed in the able hands of my brilliant friend and colleague Kate Browne. Kate not only provided me with a set of thoughtful comments; she also encouraged, supported, inspired, and guided me through the entire process.

I owe a great deal to the three anonymous reviewers who offered feedback on my book proposal and three early chapters. Russell Dynes and Brenda Phillips deserve recognition and thanks for their careful review of the complete manuscript.

I offer my deepest thanks to Micah Kleit, executive editor at Temple University Press, for taking a chance on me and my work. Micah's interest and enthusiasm made me believe that a book really was hidden away in the dissertation, and his editorial expertise improved the final product considerably. I also thank Gary Kramer, Irene Imperio Kull, Joan Vidal, Heather Wilcox, and the rest of the team at Temple for all that they did to bring the book to life.

Several organizations provided financial support for this research. I thank the American Association of University Women, the Center for Humanities and the Arts and the Graduate School at the University of Colorado at Boulder, the National Science Foundation, the Natural Hazards Research and Applications Information Center, and the Public Entity Risk Institute. My participation in the Research Education in Disaster Mental Health (REDMH) Program, which the National Institutes of Mental Health funded, played a crucial role in the conceptualization and completion of this work. Fran Norris, who established REDMH, introduced me to new ways of thinking about loss and trauma. I will always be thankful for Fran and for all the knowledge and wisdom that she so generously shares.

I cannot imagine completing much of anything, let alone this book, without my family. I owe my parents, Cathy and Bud Peek, an entire lifetime of thanks. My brothers and their wives—Brad and Heather, Matt and Gina, and Zach and Laura—continue to keep me grounded and laughing. Much gratitude also goes to my in-laws, Dorothy and Chris Bell and Nora and Ron Gottschlich.

Justin Gottschlich, my husband and best friend, is a constant reminder of all the most extraordinary things in life. His sense of humor, loving patience, intelligence, and passion for knowledge continually inspire me. This book is dedicated to him for countless reasons, but most of all because he has been with me every step of the way.

Behind the Backlash

1

Introduction

The attacks that occurred on September 11, 2001, unleashed an almost unimaginable torrent of pain and destruction. Since that day, countless scholarly articles, books, edited volumes, and impressive pieces of investigative journalism have dissected and analyzed the events leading up to and the consequences of the terrible calamities that will forever mark that moment in history. This book is distinct in that its central focus is on those persons who were caught up in the extraordinary wave of hostility and backlash violence that followed the terrorist attacks.

Specifically, *Behind the Backlash* chronicles the exclusion that Muslim American men and women faced before and especially in the aftermath of 9/11. This book draws on the voices of Muslim Americans to describe the range of discrimination they experienced, to explain the personal and collective impacts of the backlash, and to shed light on the ways in which Muslims adapted in the aftermath of the terrorist attacks. To begin, I offer a brief explanation regarding the origins of this work and my encounters with the people whose experiences are the subject of this text.

Growing up, I, like the majority of Americans, knew little about the beliefs and practices of the more than one billion people around the globe who follow the religion of Islam.[1] No Muslims lived in my hometown in rural eastern Kansas, where the vast majority of the population was white and Protestant and the most serious religious divisions were between the Baptists and the Methodists. I was first exposed, albeit briefly, to Islam when I went away to college and took a class on world religions. The course description promised an introduction to the histories and central beliefs of the world's major religions, including the three great monotheistic faiths—Judaism, Christianity, and Islam. Three fifty-minute class sessions were dedicated to Islam as part of the larger section on "Eastern Religions." Although educational in some respects, these lessons also served to promote the incorrect view of Islam as a foreign religion practiced only in distant lands.

My first serious introduction to Islam came a few years later, when I moved to the mid-size city of Fort Collins, Colorado. It was 1997, and I had accepted a position to coordinate a program aimed at retaining ethnic minority university students who were pursuing degrees in the natural sciences. Aisha—a native of Afghanistan—was one of the undergraduates selected to participate in that program. She was a sophomore in college at the time and was working on her bachelor's degree in computer science. When I first met Aisha, I had no idea that she was Muslim. She wore no headscarf or other visible signifier that might have offered some clue to her religious beliefs, and I was not yet savvy enough about the world to know that nearly all Afghans are Muslim.[2]

Soon after I started my job, Aisha approached me and asked if she could use one of the vacant offices so that she could pray between classes and work. She explained that she was Muslim and that one of the requirements of her faith was that she pray facing toward the holy city of Mecca five times each day. Because she spent long hours on campus, it was difficult for her to find a private space to perform her noon and midday prayers. I readily agreed to Aisha's request but then quickly admitted my ignorance when it came to virtually everything associated with Islam. Aisha laughed and, in her usual good-natured way, assured me that I was not alone. She then asked if I might like to have dinner at her house one evening so that I could meet her family and try some of her mother's homemade Afghan food. I did not know it at the time, but Aisha would become the first of many who would teach me about what it means to be a Muslim in America.

Looking back, I suppose that, in some respects, I was drawn to Aisha because of our differences. Although only a few years separated us in age, our lives had unfolded half a world apart and in extraordinarily different ways. Aisha was born in Kabul, Afghanistan, just before the Soviet invasion in December 1979. Like all other Afghans, Aisha and her family suffered tremendous losses in the protracted and bloody ten-year war that followed. Aisha's father, both of her grandfathers, and several other family members died in the fighting. One of her uncles and several other family friends were taken by the Communist-controlled government and were never heard from again. Aisha's mother was forced to quit her job as a teacher after she and the other women at the school received death threats. Soon thereafter, Aisha and her three siblings had to stop attending school because of the growing risks that daily bombings and frequent landmine explosions posed. Aisha's immediate family was financially well-off before the war started, but they would eventually lose the land that they owned, their home, and all their material possessions.

Aisha was nearly ten years old when she, her two sisters, her younger brother, their mother, and four other female family members fled Kabul. The nine of them—like the millions of other Afghans who were displaced as a result of the conflict—left everything that they had behind and boarded a bus headed to Pakistan. They traveled for days through the treacherous mountains of their war-torn country, only to be turned back by Soviet guards at the border. Aisha and her family returned to the bus devastated, but a sympathetic driver encouraged them to find another way to pass the checkpoint. Two days later, under the cover of night and hidden in a rice truck, Aisha's family slipped across the Afghan border and into the city of Peshawar, Pakistan.

Upon their arrival in Pakistan, the family managed to rent a tiny apartment with the help of Aisha's grandparents and an uncle who had emigrated to the United States. Aisha attended a school in Pakistan that was opened specifically for Afghan refugees. The students sat on cold, dirt floors in the unheated and overcrowded building. They had no desks, books, paper, or pencils, and the teacher was forced to write the day's lessons in chalk on the dirt classroom walls. Aisha and the other children didn't mind, though, as they were thankful to be alive and in school. They had seen too many of their former classmates killed or maimed in landmine explosions back in Kabul.

As a child, Aisha often fantasized about living in the United States, and, after nearly three years in Pakistan, her dream came true. Aisha's uncle, who had recently married and moved to Fort Collins, sent word that the family had been granted immigration papers. Plane tickets were waiting for Aisha and her eight other family members who had survived the war and escaped Afghanistan. Upon receiving the incredible news, the family closed the door on their apartment in Pakistan and never looked back.

Aisha and her family arrived in Colorado in 1992. School officials were not sure what to do with her and her siblings, because the children did not speak any English and no school district employees spoke their native Farsi language. Aisha was thirteen years old at the time, and, because of her age, she was ultimately placed in the eighth grade. For the first several months of school, however, she had absolutely no idea what the teachers or the other students were saying. But she was determined to learn. To pass her exams,

Aisha would memorize the shapes of letters and words and then would write the answers based on the images stored in her mind. Every afternoon she would watch Barney, the beloved purple dinosaur, on television. Aisha learned some of her first words in English by repeating the catchy tunes that Barney would sing to his predominantly preschool-age viewing audience. After eating dinner with her family, Aisha would spend what was left of the evening studying and doing homework in her cramped bedroom. She would often struggle with writing assignments late into the night, looking up words in the dictionary until she could string them together in a coherent sentence.

After about six months, Aisha was able to speak a limited amount of English, although her heavy accent left her vulnerable to the taunts of her peers. A few years later, it was impossible to tell that Aisha was not a native English speaker. After she had mastered the language, Aisha continued with her rigorous study habits, now turning her efforts toward math and science. She maintained a 4.0 grade point average throughout high school and eventually went on to earn several scholarships to attend the local university.

Aisha had always been a believer, and she had relied on her faith to make it through the most difficult times in her life. As she reached adulthood and started college, the pull toward Islam and the importance of asserting her Muslim identity became even stronger.[3] Aisha became more involved in the local mosque and also led several initiatives on her university campus to educate the public regarding Islam and the plight of Afghan refugees. During her senior year of college, Aisha began wearing the hijab, or headscarf, as a symbol of her devotion to her faith. Several of her family members had discouraged her from wearing the headscarf, as they feared she would be harassed and would not be able to get a job. Aisha defied her family and insisted on wearing the scarf. She was proud that she could represent Islam and was relieved when she was hired to work as a computer programmer soon after her graduation in the spring of 2001.

Then, four months later, the 9/11 hijackers carried out the coordinated air assaults on the World Trade Center and the Pentagon. As Aisha watched the Twin Towers collapse over and over again on television, she was overwhelmed with sorrow. She had spent the first decade of her life living in the midst of terrible violence, and she had never imagined that the United States—a place where she had always felt safe—would become the target of such hateful destruction. The blow was worsened when she learned that the men who committed the atrocities claimed to practice the same religion she did and that Osama bin Laden, the leader of the al Qaeda terrorist network responsible for the attacks, had apparently sought refuge in her native Afghanistan.

Aisha could not help but wonder about her future in the United States. Her teachers, co-workers, and others in the community had always held her up as a source of inspiration and hope: Aisha was living proof that the American dream was alive and well. Would she now be viewed by those very same people as a threat? Would strangers believe that she was a terrorist who wished to do them harm? Would the doors that had previously been open to her now be closed indefinitely?

The Islamic faith has long been misunderstood, misrepresented, and viewed with suspicion in the United States and throughout much of the Western world.[4] Yet nothing could have prepared Muslim Americans for the response that followed 9/11. Although some members of the public issued calls for tolerance and restraint, fearmongers seemed to drown out the voices of reason. In the aftermath of 9/11, religious leaders, politicians, media pundits, and self-proclaimed terrorism experts exploited the feelings of an already-terrified citizenry by offering gross overgeneralizations and blatantly incorrect depictions of Muslims as monoliths of extremism and hatred.[5]

Franklin Graham, an evangelical Christian leader who delivered the invocation and sermon at President George W. Bush's 2001 inauguration, described Islam as "a very evil and wicked religion" after the terrorist attacks.[6] Jerry Vines, former president of the Southern Baptist Convention, referred to the Prophet Muhammad (whom Muslims revere and believe was the last messenger of God) as a "demon-possessed pedophile" and added that "Allah is not Jehovah either. Jehovah's not going to turn you into a terrorist that'll try to bomb people and take the lives of thousands and thousands of people."[7] In his 2002 book, *The Everlasting Hatred,* Christian prophetic writer Hal Lindsey warned Americans that "Islam represents the single greatest threat to the continued survival of the planet that the world has ever seen."[8] John Hagee, an evangelical pastor whose weekly sermons are broadcast to millions of homes, has long been an outspoken critic of the Islamic faith. In a post-9/11 radio interview, he stated that "those who live by the Qur'an have a scriptural mandate to kill Christians and Jews. . . . [I]t teaches that very clearly." Yet, for a man who purportedly knows so much about Islam, Hagee repeatedly and incorrectly refers to Muslims as "Islamics."

Soon after 9/11, Saxby Chambliss, a Republican congressional representative and future senator of Georgia, informed a group of law enforcement officers that the best antiterrorist measure for his district would be to "turn loose" the local sheriff and "let him arrest every Muslim that crosses the state line."[9] Chambliss seemed to be simply echoing the calls for racial and religious profiling that Republican Representative John Cooksey had previously expressed, telling a talk radio show host that "someone who comes in that's got a diaper on his head and a fan belt wrapped around that diaper on his head, that guy needs to be pulled over."[10]

On separate occasions, television commentators Bill O'Reilly and Sean Hannity compared the Qur'an, the Islamic holy book, to Adolf Hitler's *Mein Kampf*.[11] Talk radio host Michael Savage told listeners that to "save the United States," lawmakers should institute an "outright ban on Muslim immigration." Savage also recommended making "the construction of mosques illegal in America."[12]

More than twenty books on the "Islamic menace" were published in the one-year period following the 9/11 attacks.[13] Two of those books became best-selling titles among the thousands of books on Islam at Amazon.com: *American Jihad: The Terrorists among Us*, by Steven Emerson, and *Militant Islam Reaches America*, by Daniel Pipes. In his writings on the threat that the growing Muslim population allegedly poses in the United States, newspaper columnist Cal Thomas advises his readers that "it is past time to stop worrying about political correctness . . . and [time] to start telling the truth. America's enemies are among us. They are here to kill us."[14]

Never before had Muslims been subject to such overt hostility from so many different corners. Not surprisingly, violent outbursts and discriminatory actions followed: Civil-rights organizations recorded thousands of incidents of anti-Islamic and anti-Arab harassment, hate crimes, and vandalism in the months following 9/11 (see Chapter 2). In addition to the attacks on Muslims and Arabs, public anger was directed at other religious and ethnic minorities who were mistakenly identified as "Middle Eastern." Federal officers raided mosques and froze the assets of several major Islamic charities that regularly sent donations overseas. Arab and Muslim men were questioned and arrested. Some were deported without their family members' knowledge of their whereabouts. Others were detained indefinitely and denied access to legal counsel. Members of religious and ethnic minority communities were barred from boarding airplanes based solely on their names, appearances, or countries of origin. Muslim children were bullied by their peers, and adults were fired from their jobs.

It was during the dark days immediately after 9/11 that I decided to document and to analyze the reactions of Muslim Americans to the terrorist attacks. Sociologists have long recognized that crisis events offer important opportunities for learning about human behavior and group life. In 1969, Robert Merton argued that disasters bring out, in bold relief, aspects of social systems that are not so readily apparent during less stressful periods.[15] Nearly a decade earlier, Charles Fritz noted that disasters make normally private behaviors and interactions visible for public observation by compressing vital social processes into a brief time span.[16] But disasters do more than simply reveal the inner workings of society. These events may also further unravel the weakest seams in the larger social fabric, intensifying preexisting inequalities and prejudices.

The 9/11 assaults have become a historical marker, seared into the consciousness of all Americans. Most citizens are likely to remember where they were and what they were doing when they first learned that the United States was under attack on the morning of September 11, 2001. Muslim Americans are no different. For them, however, the tragic events represent a dividing line not only in American history but also in their own collective religious history.

I spent just over two years, from late September 2001 through the end of December 2003, gathering the stories of 140 Muslim American women and men. All these individuals were practicing Muslims who were active in their local faith communities. They were relatively young, ranging in age from eighteen to thirty-five years, and almost all were pursuing undergraduate or graduate degrees or had recently graduated from college.[17] These students and young professionals had their feet firmly planted in the United States, although many had traveled abroad or had lived in other countries for extended stretches of time. Most (82 percent) were born in the United States as the children of recent immigrants or they had migrated at a very young age.[18] The remaining respondents had come to the United States to pursue educational or work opportunities (11 percent) or had converted to Islam as young adults (7 percent).

Because some spaces associated with Islam are segregated by gender, my position as a female researcher allowed me more access to women than men. Consequently, women made up the majority of my informants ($n = 93$), although I interviewed a number of men as well ($n = 47$). The participants were predominantly of South Asian ($n = 69$) or Arab ($n = 46$) descent, and I also interviewed white ($n = 13$), Latino ($n = 6$), and African American ($n = 6$) Muslims.[19] All were fluent in English, and more than 70 percent spoke at least one other language (including Arabic, Farsi, Urdu, Pashto, Punjabi, Bengali, Turkish, Cambodian, French, Indonesian, and Japanese). I conducted all the interviews, which lasted between one and four hours, tape recorded them, and later had them transcribed verbatim. This process produced thousands of pages of qualitative data. My analysis of the data is based on numerous close readings of the typewritten transcripts, which I coded using a qualitative software program.

In the first three months after 9/11, I organized small group interviews with all those who had agreed to participate in the study. These interviews allowed me to capture a wide range of perspectives from a relatively large and ethnically diverse sample of Muslims.[20] In the subsequent months and years, I followed up on the focus groups by interviewing participants one on one. I interviewed many of the people who appear in this book three to four times over the period of this research. In addition, I kept in touch with several of the participants via telephone and e-mail and thus was able to pursue various themes and issues after the years of systematic data gathering were completed. Longitudinal studies of this sort are rare in the field of disaster research, where the one-time case-study method predominates.[21] Yet, as sociologist Brenda Phillips has argued, it is exactly this sort of long-term, intensive immersion in the field that is required to acquire a thorough understanding of human behavior in postdisaster settings.[22]

Most of the people who participated in this project lived in New York City at the time of the terrorist attacks. I also drew a smaller sample of interviewees from Colorado (where I lived in 2001). This other group allowed me more frequent access to a number of respondents and enabled me to compare their experiences with those who resided at the physical epicenter of the disaster.

I launched this study less than three weeks after the 9/11 attacks. I understood that it was vital that I get into the field quickly to collect valuable information, which would be lost if it were not captured in the short time frame following the attacks (disaster researchers refer to this as "perishable data").[23] This methodological decision was not without consequences, however. The community that I set out to study was in the midst of the worst public and political backlash in its collective history. By the time I began collecting data in New York City on September 29, 2001, a rash of anti-Muslim hate crimes had already been recorded, and hundreds of Middle Eastern and Muslim men had been detained by federal authorities.

Given the magnitude of the 9/11 catastrophe and the shockwaves that it sent through the Muslim American community, I was concerned about my ability to access individuals who would agree to be interviewed. I also recognized that my status as an outsider to the religious faith could present various methodological barriers.[24] Therefore, I worked to foster relationships with a number of key informants in various Islamic student and professional organizations. I identified these organizations through Internet searches and based on the suggestions of colleagues and Muslim acquaintances. I made telephone calls and sent letters and e-mails until I made contact with at least one leader within each organization who was interested in the study. These key informants were crucial to the success of this project, as they introduced me to their friends, assisted with scheduling interviews, and vouched for me as a trustworthy person and researcher.

Much to my relief, once I actually began conducting interviews, I found that the young women and men were eager to tell me their stories. In fact, of all the people I approached after 9/11, only one individual declined to participate in the study. Some said that they felt it was their "obligation" to speak out, as they wanted their voices heard at a time when they felt vilified by the media and much of the public. Others simply appreciated having the opportunity to share their experiences with someone who was genuinely interested in learning more. The research seemed to have a cathartic effect for many, as the extended qualitative interview format allowed the participants to talk freely about various issues relevant to their lives.[25] Throughout the text, I have changed the names and some identifying characteristics of the participants, to protect their privacy.

These men and women invited me into their homes, classrooms, and places of work and worship. I accompanied them to political and religious speeches and peace rallies, sat through college classes, shadowed them at their jobs, attended Muslim Students Association (MSA) meetings, observed Friday prayers at mosques, and ate Ramadan dinners at Islamic centers. I was invited to and attended several weddings and graduation parties, which allowed me the opportunity to interact with the friends and family members of the respondents. When participating in these various events, I always attempted to follow Islamic norms of social interaction (removing my shoes before entering someone's house, avoiding touching members of the opposite sex, wearing modest clothing, observing gender-segregated seating patterns, and so forth). I adhered to these rules of etiquette out of cultural and religious respect, and because I believed it would have been methodologically irresponsible and inappropriate to have behaved otherwise.

Spending time with the respondents helped me verify and better understand the experiences and information that came to light in the qualitative interviews. For instance, one of the greatest fears that the participants expressed immediately following 9/11, particularly among the women, was traveling on public transportation alone. As I walked through subway stations and sat on trains with these young women, it quickly became clear that the suspicious and angry looks they reported were not exaggerations.

Interest in the size and characteristics of the Muslim American population has risen sharply in the aftermath of 9/11. However, estimating the number of Muslims in the United States has proven difficult. The U.S. Census Bureau and the Immigration and Naturalization Service are not legally allowed to collect data on the religious affiliations of citizens or immigrants—due in large part to the principle of church-state separation—and therefore precise figures for the number or demographic characteristics of Muslims living in the United States do not exist. Moreover, because Muslims represent a very small percentage of the overall American population, figures drawn from general population surveys tend to be unreliable or overlook Muslims altogether.[26] Additional difficulties in counting the number of American Muslims emerge from the diverse nature of the population itself. Muslims can be of any race or geographic origin, and immigrants from dozens of different countries, native-born Muslims, and converts to the faith make up the Muslim American community.[27]

As a result of these and other barriers to reliable data collection, estimates vary widely regarding the size of the population, and at times disagreement develops concerning who should be identified and counted as Muslim. The media, drawing on a variety of sources, commonly characterize the size of the Muslim population in the United States as ranging somewhere between three and nine million persons.[28] The Hartford Institute for Religious Research coordinated a 2001 study that estimated a population of between six and seven million Muslim Americans.[29] More recently, the Pew Research Center conducted a 2007 study that concluded that approximately 2.35 million Muslims lived in the United States. The Pew study, which was based on a nationwide survey of a representative sample of Muslim Americans, found that roughly 65 percent of adult Muslims living in the United States were born elsewhere and that slightly more than half of all native-born Muslims converted to Islam.

One thing that is certain is that the size of the Muslim American community is increasing steadily. Islam is the fastest growing religion in the United States, and some scholars predict that by the middle of the twenty-first century it will become the nation's second-largest religion—surpassed only by Christianity in terms of its number of adherents.[30]

The growth of the Muslim population in America can be divided into several distinct phases. The first Muslims in North America may have been seafarers who made the perilous voyage across the Atlantic Ocean before Christopher Columbus.[31] Later, between the sixteenth and eighteenth centuries, an undetermined number of African Muslims were brought to America under the brutal slave trade. These individuals were largely forced to abandon their faith, their traditions, their native languages, and their friends and families.[32] The adoption of Islam by some twentieth-century African Americans has been linked, in part, to an emotional tie to this early New World history.[33]

The earliest voluntary migration of Muslims to the United States began during the late 1800s and consisted mostly of individuals from Eastern Europe and parts of the Ottoman Empire, including modern Lebanon, Syria, Jordan, and Palestine.[34] Around the middle of the twentieth century, significant numbers of Muslim students from developing countries began attending American universities.[35] These individuals, many of whom eventually settled in the United States, helped establish some of the first national Muslim organizations and major Islamic centers and mosques in American cities.

Three primary factors drive the more recent and rapid expansion of the Muslim American community: (1) birth rates, (2) religious conversion (especially among African Americans and whites), and, most significantly, (3) changing immigration trends and patterns.[36] In 1965, the U.S. Congress passed the Immigration and Nationality Act, which repealed highly restrictive country-of-origin quotas established in the 1920s that favored Western European, mostly Judeo-Christian, immigrants. This post-1965 change in federal immigration policy led to an unprecedented diversification of the American population over subsequent decades, as millions of immigrants and refugees arrived from around the world, pulled here by economic and educational opportunities or pushed from their homelands as a result of political turmoil, wars, revolutions, and environmental disasters.[37] These and other social, political, and economic forces have made the United States the most religiously diverse nation on earth, and Muslim Americans represent an increasingly important segment of society.[38]

In the aftermath of 9/11, the media and public officials often used the terms "Muslim" and "Arab" interchangeably. This conflation of categories led to the perception among many that all Muslims are Arab and that all Arabs are Muslim.[39] This is certainly not the case. Muslim is an identifier used to describe those who believe in the religion of Islam, and thus Muslims can come from any nation and be of any racial or ethnic background. An estimated 1.57 billion Muslims live in countries spanning the globe, and only about 20 percent of the world's Muslims reside in Arabic-speaking countries.[40] In fact, the four nations with the largest Muslim populations—Indonesia (203 million), Pakistan (174 million), India (161 million), and Bangladesh (145 million)—are all located outside the Arab world.[41]

Approximately 300 million Arabs live in the world today. Arabs represent a heterogeneous ethnic population that shares a cultural and linguistic heritage and includes people who live in or trace their ancestries to countries in northern Africa and southwestern Asia where the primary language is Arabic.[42] The 2000 U.S. Census identified 1.2 million Americans who reported ancestry in one of the 22 Arab countries, but Arab American advocacy organizations claim the population may be three times that size.[43] Arabs may be of any religious background; in the United States, an estimated two-thirds of all Arab Americans are Christian, with the remaining one-third being Muslim.[44]

The Muslim American community is strikingly diverse. Muslim immigrants to the United States, who make up nearly two-thirds of the entire Muslim American population, come from at least 68 countries, and these individuals have different traditions, practices, doctrines, languages, and beliefs.[45] According to the Pew Research Center, more than one-third (37 percent) of all foreign-born Muslims are from Arabic-speaking countries. An additional 27 percent emigrated from South Asian countries, including Pakistan, India, Bangladesh, and Afghanistan. A substantial number of Muslims have also arrived from Iran (12 percent), Europe (8 percent), and sub-Saharan Africa (6 percent). Even with the heavy presence of immigrants among the Muslim population, more than three-quarters (77 percent) of all American Muslims are U.S. citizens. Just over one-third of all Muslim Americans were born in the United States, and, of these individuals, most identify as black or African American (56 percent), white (31 percent), or Hispanic (10 percent).[46]

Muslims live in every state in the United States, although they tend to be concentrated in large cities and traditional immigrant-receiving centers. The ten metropolitan areas with the largest populations of Muslim Americans include Los Angeles; New York City; Detroit; Washington, D.C.; Chicago; Orange County, California; Houston; Oakland; San Diego; and Boston.[47] Despite their predominantly immigrant and ethnic minority status, Muslims are actually less residentially segregated than many other groups. Most Muslims live in neighborhoods where they form a distinct minority amid a mostly white majority (notable exceptions exist in such places as Detroit and New York City, and, as their numbers continue to grow, it is likely that Muslims will begin to create enclaves elsewhere).[48]

Socioeconomic factors may help explain the high rates of residential integration among the Muslim population. With the exception of African American Muslims, America's Muslims are generally better educated and more affluent than the nation as a whole. Nearly 60 percent of Muslim Americans hold college degrees, which is more than double the national average.[49] Muslim American women are one of the most highly educated female religious groups, second only to Jewish American women.[50] Muslim Americans also have the highest degree of economic gender parity—meaning that men and women tend to be more on "equal footing" in terms of earnings—of any religious group in the United States.[51]

Muslim Americans experience lower poverty rates than most other religious or ethnic minority groups in the United States, which is not surprising given their generally high rates of educational attainment. More than half of all Muslims have incomes in excess of $50,000 a year, and their average overall annual income is about $55,000.[52] These statistics reflect the fact that nearly 50 percent of all Muslim Americans earn their living in such professions as engineering, medicine, teaching, and business management.[53] Muslims also represent a relatively young segment of American society: Three-quarters of adult Muslims are younger than fifty years old.[54]

Religion plays an important role in the lives of many Americans, and this is especially true for Muslim Americans. A nationally representative survey found that 80 percent of Muslim Americans acknowledge the importance of faith in their lives.[55] About 60 percent of Muslim Americans say that they pray every day,[56] and just over 40 percent attend services at a mosque at least once a week.[57] Younger Muslim Americans (those under age thirty) report attending religious services more frequently than do older Muslims.[58] Muslim American women are as likely as Muslim American men to attend mosque at least once a week.[59] This is in sharp contrast with the gender pattern observed in many Muslim majority countries, where men are more likely than women to regularly attend religious services.[60]

In 2003, the Washington-based Council on American-Islamic Relations (CAIR) launched a national "Islam in America" ad campaign. In running the series of advertisements, CAIR, which is one of the largest and most active Islamic civil-rights and advocacy organizations in the United States, hoped to address common misperceptions about Islam while also underscoring the significant diversity of its followers. The campaign kicked off with a full-page ad in the *New York Times,* headlined with the words, "We're all Americans." Just below the headline, the ad featured photographs of a white man, an African American girl, and an Asian man and asked the question "But, which one of us is a Muslim?" The response, "We all are. . . . [W]e're American Muslims," was followed by three paragraphs of text that outlined a number of basic facts about Islam and Muslims. Other major Islamic organizations, including the MSA national office, the Islamic Circle of North America, and the Islamic Society of North America, have embarked on similar campaigns to educate the public regarding the basic tenets of the faith.

Even before the 9/11 attacks, Muslim Americans faced an uphill battle in their quest to enlighten a mostly non-Muslim public. For decades, Americans have been bombarded with derogatory images of Muslims in film and television. On the big and the small screen, the Islamic faith is regularly linked with the oppression of women, holy war, and terrorist attacks. Jack Shaheen, who reviewed more than 900 Hollywood movies for his book *Reel Bad Arabs,* notes that when mosques are displayed onscreen, the camera inevitably cuts to men praying and then gunning down civilians.[61] Mainstream American and Western print and broadcast media also regularly, and unapologetically, reinforce the worst stereotypes about Islam—that it is a violent, primitive, and imminently hateful religion.[62]

Since 9/11, negative perceptions of Muslims have been on the rise. For example, an *ABC News* poll found that four months after the terrorist attacks, 14 percent of Americans believed that mainstream Islam encourages violence. A year and a half later, that number had jumped to 34 percent.[63] In the same *ABC News* follow-up survey, 43 percent of Americans expressed the view that Islam does not teach respect for the beliefs of non-Muslims. In 2004 and 2005, CAIR commissioned two national surveys to gauge public sentiment about Islam and Muslims. Both surveys concluded that about one in four Americans harbors prejudice against Muslims. Specifically, in 2004, the survey found that 26 percent of respondents agreed that Islam teaches violence and hatred; 27 percent agreed that Muslims value life less than other people; 29 percent said that Muslims teach their children to hate nonbelievers; and just over half, 51 percent, agreed that Islam encourages the oppression of women.[64] These numbers remained virtually unchanged in the 2005 survey.[65]

In 2006, *ABC News* conducted a survey of 1,000 adults across the United States. The results showed that nearly six in ten Americans think Islam is prone to violent extremism, almost half regard the religion unfavorably, and about one-quarter of respondents openly admitted to harboring prejudicial feelings against Muslims and Arabs alike.[66] A *USA Today*/Gallup poll, also conducted in 2006, found that more than one-third of Americans (39 percent) feel some prejudice against Muslims. The same percentage favored requiring Muslims, including those who are U.S. citizens, to carry a special identification card "as a means of preventing terrorist attacks in the United States." About one-third said American Muslims were sympathetic to al Qaeda, and 22 percent indicated that they would not want Muslims as neighbors.[67] By 2009, a majority of Americans had a negative impression of Islam, with 53 percent of Gallup survey respondents reporting that they viewed Islam unfavorably.[68]

Americans' attitudes toward Islam and Muslims are undoubtedly shaped, at least in part, by their lack of familiarity with the faith and its followers: Approximately six in ten Americans acknowledge that they do not have even a basic understanding of Islam.[69] In addition, many of those who report some knowledge of Islam actually hold incorrect beliefs about the faith. For example, about 10 percent of Americans think that Muslims worship a "moon god," a notion that most Muslims would find not only false but also offensive.[70] These issues are further compounded by the fact that most Americans have no close relationships with Muslims. According to one study, only about one in five non-Muslim Americans has Muslim friends or colleagues.[71] Several surveys have shown that those who are more knowledgeable about Islam—either through education or personal contact with Muslims—are a good deal more likely to view the faith in a favorable light.[72] Research has also found that familiarity and contact with Arabs and Muslims leads to more willingness to defend the civil liberties of these persons.[73]

The aforementioned survey data point to two troubling trends: First, most Americans have very little knowledge of the Islamic faith; and second, public opinion has grown increasingly negative toward Muslims in the years since the 9/11 attacks. If history has taught us anything, it is that ignorance and hostility make for very dangerous bedfellows, especially during times of war and national insecurity.

Indeed, the United States has a long record of demonizing immigrants and ethnic minorities from enemy countries during times of conflict. With the U.S. declaration of war against Imperial Germany on April 6, 1917, approximately half a million German immigrants were classified as "enemy aliens."[74] During World War I, the federal government conducted round-ups of Germans, registered more than 260,000 male and 220,000 female enemy aliens, and arrested and subsequently detained roughly 6,300 Germans in internment camps.[75]

Just over twenty years after the last German internees had been released, the United States entered World War II. This time, almost a million immigrants and American citizens who traced their roots to the Axis powers—Germany, Italy, and Japan—were labeled enemy aliens, fingerprinted, and registered. Approximately 2,300 Germans and an estimated 200 Italians in the United States were interned in camps during World War II.[76] Race prejudice and war-time hysteria resulted in the incarceration of more than 120,000 Japanese American men, women, and children for the duration of World War II.[77] More than two-thirds of the Japanese detainees were native-born American citizens, although this status was meaningless in the face of mass arrests and forced removal from their homes and communities. Ultimately, none of the Japanese detainees was incriminated for any involvement in sabotage or espionage.

In one of many belated apologies issued to Japanese Americans, President George H. W. Bush promised that the atrocities committed by the federal government would "never be repeated."[78] Yet, in 1986, the Reagan-Bush administration considered using two military compounds in the southern United States for the possible internment of Arab Americans.[79] A few years prior to that, the Carter administration contemplated the arrest and incarceration of Iranian students at U.S. universities as a result of the hostage crisis growing out of the seizure of the American embassy in Tehran.[80] The Federal Bureau of Investigation launched one of its first national campaigns to interview and to deport Arab Americans following the Munich massacre.[81] The crisis began when Palestinian militants kidnapped eleven Israeli athletes and coaches during the 1972 Olympic Games in Munich. The militants murdered all eleven hostages, and five of the eight terrorists were killed when German authorities attempted to rescue the hostages.

Since 1999, the U.S. government has entered into a series of contracts with major corporations to build detention camps at undisclosed locations within the United States. The government has also contracted with several companies to manufacture thousands of railcars, some reportedly equipped with shackles, apparently to transport detainees.[82] In the aftermath of the 9/11 attacks, calls for the internment and mass deportation of Muslims abounded, and a provision in the USA PATRIOT Act of 2001 (introduced as the Provide Appropriate Tools Required to Intercept and Obstruct Terrorism Act of 2001) created a legal framework for establishing detention centers to incarcerate U.S. citizens and foreign nationals.[83] Understandably, promises of "never again" offer little consolation to Middle Eastern and Muslim

Americans, who are keenly aware that they are the latest minority group to be defined as threatening outsiders following a national tragedy. With that awareness comes heightened levels of anxiety and mistrust.

The purpose of the chapters that follow is threefold. First, drawing on official statistics and in-depth interviews, I examine the character and breadth of discrimination that Muslim Americans have endured before and especially after the 9/11 attacks. As this book shows, Muslim Americans were confronted with stereotypes and harassment prior to 9/11. In the aftermath of the terrorist attacks, Muslims experienced a dramatic increase in the frequency and intensity of these hostile encounters. *Behind the Backlash* documents the verbal harassment; violent threats and intimidation; physical assault; religious profiling; and employment, educational, and housing discrimination that Muslims faced following 9/11. Second, I explore the personal and social impacts of the backlash. The first-hand accounts provide a glimpse into the personal and collective trauma that can arise when religious minorities are subjected to extreme prejudice and exclusion. Third, I discuss the ways that Muslim Americans have coped with and responded to assaults on their faith, families, and personal identities. I draw on sociological insights to explain the struggles of young Muslim adults to establish community and to define their identities during a time of national crisis. Ultimately, this book explores how disasters and other crisis events impact the most marginalized members of our society.

2

Under Attack

During the early morning hours of Tuesday, September 11, 2001, nineteen men took control of four commercial airliners en route to Los Angeles and San Francisco from Boston, Newark, and Washington, D.C. The first hijacked aircraft struck the north tower of the World Trade Center at 8:46 A.M. Eyewitnesses flooded New York City's 9-1-1 call system with reports of the plane crash as the media and amateur photographers turned their cameras toward the World Trade Center. Almost immediately after the plane collided with the tower, television stations began broadcasting images of black smoke pouring out of a gaping hole in the massive building. News anchors offered conflicting accounts: Some reported that a small, twin-engine commuter plane had hit the World Trade Center; others indicated that a commercial airliner had veered off course and had struck the tower. At this point, few reporters speculated that the crash had been deliberate.[1]

As stunned observers stared up at the inferno, emergency response personnel from New York City and the Port Authority of New York and New Jersey began mobilizing what would become the largest rescue operation in the nation's history. Well over a thousand first responders—firefighters, police officers, and paramedics—were deployed to the scene of the first crash.[2] Medical workers set up triage areas around the perimeter of the World Trade Center as they attempted to aid those who had been injured when the plane hit the building. Police units began shutting down subway stations as fire teams evacuated civilians from the north tower and its surrounding area.

Then, at 9:03 A.M., a second airliner, traveling at more than five hundred miles per hour, slammed into the side of the south tower. Camera crews from across the city captured the impact and subsequent explosion on film. The force of the plane crash rocked the building, and two huge fireballs erupted from the south tower as several floors became engulfed in flames. Thick smoke billowed from the tower as ash and debris fell to the ground.

President George W. Bush first addressed the nation at 9:30 A.M. on the morning of September 11. In his brief remarks, the president confirmed that a terrorist incident had indeed taken place: "Today we've had a national tragedy," Bush said from an elementary school he was visiting in Sarasota, Florida. "Two airplanes have crashed into the World Trade Center in an apparent terrorist attack on our country." Bush then promised "to hunt down and to find those folks" who committed the atrocities.[3] Only minutes after the president finished his address, the third hijacked airliner hit the Pentagon in Arlington, Virginia. At 10:03 A.M., the fourth hijacked plane crashed in a field in rural Pennsylvania.

The violent assaults were designed to be spectacular in their destruction of symbols of U.S. economic, military, and political power. The first two hijacked commercial airliners brought down the 110-story twin towers of the World Trade Center and led to the partial or total collapse of seven other buildings in the financial district of lower Manhattan. The third airliner heavily damaged part of the Pentagon, which serves as the headquarters for the U.S. Department of Defense. The fourth plane was destined for either the U.S. Capitol or the White House but was forced down by several passengers before it could reach its intended target.

These deliberate acts claimed the lives of more people on American soil than any other hostile attack in the nation's history.[4] The death toll stands at 2,973, which includes all 246 passengers and crew members on the four hijacked airplanes; 55 military personnel and 70 civilians at the Pentagon; and 2,602 civilians and first responders in New York City who were in the towers at the time of the aerial assaults or when the buildings collapsed.[5] All told, citizens from more than ninety nations perished as a consequence of 9/11. The nineteen individuals who hijacked the planes also died on impact, although their names are typically not included among the official rosters of the deceased.

In addition to those persons who lost their lives, many more suffered various wounds to the body and mind as a result of the disaster. Soon after the collapse of the enormous blazing towers, which sent walls of dust and debris surging down narrow city streets, several thousand people in New York received medical care for burns, lacerations, broken bones, and other afflictions.[6] In the weeks and months to follow, a considerable number of people who were close enough to the epicenter to inhale the smoke and noxious fumes sought treatment for respiratory problems, such as wheezing, shortness of breath, asthma, and a new syndrome aptly named "World Trade Center cough."[7]

The children and adults who lived, went to school, or worked near the disaster-affected areas were exposed to an extraordinary array of stressors (life threats, bereavement, disruption of normal routines, and displacement), which provoked fear, nightmares, and other forms of worry that persisted for long periods of time.[8] The rescue and recovery workers who labored at the sites of the attacks—putting out fires, cleaning up debris, and salvaging human remains—witnessed scenes of unspeakable destruction and subsequently experienced high rates of depression and anxiety.[9] Mental health professionals who consoled the families of the deceased, comforted those who searched for the missing, and provided support for survivors and volunteers were vulnerable to various psychological disturbances arising from their regular confrontation with human tragedy.[10]

It is clear that the emotional distress that the attacks generated was not confined to the impact zones but instead rippled outward across the United States. The Pew Research Center estimated that roughly 20 percent of Americans knew someone (or had a friend or relative who knew someone) who was injured or killed on 9/11. A national survey revealed that the vast majority of American adults—about 90 percent—exhibited at least one symptom of post-traumatic stress in the week following the attacks, and nearly half—44 percent—displayed substantial symptoms of stress.[11] A series of follow-up polls documented ongoing adverse emotional and physical health reactions among the general population.[12] As the months passed and people attempted to come to terms with the many losses associated with the disaster, the immediate trauma seemed to settle into a kind of generalized mass anxiety. In one survey, taken almost a year after the tragedy, nearly two-thirds of the respondents said that they thought about 9/11 at least several times a week.[13]

The 9/11 attacks also caused staggering financial losses. The U.S. Government Accountability Office contends that the costs associated with the attacks were somewhere in the range of $80 to $100 billion (in 2001 dollars).[14] This figure includes, among other things, the "direct costs" resulting from the loss of human life; the destruction of physical property, including a large section of the Pentagon and fifteen million square feet of prime office space in lower Manhattan; the expense of responding to the disaster during the emergency period; the cost of removing two million tons of rubble; and the economic toll of recovery. The "indirect costs" represent losses that are far more difficult to estimate, such as diminished business profits, the loss of employee income, and reduced tax revenues. The business travel and tourism industries were severely affected as well, and in September 2001, domestic and international air travel fell by 30 percent nationwide. Economic activity in Manhattan's financial district all but ceased after the attacks, and between 75,000 and 100,000 jobs were lost in New York City in the last three months of 2001.[15]

The coordinated assaults on New York and Washington, D.C., generated widespread disruption across the United States. Less than an hour after the first airplane struck the north tower of the World Trade Center, the Federal Aviation Administration ordered a halt to all nonemergency civilian flight operations, stranding tens of thousands of passengers at airports across the country. This order represented the first time in American history that air traffic nationwide had been grounded. Shortly thereafter, Secret Service agents were deployed to the White House, and the U.S. military was placed on high alert worldwide. All federal office buildings in Washington, D.C., were evacuated, and New York state government offices were closed. Trading on Wall Street was suspended, and every bridge and tunnel leading into Manhattan was shut down. Los Angeles International Airport, the destination of three of the hijacked airplanes, was evacuated and shut down, as was San Francisco International Airport, the destination of the fourth airliner that crashed in Pennsylvania. Schools, businesses, and other organizations across the nation closed for days, and in some cases for weeks, after the attacks.

In the wake of the tragedy, many people experienced an overwhelming desire to help. Tens of thousands of emergency response personnel and private citizens spontaneously converged at the scene of the attacks.[16] Concerned individuals lined up at blood donation stations across the United States, and volunteers overwhelmed community service agencies with offers to assist. Open displays of patriotism were evident everywhere, as Americans bought out every U.S. flag in the nation.[17] Individuals and organizations donated nearly $2 billion and an extraordinary amount of food, clothing, and supplies to the relief efforts.[18]

All the while, survivors in New York City desperately hunted for the disappeared. Frantic family members and friends presented photos of missing loved ones to hospital employees, Red Cross staff, strangers on the street, and anyone else whom they thought might be able to aid them in their search. Thousands of handmade fliers that asked, "Have you seen this person?" were posted on lampposts, in restaurants, and all along the walls of Grand Central and Penn Stations.[19] Countless candlelight vigils, communal interfaith services, teach-ins on university campuses, and other events were organized to help people cope with the events. Despite some apprehension, no panic, no rioting, and no real looting occurred in New York City following the attacks.[20]

In many ways, the outpouring of warmth and goodwill closely resembled the reactions that have long been observed in the aftermath of natural disasters and other catastrophes. Samuel Henry Prince, one of the earliest scholars of disaster, writes of a "city of comrades" coming together after the deadly 1917 Halifax ship explosion.[21] In his report on a major flood, Robert I. Kutak references the "democracy of distress," which he says led to a temporary breakdown of race and class divisions among affected citizens.[22] Anthony F. C. Wallace[23] describes a "stage of euphoria" that brought together those who survived a catastrophic tornado, and Martha Wolfenstein[24] calls the more general phenomenon a "post-disaster utopia." Allen Barton uses the concept of the "altruistic community" to explain how human suffering could generate such supportive behavior among populations devastated by disaster.[25] After reviewing a significant number of case studies of disaster, Charles E. Fritz concludes that the emergence of a "community of sufferers" is a nearly universal feature of large-scale crises.[26]

Following 9/11, a number of seasoned disaster researchers drew on these past studies and argued that the response to the terrorist attacks essentially affirmed what we already know about human reactions to catastrophe.[27] Their argument, in effect, was that decades of research on earthquakes, tornados, hurricanes, and floods has shown that regardless of the type of event, human beings react fundamentally the same. During the emergency period, survivors rush to rescue the injured from the rubble. Crime and other acts of deviance decline as community members concentrate on promoting public safety and restoring community life. Neighbors come together to help one another clean up the debris and to begin the process of rebuilding damaged homes. Individual differences and status distinctions are forgotten, even if only temporarily, as the good of the collective becomes paramount. From this perspective, disasters bring out the best in humanity, not the worst.

The national and international media offered a similar frame in much of their initial reporting on the events of 9/11. The day after the terrorist attacks, the French daily newspaper *Le Monde*, which is frequently critical of U.S. foreign policy, ran the headline "Nous sommes tous Americaines" ("We are all Americans") on the front page of its morning edition. The motto "United We Stand" appeared on the cover of numerous U.S. newspapers and magazines. Radio and television commentators periodically uttered the phrase "Today we are all New Yorkers." Images of death and destruction were juxtaposed with stories of ordinary heroes and remarkable acts of generosity. New York was depicted as a city transformed. It was no longer an urban metropolis filled with self-interested individuals; it had become a single human community bound together by a horrible tragedy.

These academic and popular interpretations of the events speak to one reality, a reality of social solidarity, of bravery, of good deeds, and of kindness. But a second powerful reality also exists that the very notion of a single, unified "altruistic community" serves to obscure.

After 9/11, the national mood swung quickly from shock to outrage. Americans had watched in horror as men and women, faced with insufferable heat and smoke, plunged to their deaths from the burning World Trade Center. Then the two tallest buildings in New York City crumbled to the ground like a house of cards. And just as quickly as those buildings disappeared from the skyline, so too did the belief that an attack of this magnitude could be carried out on American soil. Foreign extremists had infiltrated the United States, and Americans feared that terrorist cells were hidden among the population, waiting to strike again. The anger in the United States at that time was palpable, and anger needs an outlet.

President Bush addressed the nation again on the evening of September 11, 2001. He solemnly assured the American people that the search was already underway for those who perpetrated the acts of mass murder. The pledge to find those who were responsible and to bring them to justice was understandable, given the utter ruthlessness of the attacks and the catastrophic losses they caused. However, the attribution of blame and the subsequent scapegoating that followed 9/11 left those who shared a common ethnic or religious identity with the hijackers—who, it would quickly be discovered, were all Arab Muslim men—feeling fearful and isolated. As a consequence of the terrorist attacks, Arab and Muslim Americans became the targets of hate crimes, harassment, and government surveillance. Thus, although the events of 9/11 brought together many Americans and led to increased feelings of patriotism and national unity, the public and political response that followed the attacks alienated and further marginalized millions of others. In fact, we were really not "all Americans" on that day.

In his book *A New Species of Trouble,* Kai Erikson argues that a profound difference exists between those disasters that can be understood as the work of nature and those that are recognized as the product of humankind.[28] Although Erikson is mostly concerned with a category of events known as "technological" or "toxic" disasters, rather than terrorism, his central ideas are still important in understanding the public response to 9/11. In natural disasters, such as floods, tornadoes, and earthquakes, people usually blame "Mother Nature" or an "act of God" rather than hold government officials, building contractors, or other citizens accountable for individual and collective choices that may have placed victims in harm's way. The ability to attribute losses to some higher power, in many cases, allows survivors to move forward and to mobilize necessary resources to begin the process of recovery. At the other end of the spectrum are calamities that other human beings unmistakably bring about. Oil spills, chemical releases, nuclear meltdowns, and other disasters of overtly human origin are, in principle, preventable, and thus victims can always assign some blame. For this reason, emergencies that result from human actions are more likely to provoke fear, anger, and outrage rather than passive acceptance or resignation.

The events of 9/11 certainly share many characteristics with the toxic calamities that Erikson so carefully describes. Yet what distinguishes the terrorist attacks—and places them on a scale entirely their own—is that they were deliberate acts of malice. Under no circumstance could the death and destruction be attributed to human negligence, technological error, scientific miscalculation, or even greed. These were carefully coordinated attacks, designed to maximize the loss of life among civilians, to destroy symbols of American prosperity and strength, and to terrify an entire nation.

Arab and Muslim Americans quickly recognized the magnitude and significance of the 9/11 attacks and anticipated the likelihood of serious repercussions.[29] This anticipation reflected their awareness of a history of backlash violence and government-sanctioned discrimination against Arabs and Muslims in the United States following previous crises. Conflicts in the Middle East and acts of terrorism associated (rightly or wrongly) with Arabs or Muslims have triggered most of the hostile acts aimed at these groups. For example, the 1973 Arab-Israeli war and oil embargo heightened negative stereotypes against Arab and Muslim communities in the United States, as did the 1979 Iran hostage crisis.[30] In 1985, the American-Arab Anti-Discrimination Committee (ADC) documented a spate of violent crimes against Arab Americans and their businesses following the hijacking of TWA Flight 847 by Shiite militants in Lebanon.[31] When the United States bombed Libya in 1986, Arab students were harassed and beaten, and Arab American homes, community centers, and other ethnic and religious institutions were vandalized.[32]

In the eight months prior to Iraq's invasion of Kuwait in August 1990, ADC recorded just four anti-Arab incidents. However, as U.S. troops were deployed to the Persian Gulf, political rhetoric escalated, and levels of public anxiety increased, so too did assaults against Arab Americans. In the last three months of 1990 and throughout 1991, ADC logged more than 150 confirmed hate crimes perpetrated against Arab Americans.[33] During this same period, threats against Arab and Muslim Americans grew so numerous that the mayor of Detroit asked Michigan's governor to assign National Guard troops to protect the city's large Arab American community. As the nationwide wave of hate crimes grew more severe, President George H. W. Bush called for an end to religiously and ethnically motivated aggression, insisting that "death threats, physical attacks, vandalism, religious violence, and discrimination against Arab Americans must end."[34]

The Council on American-Islamic Relations (CAIR) recorded 296 occurrences of harassment and violence against Muslim Americans in the year following the 1995 Oklahoma City bombing.[35] Nearly three-quarters of the attacks, which included shootings, mob violence, and the burning and desecration of mosques, happened during the one-week period immediately after the April 19 bombing. These incidents occurred across the United States and were precipitated in large part by false media reports regarding the involvement of "Middle Eastern–looking men" and "Islamic fundamentalists" in the destruction of the Alfred P. Murrah Federal Building. The day after the attack, the *New York Times* questioned whether the bombing could have been the work of "Islamic militants," noting that "some Middle Eastern groups have held meetings there, and the city is home to at least three mosques." This media speculation continued for months, despite the fact that Timothy McVeigh, a white man who was affiliated with the radical Christian Identity movement, was apprehended an hour after the bombing took place and was named by the Federal Bureau of Investigation (FBI) as the prime suspect within a matter of days of his arrest.[36]

The government response that followed the Oklahoma City bombing was perhaps even more startling than the surge in anti-Muslim hate crimes. Soon after the bombing, the U.S. Congress passed the Comprehensive Anti-Terrorism Act of 1995. Even though both of the Oklahoma City bombers were American-born and American-raised, the bill established a special measure for deporting "alien terrorists." It also sanctioned, among other security measures, airport profiling of potential terrorists. The profile was not of a blond-haired, blue-eyed Timothy McVeigh but of a brown-skinned Arab or Muslim.[37]

Following the 1996 explosion of TWA Flight 800 over the Atlantic Ocean, law enforcement agents quickly asserted, apparently without evidence, that the plane was brought down by terrorists with ties to the Middle East. Consequently, significant numbers of Arab Americans, Muslim Americans, and others who simply appeared to be Middle Eastern were subjected to harsh questioning, demeaning treatment, and intrusive searches of their personal possessions and bodies. Some were even told that they were being interrogated more extensively than others because they "fit a profile."[38] In the end, the crash was attributed to faulty wiring.

Retaliatory attacks in the aftermath of crisis have become part of the Muslim American collective consciousness. Thus, it is no surprise that in the wake of 9/11, almost like a startle reflex, Muslims moved swiftly into action as they attempted to avert antagonistic responses. Just hours after the first airplane collided with the World Trade Center, Muslim American groups condemned the acts of terror. The joint statement, which every major Islamic organization in the United States endorsed, read in part, "American

Muslims utterly condemn what are vicious and cowardly acts of terrorism against innocent civilians. We join with all Americans in calling for the swift apprehension and punishment of the perpetrators. No political cause could ever be assisted by such immoral acts."[39]

Days later, CAIR purchased and ran a full-page advertisement in the *Washington Post* that stated, "Our thoughts and prayers are with the families, friends, and loved ones of those who have been killed or injured. May we all stand together through these difficult times to promote peace and love over violence and hate." Similarly, the Muslim Public Affairs Council issued the following statement: "We feel that our country, the United States, is under attack. All Americans should stand together to bring the perpetrators to justice. We warn against any generalizations that will only serve to help the criminals and incriminate the innocent. We offer our resources and resolve to help the victims of these intolerable acts, and we pray to God to protect and bless America." Muslim Students Association (MSA) National, which represents more than seven hundred affiliated chapters on college and university campuses across the United States, issued several press releases expressing grief and support for the larger American community.[40]

Muslim and Arab leaders abroad also condemned the attacks and offered their condolences. For example, on the morning of September 11, Palestinian leader Yasser Arafat spoke out against the terrorists and sent his sympathy to the American people. One of Sunni Islam's highest religious authorities, Sheikh Mohammed Sayed Tantawi of Al-Azhar mosque in Cairo, said that the terrible acts would be punished on judgment day. President Mohammad Khatami of Iran stated that attacking innocent people is not tolerated in Islam. And, in October 2001, representatives of fifty-seven nations at the Organization of Islamic Conferences declared that "such shameful terror acts are opposed to the tolerant divine message of Islam, which spurns aggression, calls for peace, coexistence, tolerance, and respect among people, highly prizes the dignity of human life, and prohibits the killing of the innocent."[41]

Prominent Islamic religious leaders in the United States, including Imam Hamza Yusuf and Imam Siraj Wahhaj, offered dozens of interviews to print media and appeared on national television to present the faith's prohibition of terrorism. On September 20, 2001, President George W. Bush invited Imam Yusuf to the Oval Office, where the two men met privately and later stood side by side and sang "God Bless America."[42] Islamic scholars called the attacks a distortion of Islam and argued that no religious justification exists for such violent actions. Ingrid Mattson, a professor of Islamic Studies and Christian-Muslim Relations at Hartford Seminary, said, "Islamic law is very clear: Terrorism is not permitted." She added, "Even in a legitimate war—even if Osama bin Laden were a legitimate head of state, which he's not—you're not permitted to indiscriminately kill civilians, just to create terror in the general population."[43]

Major Arab and Muslim American advocacy groups prepared resource packets and posted information on their Web sites that answered common questions about Arab Americans, Islam, and the Middle East. Representatives from these organizations also spoke at forums that professional associations and federal and state agencies sponsored. Members of MSAs organized educational forums, film screenings, and guest lectures on university campuses across the nation. Individual Arabs and Muslims gave countless talks to religious groups, schools, businesses, and local organizations about the impact of 9/11 on their lives and communities. Muslims began holding "open mosque" events designed to offer the public an introduction to Islam and to connect people of different faiths. Christians, Jews, and other people of faith were invited to join Muslims in breaking the fast during the Islamic holy month of Ramadan. CAIR initiated a campaign to provide informational books on Islam to thousands of libraries nationwide.

As Muslims attempted to convince the American people that those men who hijacked the airplanes on September 11 also hijacked their faith, others began to stand up in defense of the Islamic community. During the fall of 2001, hundreds of non-Muslim women across the United States volunteered to wear the hijab for a day to support their Muslim sisters. The campaign, which was named "Scarves for Solidarity," was largely organized via the Internet.[44] Volunteers offered to escort Muslim families to the grocery store and on other errands to ensure their safety. Individuals sent cards, flowers, and cash donations to mosques, and callers flooded their voicemails with messages of support. In some cities, members of the public formed human chains around mosques to discourage vandalism and to promote tolerance and solidarity. The media ran numerous stories on the beliefs and practices of Muslim Americans and on their historical and contemporary contributions to society. Religious leaders from various faiths opened the doors to their houses of worship and invited Muslims to share an Islamic perspective on the events of 9/11. Leading advocacy groups for Latinos, Sikhs, Asian Americans, Arab Americans, and other minority communities formed civil-rights coalitions with Islamic organizations. In addition, new educational and community outreach groups—such as Hate Free Zone, Neighbors for Peace, and Muslims Against Terrorism—were launched after the 9/11 attacks to encourage dialogue across racial and religious divides and to oppose bias-based harassment.[45]

Some public officials and government agencies also took proactive steps in attempts to thwart backlash violence. On September 12, 2001, the U.S. Congress passed a resolution affirming the need to protect the civil liberties of all Americans and condemning bigotry against Arabs, Muslims, and South Asians. The resolution stated:

> Be it resolved that Congress (1) declares that in the quest to identify, bring to justice, and punish the perpetrators and sponsors of the terrorist attacks on the United States of September 11, 2001, that the civil rights and civil liberties of all Americans, including Arab Americans, American Muslims, and Americans from South Asia, should be protected and (2) condemns any acts of violence or discrimination against any Americans, including Arab Americans, American Muslims, and Americans from South Asia.

On September 13, 2001, the U.S. Commission on Civil Rights made a hate crimes hotline available. At the height of the backlash, the hotline reportedly received up to 70 calls per hour.[46] The Equal Employment Opportunity Commission (EEOC) introduced a new category designed to track instances of employment discrimination against Muslims, Arabs, Middle Easterners, South Asians, and Sikhs.[47] The EEOC also posted a special "9/11 Information" section with resources on its Web site and issued fact sheets for employers and employees about workplace rights for religious and ethnic minorities.

Soon after 9/11, Secretary of Education Rod Paige sent a letter to every school superintendent and college president in the country. Paige called on educators to take preventative measures against incidents of anti-Arab and anti-Muslim harassment, which he deemed "unconditionally wrong" and intolerable in our nation's schools.

The U.S. Department of Justice created the Initiative to Combat Post-9/11 Discriminatory Backlash with the stated goals of reducing the incidence of bias-related attacks and ensuring that perpetrators of hate crimes would be brought to justice.[48] The Justice Department's Civil Rights Division announced in a September 13, 2001, press release that "any threats of violence or discrimination against Arab or Muslim Americans or Americans of South Asian descent are not just wrong and un-American, but also are unlawful and will be treated as such."

Six days after the terrorist attacks, President Bush visited the Islamic center on Massachusetts Avenue in Washington, D.C. In a highly publicized address, President Bush proclaimed, "Islam is peace." He pointed out that "America counts millions of Muslims amongst our citizens" who are "doctors, lawyers, law professors, members of the military, entrepreneurs, shopkeepers, moms, and dads," and "they need to be treated with respect." He continued, "Those who feel like they can intimidate our fellow citizens to take out their anger don't represent the best of America, they represent the worst of humankind, and they should be ashamed of that kind of behavior."[49]

Despite efforts to combat intolerance in the weeks and months following 9/11, many individuals in the United States became the targets of hostility. Arabs and Muslims (as well as Latinos, South Asians, and other individuals who were mistakenly perceived to be Arab or Muslim based on their skin color, dress, or organizational affiliations) suffered an unprecedented outbreak of backlash violence.

The FBI—which is the government entity tasked with compiling and publishing data on hate crimes motivated by religious, racial, ethnicity/national origin, sexual orientation, or disability bias—received 481 reports of anti-Islamic hate crimes in 2001. This represents a 1,600 percent increase over the 28 incidents recorded in the year 2000.[50] The sharp rise in hate crimes is even more staggering when considering that almost all the incidents recorded in 2001 occurred in the less-than-four-month period *after* the 9/11 attacks.[51]

No documentation is available from the FBI, or any other federal agency, regarding the prevalence of anti-Arab hate crimes either prior to or in the aftermath of 9/11. This is because FBI hate-crime statistics do not include a separate category for anti-Arab incidents. Most government definitions actually classify Arab Americans racially as "white," a fact that many Americans are surprised to learn, since popular representations tend to depict Arabs as racial and cultural outsiders. It is worth noting, though, that the number of recorded "anti-other ethnicity/national origin" hate crime incidents more than quadrupled from 354 in 2000 to 1,501 in 2001. The dramatic increase presumably resulted from the post-9/11 backlash against South Asians and Middle Easterners.[52]

Government prosecutors contend that most of the 481 anti-Islamic hate crimes recorded in 2001, which included assaults, bombing plots, acts of vandalism, arson, violent threats and intimidation, and shootings, were in direct retaliation for the attacks on the World Trade Center and the Pentagon. At least twelve people, and perhaps as many as nineteen, were murdered as a result of anti-Arab and anti-Muslim hatred.[53]

The first confirmed backlash-related homicide occurred on September 15, 2001, just four days after the 9/11 attacks. Balbir Singh Sodhi, a native of Punjab, India, was shot five times while he was planting flowers in front of his Mesa, Arizona, gas station. Sodhi was neither Arab nor Muslim but was apparently targeted because he had a beard and wore a turban as part of his Sikh faith. Sodhi's killer, Frank Roque, left the scene and shot and wounded a Lebanese American clerk at another gas station and later opened fire on the home of a family of Afghan descent. As Roque was being apprehended for Sodhi's murder, he shouted, "I stand for America all the way! I'm an American. Go ahead. Arrest me and let those terrorists run wild!"[54] Law enforcement records indicate that before the slaying, Roque had bragged at a local bar that he was going to "kill the ragheads responsible for September 11."[55] Roque was obviously incapable of distinguishing his victim from the turbaned images of bin Laden that the media widely broadcast after the World Trade Center collapse.

Waqar Hasan, a Pakistani Muslim, was also shot and killed on September 15, 2001, as he stood cooking hamburgers at his grocery store near Dallas, Texas.[56] Mark Stroman, who was convicted of killing Hasan, later admitted to murdering Vasudev Patel, an Indian man who owned a convenience store in Mesquite, Texas, and to shooting and blinding Rais Uddin, a Pakistani immigrant and gas station attendant. Stroman attributed the violent acts to his rage over the 9/11 attacks.[57] After his arrest, Stroman said, "I did what every American wanted to do but didn't. They didn't have the nerve."[58]

In the spring of 2003, Larme Price, a thirty-year-old man with a history of drug abuse and mental health problems, went on a violent crime spree in Brooklyn and Queens. Over a seven-week period, he shot five men in the head at point-blank range, killing four of them and seriously wounding the fifth. All the deceased were immigrants—from Russia, Guyana, India, and Yemen. Price eventually broke down and turned himself in to the police. In his confession, Price told officers that he had targeted people from the Middle East in his quest for revenge for the World Trade Center attacks. Only one of the four slaying victims was actually from the Middle East, although Price was apparently under the impression that they all were.[59]

Large metropolitan areas with highly visible Muslim populations were especially prone to surges in hate-crime activity. In Chicago and Los Angeles, for example, law enforcement officials reported fifteen times the number of anti-Arab and anti-Muslim bias incidents in 2001 compared to the preceding year. The city of Phoenix recorded no anti-Arab or anti-Muslim hate crimes in the eight months prior to 9/11 but logged forty-six such hate crimes in the last four months of 2001.[60] On September 12, 2001, a mob of hundreds of angry whites, some shouting, "Kill the Arabs," some wielding weapons, commenced a march to the largest predominantly Arab mosque in Chicago. More than 125 suburban police officers were called in to keep the mob from storming the mosque and the primarily Muslim residential community surrounding it. The following night, a similar march occurred, and the police were called in again. For three nights, the police were forced to form a human barricade around the neighborhood to protect the citizens.[61] One of the demonstrators told a newspaper reporter, "I'm proud to be American and I hate Arabs and I always have."[62]

Communities with fewer Muslims were also vulnerable to xenophobic attacks. In Irving, Texas, someone fired nine shots through the windows of the Islamic center, shattering the glass and damaging the furnishings. Vandals painted "Jesus is the Lord and Allah is the Devil" and other vicious comments outside a mosque in Canejo Valley, California. An angry

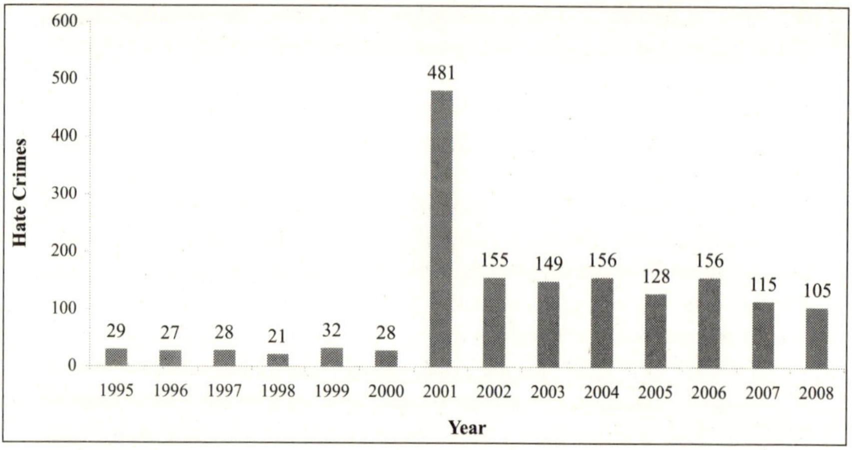

Figure 2.1. *Anti-Islamic hate crimes, 1995–2008. (Source: FBI Uniform Crime Reporting Program, "Hate Crime Statistics," 2008, www.fbi.gov/ucr/ucr.htm#hate, accessed January 23, 2010.)*

Ohio man rammed his car through the front wall of the Islamic center of Cleveland. Someone hurled bricks wrapped with hate messages through the windows of an Islamic bookstore in Alexandria, Virginia. An Islamic school for children in Charlotte, North Carolina, was forced to close down after teachers received a spate of threatening phone calls. In Huntington, New York, a man attempted to run over a Muslim woman and then threatened to kill her for "destroying my country."

FBI data indicate that the most severe wave of hate crimes occurred in the nine weeks immediately after the World Trade Center and the Pentagon were hit. Although the numbers of recorded hate crimes have decreased in the years since,[63] they remain well above the pre-9/11 levels (see Figure 2.1).

Obviously violent crimes perpetrated against Muslims increased considerably following 9/11, but the numbers do not tell the entire story. Federal hate-crime statistics only document (1) acts defined as criminal under hate-crimes legislation, which varies from state to state; (2) acts that victims have actually reported to authorities, which is problematic because hate-crime survivors often do not report bias incidents for many reasons, including fear of retaliation by the perpetrators, post-traumatic stress, feelings of self-blame or powerlessness, mistrust of the police, or fear of retribution within the criminal justice system; (3) acts that local and state law enforcement officials have recorded as hate crimes and have submitted to the federal authorities; and (4) in most cases, the most heinous of crimes.

Underreporting of hate crime is clearly an issue. But how significant is the problem? The FBI has tallied somewhere between about six thousand

and ten thousand hate-crime incidents annually since it began publishing the numbers in 1992. Yet, a 2005 special report by the U.S. Department of Justice, based on an analysis of detailed National Crime Victimization Surveys, found that the actual annual level of hate crime in the United States averaged some 191,000 incidents—in other words, approximately twenty to thirty times higher than the numbers that the FBI reported each year.[64] Official hate-crime statistics simply do not reflect the true number of incidents committed against any given minority population, nor do these numbers capture the full psychological and social impact of these crimes on the targeted community.

Other federal agencies noted significant increases in complaints involving acts of discrimination and racial profiling after 9/11. The EEOC investigated 654 cases alleging 9/11-related workplace discrimination based on ethnicity, race, or national origin and 706 charges of religious bias against Muslims in the year following the attacks. More than 75 percent of these EEOC cases involved persons, most of whom were Arab, South Asian, and/or Muslim, who were wrongfully terminated from their jobs.[65] During the first eight months after the attacks, the U.S. Department of Transportation (DOT) investigated 111 complaints from airline passengers who were singled out at security screenings for interrogations or full-body searches because of their ethnic or religious appearance. The DOT reported that it was also investigating an additional thirty-one complaints by persons who were barred altogether from boarding airplanes.[66] Arab American Congressional Representative Darrell Issa and a Muslim American Secret Service agent on President Bush's security detail were among those not allowed to fly.

Traditional popular and legal discourse on racial profiling has focused on "Driving While Black" and, more recently, "Driving While Brown." These expressions are used to draw attention to the frequency with which police use traffic stops as a pretext to pull over and search African Americans and Latinos. After 9/11, Arab and Muslim American advocates coined the phrases "Flying While Arab" and "Flying While Muslim" to highlight the ways that members of their communities were being profiled and subjected to humiliating security procedures based solely on their skin colors, religious attire, countries of origin, or ethnic-sounding names.

A number of advocacy and human-rights groups issued their own reports on the prevalence of hate crimes and discrimination perpetrated against religious and ethnic minorities in the aftermath of 9/11. These documents illustrate the difficulty associated with separating anti-Arab and anti-Muslim incidents; the hostility encountered is often directed indiscriminately at either or both Arabs and Muslims—or anyone mistaken for them. Even so, the available reports suggest a clearly identifiable pattern of post-9/11 retaliatory attacks.

The group South Asian American Leaders of Tomorrow (SAALT) reviewed newspapers and other media serving major cities throughout the United States and found that in the first week after the terrorist attacks, 645 separate bias incidents were directed toward Americans perceived to be of Middle Eastern descent.[67] ADC documented more than 700 violent incidents targeting Arab Americans and other minorities in the first nine weeks following the attacks. ADC also verified more than 80 instances of discriminatory removal of passengers from airplanes and more than 800 cases of employment discrimination against Arab Americans.[68] The Sikh American Legal Defense and Educational Fund estimated that 250 post-9/11 hate crimes were perpetrated against Sikhs, who are often misidentified as Muslim or of Middle Eastern descent due to their appearance.[69] The National Asian Pacific American Legal Consortium confirmed nearly 250 bias-motivated attacks and 2 murders targeting Asian Pacific Americans in the three months following 9/11.[70] Human Rights Watch cited more than 2,000 backlash-related crimes against Arabs, Muslims, and other minority citizens and immigrants.[71]

CAIR issued a special report in the aftermath of the 9/11 attacks. The report documented 1,717 cases of anti-Muslim harassment in the first six months following 9/11.[72] CAIR also publishes annual civil-rights reports that track incidents of anti-Muslim bias in the United States. As illustrated in Figure 2.2, reported acts of discrimination committed against Muslim Americans have steadily and consistently risen since 1995, the year when CAIR first began tracking anti-Muslim abuses in response to the rash of hate crimes that followed the Oklahoma City bombing. Although the most striking increase in violent incidents followed the 9/11 attacks, the data show that anger and acts of discrimination directed against Muslim Americans have continued to escalate. These trends likely signify the lasting imprint of 9/11 as well as new hostilities stoked by the wars in Afghanistan and Iraq, conflicts erupting in the Middle East, and the focus on the threat of Islamic fundamentalism in the rhetoric surrounding the global War on Terror.

In addition to enduring ill-treatment at the hands of fellow citizens and private entities, Arab and Muslim Americans became the targets of special governmental legislation and other law enforcement measures adopted after 9/11.[73] These measures, which were ostensibly designed to combat terrorism, have led to a systematic erosion of civil rights for all Americans but have been especially devastating to Arab and Muslim communities. Portions of the USA PATRIOT Act and other post-9/11 federal legislation empower law enforcement officials to (1) arbitrarily choose foreign or domestic organizations suspected of supporting terrorism, and then—using secret evidence—jail or deport anyone who gives them material support; (2) jail those who commit even minor criminal offenses deemed "dangers to human

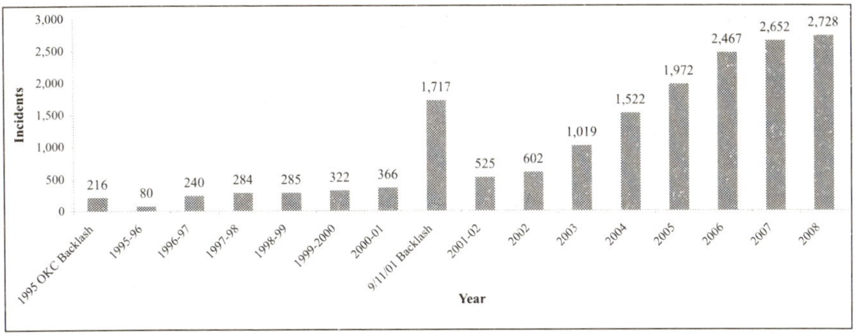

Figure 2.2. *Anti-Muslim bias incidents, 1995–2008. (Source: Council on American-Islamic Relations, "The Status of Muslim Civil Rights in the United States: Seeking Full Inclusion," Washington, D.C., 2009.)*

life" whose intent is to "intimidate society" or "influence government policy"; (3) detain U.S. citizens and noncitizens suspected of being enemy combatants without bail and without access to attorneys; (4) try such individuals in secret before military tribunals; and (5) prepare detention camps to incarcerate U.S. citizens and foreign nationals for prolonged periods of time.[74]

After the passage of the USA PATRIOT Act, Attorney General John Ashcroft announced further measures authorizing FBI agents to spy on domestic groups without having to show evidence of a crime. Agents were permitted to covertly monitor public meetings and religious assemblies for the first time in decades.[75] In 2006, the U.S. Congress passed the Military Commissions Act, which allows for the indefinite imprisonment of anyone who donates money to a charity that turns up on a list of "terrorist organizations" or who speaks out against the government's policies. The law also calls for secret trials for citizens and noncitizens alike.[76]

In the weeks immediately following the 9/11 terrorist attacks, local, state, and federal law enforcement agencies rounded up and imprisoned between 1,200 and 5,000 Muslim and Arab men.[77] The government refused to reveal the detainees' identities, give them access to lawyers, disclose information regarding the charges against them, or allow them to have contact with their families.[78] According to a report from the U.S. Department of Justice, the men were subjected to "a pattern of physical and verbal abuse by some correctional officers" in the detention facilities.[79] Under the threat of a lawsuit, the federal government eventually released the names of some of the men who had been swept up in the post-9/11 mass arrests. Most of the men were picked up on minor immigration violations, and many were quietly deported after months or years in detention. None of the men was charged with any terror-related activity.[80]

In the fall of 2001 and spring of 2002, representatives from the FBI and other law enforcement agencies began visiting mosques, universities, and homes to conduct "voluntary" interviews with nearly eight thousand Middle Eastern and South Asian men between the ages of eighteen and thirty-three who were legally residing in the United States as students or visitors.[81] The government acknowledged that none of the men selected for interviews was individually suspected of wrongdoing; instead, the interrogations were meant only to uncover leads that might prove useful in the antiterrorism campaign.[82] During the interviews, 90 percent of those questioned were asked about their political and religious beliefs, whether they sympathized with the 9/11 terrorists, whether they had any scientific or weapons training, and where they had traveled in the past.[83] Of the thousands of men interviewed, none was found to have any connections to terrorist activity.

Also in the wake of 9/11, Islamic charities, businesses, and homes were raided, and assets and private property were seized pending investigation.[84] In December 2002, more than seven hundred Muslim men were arrested after they had waited in line for several hours at Immigration and Naturalization Service offices to register under the newly established National Security Entry-Exit Registration System (NSEERS).[85] After this incident, the Associated Press reported that Muslim families from across the United States were seeking refuge in Canada. Dozens of civil-liberties and human-rights organizations subsequently called on the Bush administration to eliminate the mandatory NSEERS registration program on the grounds that it "appears to target people based on national origin, race, and religion rather than intelligence information."[86]

The post-9/11 arrests, detentions, and deportations of thousands of young Muslim men resulted in several high-profile cases. These incidents sent shockwaves of fear through the entire Muslim community. For example, the media offered extensive coverage of the cases of U.S. Army Captain James Yee, Portland attorney Brandon Mayfield, and University of Idaho doctoral student Sami al-Hussayen. These three Muslim men were arrested, held in solitary confinement for weeks, and labeled "terrorists." All three were eventually exonerated of all charges brought against them (in the Mayfield case, the FBI even issued a rare formal apology for its egregious investigative errors regarding a false fingerprint match that allegedly connected Mayfield to the March 11, 2004, Madrid, Spain, train bombings). Despite the legal victories for the defendants, the damage to their personal reputations and to the image of the Muslim community was done.

The statistics presented in this chapter offer a general sense of the contours of the post-9/11 backlash. Yet when we merely examine the numerical estimates of acts of discrimination, hate crimes, and profiling incidents, they fail, as statistics often do, to describe what these forms of exclusion and violence meant to the people most affected. These numbers tell us nothing of what the discrimination looked or felt like on the ground, nor do they offer even a hint of the isolation and fear that Muslim Americans experienced after the attacks. The numbers shed no light on the ways that the backlash impacted the daily lives, routines, and relationships of Muslims. It is only through listening to the voices of Muslim Americans that we can begin to comprehend the scope and severity of the backlash as well as to appreciate the sometimes remarkable ways that Muslims adapted to the exclusion. With that in mind, the subsequent chapters in this book draw on qualitative data to give voice to the lived experiences of a sample of Muslim men and women whom the post-9/11 backlash directly affected.[87]

3

Encountering Intolerance

Over the two decades prior to the 9/11 terrorist attacks, several scholars of Islam began to write with an increasing degree of urgency about the rise of anti-Muslim hostility in the United States. This work focused on negative representations of Muslims in the news and popular culture,[1] the post–Cold War construction of the "Islamic threat" by U.S. political leaders,[2] the selective targeting of Muslim immigrants by law enforcement officials,[3] and the growing number of religious-discrimination lawsuits filed in state and federal courts.[4] In 1991, the word *Islamophobia*—which refers to a hatred of Islam and the resultant fear or dislike of Muslims—first appeared in print in an American periodical.[5] It has been included in the *Oxford English Dictionary* every year since 1997.[6] The Council on American-Islamic Relations (CAIR) issued its initial report on bias crimes committed against Muslim people and their places of work and worship in 1995. CAIR has since published a series of annual reports that chronicle a disturbing upward trend in instances of discrimination and civil-rights violations. Jane Smith, a respected scholar of Islam, argued in 1999, "Prejudice against their religion is a reality with which all American Muslims must deal in one way or another."[7]

The persons represented in *Behind the Backlash* were born between the years 1966 and 1983. Thus, the individuals who participated in this study grew up during a period when the vilification and victimization of Muslims in the United States was becoming more common. This era was also a time of rapid growth among the Muslim American community. From 1990 to 2000, the Muslim American population increased by nearly 40 percent, and a significant number of new mosques and Islamic schools were founded in rural and metropolitan areas.[8] The face of Islam in America began to change as well. With the post-1965 influx of new arrivals from South Asia and the Middle East, immigrant Muslims soon outnumbered converts among African Americans.[9] The rising visibility of Islam has sparked an intense and ongoing debate concerning the role of religion in American public life and the potential "assimilability"—or ability to adapt to the dominant culture—of Muslims.

This chapter explores the challenges that the interviewees faced prior to the 9/11 attacks. Understanding this predisaster context is important for two reasons. First, it explains, at least in part, *why* the post-9/11 backlash against Muslim Americans was so swift and severe. Second, it helps put in perspective the various strategies that Muslims drew on as they attempted to respond to and recover from the unprecedented outbreak of bias-related incidents after 9/11. (I take up these points in later chapters.) As the narratives presented below illustrate, Muslim Americans were no strangers to hostile treatment before 9/11. In fact, the persons I interviewed reported that they regularly encountered confusion, stereotypes, and harassment as a result of their minority religious status.

The data included here, which are necessarily retrospective, are based on interviews that I collected with Muslim adults in the two years following the 9/11 terrorist attacks. Undoubtedly, the time frame in which the data were gathered shaped the memories that the participants recalled and shared with me. Indeed, 9/11 was a catalytic event that caused the young men and women to reflect carefully and self-consciously on their prior experiences with mistreatment, ultimately heightening their awareness of their personal and social identities as Muslim Americans.[10] As the participants struggled to come to terms with the post-9/11 fallout, they actually had a greater capacity for insight into their present situations and past circumstances. It was through this process of critical reflection that important moments—which may have previously been taken for granted—rose to the surface. The fact that many of the experiences that the interviewees described were remarkably similar underscores the pervasiveness of anti-Muslim sentiment that was present long before the assaults on the World Trade Center and Pentagon.

Discovering Difference

Adults often imagine children to be completely unaware of status differences that mark American society. Yet social science research has shown that children as young as two years of age understand that race and gender are important characteristics that define individuals and confer certain privileges (or disadvantages) on entire groups.[11] Less attention has been devoted to children's knowledge or use of religious categorizations in everyday interaction. However, some evidence shows that American children and adolescents who practice faiths other than Christianity—the dominant religion in U.S. social life—often find that other youth and adults ignore, invalidate, and even actively contest these belief systems.[12]

Most of the respondents in this study could not identify specific moments when they realized that their Islamic faith marked them as outside the norm. Instead, they described a more general sense of "difference" from the other children in their schools and neighborhoods. Although they shared many things in common with their non-Muslim friends, they were aware that their religion made them stand out from their predominantly Christian peers. Habeel remembered how, when he was a child, his mother used to call him inside to complete his daily prayers. This practice made him feel out of the ordinary, especially when his playmates would question his actions:

> I think that I always felt different as a Muslim. Maybe not my musical taste or the TV shows I like to watch, but there's something different about us. I never felt quite the same as every other average American kid. When we were little, we used to go outside and play with our friends across the street, and then our mother would call us in to pray. The kids would ask, "Why are you going in to pray?" That's one of the things, just little things that add up. So even though you don't feel totally alienated by everyone else, there's always a bit of a difference.

In addition to their religious minority status, the majority of the participants were immigrants or the children of immigrants with roots in the Middle East, South Asia, and many other parts of the world. Their membership in multiple minority groups—religious, ethnic, immigrant—meant that their faith, their cultural practices, and their physical characteristics often stood in contrast to the white, Judeo-Christian norm associated with the United States. Hafeez, a second-generation immigrant of Pakistani descent, was raised in a predominantly white neighborhood in Massachusetts. He described the period when he first began to realize how his religion and ethnic background distinguished him from his peers:

> I can remember I was pretty young, in maybe second or third grade. Most of my friends were overwhelmingly white, Protestant. It was just the little things that I noticed. My parents would fast [during the Islamic holy month of Ramadan] and no one else would. We don't

> celebrate Christmas. Christmas is so big in America. Oh yeah, and we're brown. [*Laughs.*] Do you know what I mean? I guess it was just that I knew . . . I look different from them, so I am different from them. I believe different things. I think that is when I figured out that to be American was to be Christian or Jewish. To be Muslim and brown was to be not American.

Even at a young age, Hafeez had begun to associate what it means to be "American" with specific practices (for example, celebrating Christmas) as well as with membership in the dominant racial group and most prominent faith communities in this nation.

Like the two men quoted above, many others recognized early on that numerous practices associated with their religion or culture set them apart from their peers and most of the adults in their lives. Some of the respondents began fasting (abstaining from eating or drinking anything from dawn until sunset) during Ramadan at the age of seven or eight years. This tradition meant that they went for an entire month without eating lunch at school, which sometimes drew unwanted attention from teachers and other students. The language that they spoke in their homes was usually something other than English. The food that their mothers would prepare looked, tasted, and smelled different than the dishes that were served in their school cafeterias and their friends' homes. Their Islamic names sounded unfamiliar and led to uncomfortable moments, such as when strangers would stumble over the pronunciation or classmates would tease them on the playground. The clothes that they wore tended to be less revealing and more "old-fashioned" than what their peers would wear.

Some of the respondents grew frustrated with the overwhelming sense of difference. Ameena described how her mother, who was a strong proponent of the importance of modesty in Islam, would not allow her or her siblings to wear shorts in the summer. This angered Ameena and made her feel like an outcast:

> My mom never let us wear shorts. I used to get so mad at her. I was like, "It doesn't matter. If you're young, you can do whatever you want." But she was just like that. So I was already different. When you're young, everybody notices everything about you. Everybody used to ask me, "Why aren't you wearing shorts?" It was embarrassing. When I got older, it wasn't such a big deal. But in fourth grade, it was a big deal.

Yasmin also struggled with balancing the demands of her faith and the pressure to fit in with her friends. In contrast to Ameena, however, Yasmin emphasized that she "didn't mind" dressing in more modest clothing, which meant wearing pants and long-sleeved shirts all year round. She was more concerned about the lack of availability of loose yet fashionable attire for girls and young women:

> The difficulties for me were how to dress. It's very difficult to find clothes that I would wear but that also cover my body in the right way. The only loose clothes are made for grannies. [*Laughs.*] I always had to really be creative in finding a way to dress. It doesn't sound so important, but it really is as an everyday thing. That's how people see you. I can't wear the same clothes that everyone wears. I have to dress a little bit different. I still want to fit in, at least in certain ways, just to be one with my generation and my peers. It was really hard.

Most of the women talked at some length about the external pressure—especially from their friends and the media—to wear more stylish and sexy clothing. The men, on the other hand, rarely mentioned this issue. This disparity may be due in part to the intense focus on women's dress within the Muslim community as well as a more general and pervasive societal emphasis on female beauty and sexuality. The men were more likely to remember feeling left out because they did not drink alcohol or try to "get with girls" (having sex outside the realm of marriage and consuming alcohol are prohibited in Islam). Jamil explained that when he was growing up, the pressure to engage in these sorts of activities was mostly indirect but was powerful nonetheless:

> The problem is you can't pinpoint it in one place. It's not so much because people are just peer pressuring you to drink, do drugs, whatever. Nobody's forcing you consciously. It's just when there's a whole bunch of people who are one way, it's natural for someone to want to be part of that, too. Even in junior high, like going to dances. If you didn't go, everyone asks, "Why didn't you go?" You're like, "I don't do that. I don't go to dances." Then in high school, the main thing they wanted to do is drink, party. Those are things that I don't enjoy doing, and it was always something that showed how I'm different. It was hard; it's a big barrier in this society not to drink, and it was like it came up in every conversation. It's not as simple to Muslims. We have to say, "No, I'm not going to do it." To another person, they may be like, "Why? It's just a drink." But it's not like that for us.

All the interviewees experienced pressure to assimilate to "American" values and norms. This pressure varied somewhat, however, depending on the environment in which the participant was raised. Those who grew up in predominantly white, Judeo-Christian neighborhoods described more pervasive demands to "fit in" than did those who were raised in more populous and diverse urban areas. For example, Randa grew up in a small town in upstate New York. She was the only Muslim girl in her entire school, and she was keenly aware of the impact of being a minority: "I don't know what it is about American high school and junior high that makes people want to be in the in crowd and do things that are considered cool. That pressure was there. When I was in high school, I identified much less with being Muslim than I did after high school. You don't want to stick out too much. You don't want people to think you're a weirdo."

The feelings of difference regarding their Islamic faith took a significant toll on some of the respondents. Ayesha spoke of an "inferiority complex" that she developed as a girl. Very few Muslim families lived in the community where she was raised, and she had just one close Muslim friend throughout her childhood. Thus, she had very little social support as she attempted to field a seemingly nonstop barrage of questions about Islam and life as a Muslim:

> When I was younger, I had the biggest inferiority complex. I felt like everyone was always asking me, "Why aren't you eating this?" "Why aren't you doing that?" "Why can't you be like this?" Because I'm Muslim. That was the answer to every question. It's against my religion. That's what I was taught to say. So I grew up with everyone knowing I was Muslim. But they didn't see it as something great and exotic and new. They saw it as something weird and strange, and they wanted to know why I'm like that. Why can't I just be like everyone else? So I started thinking like that. I wanted to be like everyone else, do Christmas, go out with my friends instead of coming home and doing my homework. Growing up as a Muslim girl was difficult, because I'm different. It wasn't until later that I understood what it meant to be a Muslim and to appreciate who I am and to have confidence in myself.

For Ayesha, her sense of being different and inferior emerged as a result of a normative context that privileges the dominant faith—in this case, Christianity—and marginalizes minority religions. The questions that outside members imposed, such as when her friends wanted to know why she could not eat pork or date boys, made her feel like she was being judged as "weird" or "strange." Ayesha's personal lack of knowledge of Islam further exacerbated this issue. She could not offer any theological explanation for why she was prohibited from doing certain things and instead could use only the stock answer that her parents had supplied: "It's against my religion." It was only after she reached adulthood and acquired more religious knowledge, and subsequently became more confident in responding to inquiries, that she began to feel self-assured. During her teen years, she was more concerned about being accepted and doing things that other American youth would do, such as celebrating Christmas and hanging out after school.

Given the tremendous pressure to assimilate to dominant norms, it is not surprising that some of the interviewees admitted that they cast off their religious identity in an attempt to "pass" as part of mainstream society. It was not something they were proud of, but they explained their behavior as a result of a need to fit in or as stemming from a lack of understanding of the true meaning of Islam. Maryam, a young woman who was wearing a hijab when I first interviewed her in 2001, discussed her earlier fears of being mocked for wearing religious attire: "In the beginning, when I was younger, I was like, I'm not going to be seen with the hijab. The kids are going to make fun of me. I was completely against all of this. I had to dress in the newest jeans that came out, have the nicest sneakers. . . . It really was a big deal."

In the United States, freedom of religion is a constitutionally guaranteed right that the First Amendment protects. The participants in this study recognized and were grateful for this right, although they admitted that the American context is not always as conducive to practicing their faith as they might like. Islamic holidays were rarely recognized in their schools or their parents' workplaces. For those who lived in smaller towns, few other Muslims outside their immediate families were available to celebrate holidays with, and the nearest mosque was usually miles away. Following Islamic dietary laws was difficult, as religiously permissible halal food was unavailable in most restaurants and could be acquired only in specialty grocery stores. When at school, at work, or traveling, finding a space to complete the required five daily prayers was challenging. Jinan felt that attempting to observe an Islamic lifestyle in the United States was more difficult than any hardships associated with being viewed as a religious outsider:

> Obviously, the way people view you, always being the Other, that is not good, but I don't think it's just how people look at Muslims that complicates things. It is more of a challenge just to practice my religion. There's never anywhere to eat the proper foods. There's almost never any place to pray. We pray five times a day. When you have to pray, you have to pray. I remember one time I was on a long car trip with my family. We went out into a rest stop in some woods so we wouldn't be so obvious. We were praying in there. There were secu-

> rity guards and these other people at the rest stop who were just like standing around, staring at us. It made me feel very proud, because my family, we just kept going. If I have to pray, I have to pray.

For Muslims, completing their five daily prayers involves engaging in a number of distinct postures, ranging from standing with arms crossed across the chest to kneeling and prostrating before God. Muslims face the direction of the holy city of Mecca when they pray, and they are supposed to perform their prayers at certain preestablished times each day. When forced to pray in public spaces, Muslim Americans often attract unwanted attention from a predominantly non-Muslim public. Jinan remembered feeling proud that her family continued with their prayers, even as curious onlookers gathered around, but her reaction to this incident was uncommon when compared to those of other participants. Most often, the interviewees spoke of feeling anxious or alienated when their personal faith would become public spectacles. One man told me that throughout his teen years, he had an "unconquerable anxiety about praying in public, wearing Muslim clothes, or doing anything that could be construed as Islamic." Another woman noted that she always felt "isolated" as a result of her minority religious status. She continued, "Sometimes just feeling normal, like a normal person . . . you just don't get that feeling a lot."

Recognizing Stereotypes

A stereotype is a preconceived idea that attributes certain traits, behaviors, tastes, or other characteristics to a group of people. In essence, stereotypes are the images we carry around in our minds, which may be positive or negative, about most or all persons of a particular race, ethnicity, religion, gender, or age, to name a few. Stereotypes may or may not emerge from some kernel of truth, but they always involve widely held overgeneralizations that do not take individual differences into account.[13] Misconceptions, which are closely associated with stereotypes, involve objectively false or mistaken views, ideas, or beliefs.

For the Muslims whom I interviewed, it was during their formative years when they began to realize how many misconceptions and negative stereotypes about Islam and Muslims exist. Although they did not use the language of social science, it was clear that the respondents distinguished between people who were simply uninformed and as a consequence held incorrect ideas about Islam and those who actively engaged in hostile stereotyping. Randa argued that most non-Muslims are not inherently prejudiced against Muslims; instead, she believed that they simply lack exposure to Islamic values and beliefs in everyday life. From her perspective, this lack of exposure leads to ignorance and presumably harmful misconceptions:

> What I saw early on in my life is that, generally speaking, out of all the non-Muslims that I've met, people are not genuinely hateful. They're not lashing out at Muslims out of blind fear; they don't have an inherent hate in them. But there's a lot of ignorance. Islam, Muslims haven't been in the public eye much in America. That means that a lot of people don't know about our community, who makes it up, what our religion is. I think there's always been a lot of ignorance out there.

The Muslim men and women told numerous stories about persons whom they had encountered over the years who were unaware that Islam is a religion. The lack of recognition of their faith was bewildering to many, especially given that Islam claims more followers globally than any other religion besides Christianity. Ahmad recalled having to explain to a high school classmate that Islam is not a country. He also attempted to point out the distinction between Muslims and Arabs, although he wasn't sure his fellow student understood:

> We had a student in our class. She said, "I need to know something about your religion because I have a test in world religion class. Tell me, Islam is the country?" Me and my friends, we were shocked. At first we thought she was kidding, but she kept going. "What is Arab?" She was really funny. I was like, "Wait a minute, Islam is a religion." She was like, "Okay, let me write it down. . . . Islam is a religion." This is how a lot of people work. Then when I told her there were Arab Muslims, but to be a Muslim you don't have to be an Arab, she was like, "Really? I didn't know that." She wrote that down, too, but I think she was still, um, confused.

As Ahmad's quote illustrates, the fact that Muslims can be of any nationality or ethnic background represents a source of genuine confusion for non-Muslims. One young woman remembered how surprised her friend was to learn that Muslims could be white:

> I had a pamphlet about "What Is Islam?" My friends were looking through it. They saw pictures of people showing the diversity of Islam. Then this guy says to me, "Oh, there are white Muslims?" I was like, "Yeah." It was clear they were not understanding that Islam is just a religion, just like Judaism and Christianity, not understanding

> that we are so similar. We believe in Jesus, Abraham, Adam, and Eve. Allah is just another word for God. It's how you say God in Arabic. It's not like some deity that is constructed out of wood.

South Asian Muslims also struggled to educate others about the diversity of Islam. They were faced with explaining that not all South Asians are Hindu and that millions of Muslims live on the Indian subcontinent. Leena, a second-generation immigrant, described how she tried to clarify the difference between nationality and faith:

> When I would tell people that I am Pakistani American, it seems like a lot of people know where Pakistan is and know that it was part of India and they broke up in 1947. They say, "Oh, so you're Hindu." I say, "No. I am Pakistani, and I am Muslim. I have a friend who is from India. She's not Hindu, she's Muslim." They don't understand the difference between Islam and a country, India and Hinduism as country and religion.

Some of the interviewees remembered their textbooks, ostensibly designed to educate students, as a primary source of misconceptions about Muslims, Islam, and the Middle East. For example, Ameena noted that one of her middle school textbooks incorrectly referred to Muslims as "Muhammadans." Another respondent, Mina, was put in the uncomfortable position of correcting her teacher and classmates when one of the books they were reading represented Muslim women in an overtly stereotypical way and implied that they have basically no rights when compared to Muslim men: "In class, issues came up about women and their place in Islam. They said wrong things in the textbook. I used to speak out; I was the only Muslim girl in the class. It was hard, but I had to speak out, just try to correct the stuff that was clearly not true." Mina and many other interviewees were quick to point out that in the Qur'an, women and men are viewed as equal before God.

Oversimplified and even distorted representations of Muslims and Arabs in American textbooks have been a source of concern for members of these communities for many years. In the 1970s and again in the 1990s, a team of Middle Eastern studies scholars reviewed dozens of secondary school geography and world history textbooks.[14] In a few cases, they found well-written, thoroughly researched textbooks with few discernible faults. Some books actually went out of their way to refute popular myths. Yet the majority of the books that were reviewed contained an abundance of errors in fact, emphasis, and interpretation. Rather than correcting Western stereotypes and prejudices, these books perpetuated negative images of Muslims and the

Islamic faith. Some of the most blatant examples of stereotyping included vivid descriptions of the "wild warriors of Islam" and claims that Islam "is not a gentle faith." Another book asserted, "The Moslem [*sic*] heaven is a man's heaven, where women are mainly servants." More subtle statements that were included in the texts, such as "Muslims worship a god named Allah," also encouraged the belief that Muslims worship a diety wholly different from the deity worshipped by Christians or Jews. Yet Allah is simply the Arabic word meaning "God." In fact, people who speak Arabic, be they Christians, Jews, or Muslims, often say "Allah" to describe God, just as God is called "Gott" in German and "Dieu" in French.[15]

Christian missionaries have invoked the notion that Allah is a different or pagan god for many years. For example, Robert Morey, Christian polemicist and author of the alarmingly titled *The Islamic Invasion: Confronting the World's Fastest Growing Religion,* draws on dubious evidence to assert his claim that "Allah" was an Arab "moon god." Morey's writings lie at the heart of much of the propaganda used against Islam today, including the work of Jack Chick. Over the past four decades, Chick has written and published hundreds of cartoon booklets for use by Christian missionaries attempting to spread the gospel in the United States and overseas. One of these "Chick tracts," as they are informally referred to by pastors, is titled "Allah Had No Son." The pamphlet depicts a Muslim man who threatens to kill an "infidel" Christian man for the offense of calling Allah a moon god. The Christian man pleads with the Muslim to recognize that "Satan has deceived you." The Muslim man eventually responds by acknowledging that "Allah is a false god, Muhammad is not your prophet, and the Qur'an is not your Holy Word." In the end, the Muslim converts to Christianity and concludes that he must go forth and tell his people about the moon god, even if it costs him his life. The wide reach of the publications that Morey and Chick produce may explain, in part, why 10 percent of Americans believe that Muslims worship a moon god.[16]

Sabah, a native of New York City, had a first-hand encounter with the type of religious (mis)information described above. Her neighbor received a pamphlet that subtly, but convincingly, depicted Muslims as violent people who worship a false god. Sabah attempted to show her neighbor that the information she was reading was derogatory and blatantly incorrect in certain sections:

> So we were talking, and she asked me, "Who is Allah?" I said, "Allah is the Arabic word for 'God.'" She said, "Allah is not the moon god?" She had a booklet, a comic book that somebody had given her. She gave it to me. I was like, "That is propaganda against us." This book is something that is directly done against Muslims. I said to her, "Look

> at the pictures." They have this guy with a scruffy beard, dark eyes, big shaggy eyebrows, a very scary-looking guy. If you saw him walking down the street, you'd walk . . . I would walk the other way. Then they bring the Christian peaceful guy with his son trying to teach him a calm way. They have this guy, the Muslim, saying, "I could kill you for something like that." It was frustrating, because it also said Muslims don't believe in Jesus, but we do.

Sabah's friend Natasha chimed in:

> But part of the problem is that Muslims use the word "Allah." Even when we translate things, we still say, "Allah." I think it's because it's such a beautiful name. Even in your daily language, when you say, "Thank God," you say, "Alhamdulillah." You say, "I will come, Insha'Allah" [meaning, "I will come, God willing"], because it's so ingrained in the language, you even say it when you're talking English. But the problem is that then people think, "Okay, Muslims, their god is Allah." On TV even, they'll always say, "They pray to their god, Allah."

Almost all the individuals who participated in this study were raised in the United States, and therefore they clearly understood and identified with American culture. Nevertheless, they were frequently treated as if they were strangers in their own country. Several intersecting forces have undoubtedly shaped this image of Muslims as perpetual foreigners. First, Islam has long been depicted and perceived as a "foreign religion" in the predominantly Judeo-Christian United States. Second, a large number of Muslims immigrated to the United States during the last three decades of the twentieth century. These new waves of immigrants brought with them religious, cultural, and linguistic traits that distinguished them from the rest of the majority population. Third, the ethnic origins of Muslims in the United States, whether immigrant or native-born, show an overwhelming preponderance of persons of color. Thus, racial phenotype, culture, citizenship status, and faith interact in complex ways that mark Muslims as "multiply foreign."[17]

Rashida, whose parents were from Pakistan, was born and raised in rural Illinois. She self-identified as a Midwesterner and was proud of her small-town upbringing. She spoke unaccented English and wore no visible signifiers of her religious faith. However, her "foreign-sounding" name, dark skin, brown eyes, and jet black hair led people to incorrectly assume that she was a visitor to the United States, destined one day to return to her "homeland." Rashida noted that it was mostly older persons who thought that she was a foreigner, rather than those of her own age who were presumably more accustomed to diversity:

> With the younger generation, I haven't felt like people have looked at me differently. It's been, "Yeah, it's cool because she has spirituality and culture." But with older people, sometimes they'll be like, "Do you speak your native tongue?" meaning, Urdu. "Do you want to go back to your homeland?" Would you ask a white person whose parents were from England or Switzerland, "Do you want to go back to your homeland?" No. You see them as American. The older generation will never see me as being just as American as a white American.

Rashida was essentially making the argument that light-skinned European immigrants and their children are "meltable" and thus have the opportunity to become accepted as "fully American." In contrast, South Asian Americans and other immigrants who are racially "of color" can assimilate culturally but cannot melt—that is, disappear—in the American milieu.[18]

The clothing that some of the young men and women wore also affected how they were perceived in terms of nationality and citizenship. The participants recalled that when they donned traditional or ethnic attire, such as baggy pants and long tunics (salwar kameez), people would assume they were newly arrived immigrants who did not understand the dominant culture or language. The women who wore the hijab were the most likely to be stereotyped as foreign. Indeed, as soon as they began wearing the headscarf (which most took up in high school or college, although a few started covering as early as middle school), the women noticed how differently they were treated. After Famina began wearing the headscarf, she had an embarrassing encounter with a well-intentioned student in her high school: "I was standing in the hallway, and this girl came up to me and said, 'Do—you—speak—English? Do—you—need—a—tutor?' [*Laughs and speaks in an exaggerated, drawn-out tone.*] The sad thing was she had met me before; she just didn't recognize me with the headscarf on. I had to say, 'Hey, it's me, Famina.'" Famina's friend added, "This is not uncommon. You've got to understand, a lot of people assume we can't speak English, or they speak to us more loudly."

Some strangers who would overhear the headscarf-wearing women converse seemed amazed at how fluent they were in English. These surprised persons tended to respond to the women with some variant of "You speak the language so well!" Although normally meant as a compliment, such comments highlighted an underlying belief that all Muslim women who cover are foreigners or foreign-born. Leena, who was born in the United States to parents from India, discussed this issue during one of our interviews:

> They really think we can't speak English. I was born and raised here, so it's not surprising that I speak English like the way people speak it here. This lady said, "Oh, wow, you can speak English pretty well." I was like, "Well, I was born and raised here." And they don't expect it. Sometimes when me and Farah, one of my other sisters here, when we see each other, we're like, "Yo, wassup?" People are just so shocked, like they can't believe we know what that is. [*Laughs.*]

Ariana was born overseas but moved to the United States as a young child. She self-identified as South Asian American and wore the headscarf as a symbol of her religious devotion. Soon after she began covering at the age of sixteen, she took her driver's license exam and found herself explaining to the instructor that she was not a newly arrived immigrant:

> Even when I took my road test, at the end, the instructor was very nice. He didn't mean anything mean by it; he said, "Have you driven in the country you're from?" I said, "I was three years old. I think I drove a bicycle." [*Laughs.*] Sometimes the way people talk to me, they'll think I'm from another country. They don't mean to be rude. Some people just like to talk to you. I've been here twenty years. I really do consider this home.

Even more troubling for the women was their recognition of the many negative stereotypes associated with the headscarf, which some opponents of Islam have constructed as the ultimate symbol of gender inequality and oppression within a patriarchal religious culture.[19] Much has been written from a scholarly and popular perspective about the various reasons why some Muslim women in the United States and elsewhere *choose* to adopt the headscarf as a public representation of their religious identity and devotion to Islam.[20] Nevertheless, the most common misconception that the women encountered was that some domineering male family member forced them to cover. Many women spoke passionately about this false impression:

> When people saw me wearing the hijab, they thought, oh, she's oppressed. Her husband's making her wear that, or her father. People were surprised when they saw me at school. They were like, "Aren't you supposed to be home cooking, cleaning, picking up children?" That was hard. Trying to overcome that, trying to tell people I'm not

> oppressed. I accept it. I do everything because I want to. There's no pressure or compulsion.
>
> The most interesting thing is everyone assumed that I was forced. Americans think that either my husband oppresses me, or my brother told me, or my father told me to do this. I had teachers come up to me, "Your husband did this; tell me if he did it!" I couldn't understand it. I keep telling everyone, "My mom doesn't do it." They don't even know what I went through to beg my mom to let me cover. Because they can't imagine that I took it on myself. "Are you getting married?" "Did your husband force you? Or your father?" One person thought that I had bruises on my face.
>
> The stuff about women, I'm sure every single one of us has had to explain that we're educated. No, there is no man that beats us to make us wear this. No, we do not have bruises under this. [*Points to hijab.*]

The above quotes illustrate that people who believe that Muslim women are forced to wear the headscarf also tend to assume that Islam does not value education, that the women are oppressed at home, and that they are being beaten. These particular stereotypes had dire consequences for some of the women. For instance, Dima, a second-generation Syrian American, recounted what happened to her after she began covering in high school. The school principal thought that her parents were abusing her by withholding food. He subsequently called social services to investigate her home. The unfounded allegation was devastating to Dima and caused a great deal of conflict within her family:

> The principal called me from the classroom and told my teachers, "This is really getting serious. I don't know you as the person that I knew before. Something is going on. I think you're being unhealthy." He was trying to say that I'm covering because I don't look like before; maybe I got skinny because I don't have food. I don't know what he thought. He said, "We have to send people to investigate your house to see if there's food." I looked at him, "Are you serious?" He's like, "If we see you like this. . . ." My mom, who does not cover, she was so upset. She did not want me to wear the headscarf in the first place. After this, she was literally . . . [s]he yelled at me, wanted me to stop doing this, but I want to do it.

The interviewees tended to view stereotypes about the headscarf and rampant gender inequality as emerging from media coverage of Muslim women in other countries. It is true that the American press has long focused on Muslims living nearly everywhere else but in the United States. This attention not only has reinforced the view of Islam as an imminently foreign religion but also has led to the conflation of religious and cultural practices. In his book *Covering Islam*, Edward Said argues that "Islam" defines a very small portion of what actually takes place in the vast Muslim world.[21] Nevertheless, the Western media use the label "Islam" to explain and to condemn all sorts of practices that are rooted in complex social structures, economic conditions, histories, and cultural formations. To be sure, some Muslim women do suffer very real and tragic oppression. The place of honor killing, genital mutilation, and forced childhood marriage in many cultures—although not just Muslim ones—demands attention and concern.[22] However, by focusing almost exclusively on the purported miseries of Muslim women, the diversity of their lives and experiences is rendered invisible in popular discourse. Natasha, who was born and raised in southern California, discussed how she wanted to defend the egalitarian ideals of her faith, but she felt inadequately equipped to do so given the broad range of cultures in which Islam is practiced:

> There are definitely cultures and cultural practices where women are oppressed. But it's very hard to distinguish between culture and religion, and it's especially hard to defend your religion when you don't know everything about those cultures. I've been to Egypt, but I haven't been to Iran or Afghanistan or Saudi Arabia. I know in Saudi Arabia women can't drive, and that's wrong because women and men are supposed to have equal rights, to be equal, in the Qur'an. But I couldn't tell you why these practices exist. As a Muslim, people always expect you to know why.

It is unthinkable to most Christian Americans that they would be asked to denounce injustices committed in the far corners of the world in the name of their faith. Yet as Natasha's quote indicates, Muslim Americans are regularly expected to explain (and to apologize) when wrongs are associated with Islam.

Even more nuanced educational materials were not necessarily successful in breaking down negative constructions of Islam. Iffat, a native of New York City, described what happened to her after her ninth-grade class watched a film on female circumcision:

> I remember there was one time in ninth grade, the year we were learning about the whole world, the Middle East. We were learning about female circumcision. We watched a tape about it. After the

> class, a girl was like, "Have you been circumcised?" I was like, "What? No!" I'm thinking, we just watched this whole tape and it said not all Muslims did this and this was a ritual thing; some people in Africa do this. I don't understand; was she not paying attention during the tape? People still think things. I explained it to her. That's a ritualistic thing. It has nothing to do with Islam.

The Muslim women were obviously aware that they were widely seen as passive, at best, and totally mindless and oppressed, at worst. The men also recognized these gendered stereotypes, and they understood that, by extension, they were viewed as the oppressors. Interestingly, the men were more likely than the women to acknowledge patriarchy in Islamic communities. They argued adamantly, however, that gender inequality emerges from cultural differences or limited educational opportunities rather than from something endemic to the faith itself. Hassan, who was raised in a household where his mother was the primary breadwinner and decision maker, emphasized this perspective:

> It strikes a nerve when you know people see you as against women, antiwomen. My mom's a nuclear engineer. She works and travels. We moved to Washington because of her work, even though my dad did not have a job yet. It's very normal. It really isn't something to do with the religion. It's something to do with the culture and how people are brought up. You would find that people who are less educated may oppress women.

Another young man, Ali, echoed Hassan's point and added, "People believe we have four wives, we mistreat our wives. I remember guys would ask me whether it was true that Islam says you can do this or do that with women. It's actually really offensive."

The Muslim men were painfully aware that members of their sex and faith are stereotyped as rigid, intolerant, and inherently prone to extremism. Just as Muslim women tend to appear in the news only when a story can be told about their real or perceived oppression, Muslim men are almost always portrayed as violent and fanatical. In cartoons, it is easy to spot the caricature of the Muslim man: He is the one with the wild eyes, crooked nose, unruly beard, and turban who is yelling "Allah Akbar!" and toting a gun or a bomb—or both.[23] Muslim men are depicted as villains in an alarming number of Hollywood films and television shows.[24] And, since the early 1980s, the Western media have regularly reported on the misdeeds of Muslim men throughout the Islamic world.[25] These stories rarely offer any context for the actions of these so-called Islamic extremists and thus serve to demonize and to dehumanize all Muslims.

The men who participated in this study recalled a number of early encounters with peers and adults who knew little about Islam beyond its association with terrorism. Bombings, hijackings, kidnappings, and other key events associated with Muslims or Arabs reinforced the most negative visions of the Islamic faith. One interviewee, Shadi, who immigrated with his family to the United States from Yemen, did not identify a specific incident that made him feel like he was being stereotyped. Instead, he spoke of "people" looking at him as if he were a terrorist. This general sense of being viewed as a violent extremist made him wary of identifying himself as a Muslim. He said, "Since we were kids, it's been false things. When I came to this country, it was troubling just to say I'm a Muslim. People looked at you like you were a terrorist."

Enduring Harassment

Such stereotypes as those described above are not only demeaning to Muslim Americans; they are also dangerous. Stereotypes may lead to many damaging effects, especially when the targeted group is marginalized in the larger cultural context. The persons whom I interviewed recognized that their status as religious minorities, combined with the many negative images and misconceptions of their faith, left them vulnerable to harassment. Ameena, who was of southeast Asian descent, emphasized the pervasive threat of mistreatment that she felt when growing up: "You always have that threat of being the target. You can get looks. . . . I've gotten looks ever since I was young."

In this research, I defined harassment as any nonverbal, verbal, or physical incident carried out with the intent to threaten, to intimidate, to harm, to offend, or to otherwise ostracize on the basis of the person's perceived minority religious or ethnic identity. Harassment thus encompassed many different acts, ranging from threatening stares to verbal taunts to physical altercations. Of the 140 persons whom I interviewed, just over 70 percent (n = 99) reported that they had been harassed in the pre-9/11 period. (Note: Given the relatively young age of the sample population—eighteen to thirty-five years—the probability of experiencing harassment throughout one's lifetime is possibly even higher.)

When the respondents were in elementary and high school, harassment most often took the form of teasing and name calling. Students would also tell jokes about Arabs and Muslims, which usually drew on the most common stereotypes about Arab people and the Islamic faith. Rais noted, "Every Muslim, every Arab has to live with the kidding around in school . . . [being called] camel jockey, sand roach, this kind of stuff." Muslim women who did not wear the headscarf would be asked such questions as "When is your dad going to make you put on the veil?" Those who did cover remembered being mocked for "wearing a tablecloth" on their heads. Other students frequently ridiculed Zoya, who was one of the few Pakistani American youth in her hometown in New Jersey, while she rode the bus to school:

> I lived in a mostly white town where people were pretty racist against me, especially on the school bus. Every day all the guys would call me "dot head" and "towel head" and all these things. I was always like, "You know, Islam is a religion. Go and educate yourself." They would make fun of me, call me all those names because I'm darker, because I was a different religion, because I dressed differently.

This quote highlights the fact that Muslims may be mistreated due to a complex array of factors associated with their religion, ethnic identities, and cultural practices. Zoya realized that she was being made fun of based on her status as a religious outsider and because of her dark skin and the clothing that she would wear. By calling Zoya such names as "towel head" and "dot head," the children on the school bus were invoking stereotypical terms used to disparage and to marginalize. ("Dot head" is a derogatory reference to the bindi or forehead "dot" that many Hindu women and some Hindu men wear; Zoya, as a Muslim, obviously did not wear the bindi.)

For decades, the mass media has presented the Arab and Muslim worlds overwhelmingly in the context of political violence and conflict. Consequently, Americans are accustomed to seeing images of war-torn regions throughout the Middle East and to hearing stories about extremists committing atrocities in the name of Islam. It is no surprise, then, that the respondents were subjected to the most severe harassment when violent incidents that were associated with Arabs or Islam were covered widely in the media. Marwan discussed how the 1988 bombing of Pan Am Flight 103 over Lockerbie, Scotland, which was perpetrated by a Libyan intelligence officer, resulted in a string of hostile comments from his classmates: "In grade school, it would be like, 'Don't mess with him; he's a Muslim and he'll blow up your house.' This was around the time of Lockerbie, the plane coming down, terrorists and all that stuff. I remember even in sixth grade, the other boys would say, 'Don't mess with him, he'll blow up your house.'"

The first Palestinian intifada against the Israeli occupation began in 1987 and led to anti-Muslim and anti-Arab incidents in the United States. Farook, who was from Colorado, had a part-time job in a Middle Eastern grocery and takeout deli at the time of the uprising. He described several negative encounters with persons who would enter the store just to make hateful remarks: "The deli, it was owned by Palestinians. We have always dealt with people coming in and talking crap about Islam—this is way before 9/11—people coming in saying, 'I hope we give nuclear arms to Israel so they can nuke the Palestinians' [or] 'Go back to the Middle East.'"

Some of the people I interviewed were younger than Farook, and thus they did not recall the first intifada as vividly. However, they clearly remembered and were affected when the second Palestinian uprising began in the fall of 2000. As Palestinian-Israeli violence intensified, so, too, did tensions among Muslim American youth and their Jewish American counterparts. A woman in Brooklyn discussed the conflicts that emerged on her college campus:

> When the intifada in Palestine started last year, problems broke out on campus between Palestinian and Israeli students. A few Muslim students—there was this whole issue where some Muslim students were harassed by some Jewish students. Then they were both ripping down each other's fliers [that were advertising events on behalf of Israel or Palestine]. We had a meeting with [the dean] on what we could do to prevent from being continually harassed.

When the first Persian Gulf War began in the fall of 1990, negative opinions toward Arabs and Muslims were widespread. One national poll, which was conducted in February 1991, found that 41 percent of Americans had a low opinion of Arabs. In that poll, a majority of Americans said the following terms applied to Arabs: "religious" (81 percent), "terrorists" (81 percent), "violent" (58 percent), and "religious fanatics" (56 percent).[26]

After the start of the first Persian Gulf War, the respondents in this study recalled being taunted at school about Iraq and Saddam Hussein, who was president of the country at the time. Karima, who attended a large and diverse high school in Michigan, described how other students, as well as a close friend, made comments to her after the outbreak of the Gulf War: "I'm sure people had it worse than I did during the Gulf War. I would mostly get teased about Saddam Hussein being my uncle. One of my friends who I knew really well even asked me, 'Are you related to Saddam Hussein?' Things like that. I guess it depends a lot on what's going on in the world in terms of what people are thinking and what they see in the media."

The teasing was sometimes more insidious, and, as a result, the participants felt that their patriotism and allegiance to the United States was constantly being questioned. One man, who was only ten years old when the Gulf War began, said he asked his mom to sew a yellow ribbon on his coat. He hoped that wearing that particular symbol would prove to his classmates that he did indeed support the American troops.

The interviewees tended to dismiss name calling as "stupid" or "childish" behavior. This allowed them to forgive their peers and others for being insensitive and saying hurtful things. However, the harassment escalated at times, subsequently leaving the Muslim men and women feeling scared or depressed. Latifah, who grew up in a small town in the Midwest, depicted the environment where she lived as "vicious." Some people in the town treated her as if she were going to hell because she was not a Christian, and one of her high school teachers made improper and bigoted statements about Islam in front of the entire class. In the end, Latifah could not wait to move away:

> At times it was sad to see how ignorant people were about Islam, about anything different. You really saw how afraid people were of something different. Other places embrace and respect differences, but in small-town America they're fearful of it. Being Muslim, people would think that I was going to hell because I didn't believe that Jesus was the Lord and Savior. It was really vicious. Even though I would try to talk about how there are so many similarities between Christianity and Islam, one literally evolved from the other, they didn't care. They didn't want to hear it. They would dwell on the little differences. Then they would think it's a terrorist religion and say things like, "The angels of Satan came to Muhammad and that's how the Qur'an came about." A teacher would say this. My history professor said this to our class. What that did for me was make me want to leave as soon as I possibly could. I understand how ignorant people can be, even people that are nice people by nature—these people can still be so ignorant and hateful.

Amani attended a school where she remembered the other students as mostly friendly and accepting toward her and her faith. When she was in public, however, it was a different story. Because Amani wore the headscarf, she realized she "stuck out like a sore thumb" in her home community in southern Colorado. She was frequently stared at and pointed at. And, after receiving numerous hostile comments, she eventually stopped going to certain places at night where she tended to feel unsafe:

> I got a lot of stares, a lot of negative comments before 9/11. I won't go to [the main shopping district] in the evening as a rule, because I have had comments there, and when I do have to go, I go during the day and I don't window shop. I go straight in to where I am going, and I go straight out and go to the bus or whatever. I think it really depends on how much you show up as a foreigner, or as appearing of Middle Eastern descent or as a Muslim. I have always stuck out like

> a sore thumb, because I wear a scarf. Therefore, people judge me by that, and people react to me like that.

Several of the interviewees not only were verbally harassed but also were subjected to unwelcome physical contact. The women who started wearing the headscarf in middle school or high school were the most likely to remember being bullied by their peers, which was undoubtedly a consequence of their visibility. Nearly half the young women noted that they had their headscarves yanked or pulled off by other students. Alisha, whose family immigrated to the United States from Syria when she was an infant, was kicked the first day that she wore the headscarf to high school: "I wore it, and I went to school—the first time I was getting a drink of water—and this guy kicked me. That was my first kind of experience with the scarf that I really remember." The boy who kicked Alisha was suspended from classes for a week. Alisha was grateful that the school took swift disciplinary action against him, as she believed it may have stopped other students from "picking on" her.

Although some teachers and school administrators were supportive, as evidenced by Alisha's case, others were not. For instance, Mysha and her twin brother, Ghazi, attended high school in Queens. She wore the hijab, he was dark skinned, and they had recently immigrated to the United States from Egypt. These and other factors made them stand out, and a number of students and even some of their teachers harassed them. Indeed, Mysha described several incidents that occurred soon after they arrived and began attending the school. Staff members did little to intervene on her or her brother's behalf, and, in some instances, the adults actually exacerbated the problem by making rude comments themselves. Ghazi ultimately ended up getting suspended after he confronted and fought with one of the boys who had been mercilessly harassing them. Mysha told their story:

> When I went into class, my brother started to sit down. I saw a Muslim girl covered. I tried to sit down next to her. A guy comes, "This is my seat." I stood up. I tried to sit down someplace else, and people came and sat down. I figured I can't sit down, because they wanted to have their seat. So I go to the teacher, who was writing something. I said, "Excuse me, hello. . . ." I don't remember what I said, but my question was "Where am I going to sit?" Maybe he was not in a good mood, but he said, "Outside the window." Can you imagine? I kept my tears in, but that was really not nice of him. It was really bad. When I used to go to the lunchroom with my friend, this Muslim, we were the only people who were covered. They used to throw food at us. You know, when they peel the skin off oranges? They used to throw it at

> us. I tried to tell a teacher about this and about a boy that pulled my hijab. He was no help. We had a dean's office. We used to go there and complain. Sometimes they used to come out at lunchtime, and they noticed that there was a lot of food, and we were the target. Then I had an encounter with a guy who always wanted to fight with me and my brother for no reason. My brother, he got into a fight and ended up getting removed from school for two weeks. It was the worst memories.

In addition to the verbal and physical confrontations, some of the men's and women's homes and places of worship came under attack. In fact, a quarter of the participants reported that bigots had targeted personal property (houses, cars, and so forth) or their local mosques or Islamic centers before 9/11. The assaults on the mosques, which ranged from threatening phone calls to vandalism, were obviously meant to send a message to the entire Muslim community. One man who grew up in Michigan noted that people would periodically call the mosque and say hateful things. And, late one night, someone scattered nails around the mosque parking lot in an attempt to puncture the tires of the worshippers. Another woman indicated that the mosque her family attended in Colorado had been "vandalized four or five times" in the ten-year period prior to the terrorist attacks on New York and Washington, D.C.

Before the 9/11 attacks, very little scholarship focused on Muslim Americans and their day-to-day encounters with intolerance and mistreatment. The FBI began tracking anti-Islamic hate crimes in 1995, but those figures represent only the most egregious cases that were actually reported to the police. Islamic advocacy groups released reports that offer more detailed portraits of the civil-rights violations and discrimination that Muslims were subjected to pre-9/11. However, they, too, concentrate predominantly on the most serious infringements on Muslim people's lives and civil liberties, rather than on the more chronic and ongoing problems that Muslims in this society have faced for decades.

The lack of systematic focus on the stereotyping and harassment that Muslim Americans faced *before* 9/11 has created some challenges in making sense of the severe wave of backlash violence that they experienced *after* the terrorist attacks. With only twenty-eight anti-Muslim hate crimes tallied by the federal government in the year 2000, Muslim Americans were barely on the radar screen in terms of minority groups at risk for discrimination or physical attack. Drawing on this hate-crime data, regardless of how incomplete, some commentators expressed shock that Muslim Americans, whom one journalist labeled as "the least-discriminated-against religious minority group," would experience such harsh retribution after 9/11.

The accounts included above, however, demonstrate that Muslims not only were aware of their position as religious outsiders in the United States but also recognized the numerous, and almost universally negative, stereotypes that many non-Muslims hold about them and their faith. Lack of contact between Muslims and non-Muslims, distorted educational materials in our schools, anti-Islamic propaganda, and sensationalized media coverage all ensured the perpetuation of the worst images of Islam. The verbal and physical harassment that the majority of the Muslims reported offers some insight into the ways that misconceptions about a group may translate into hostile actions.

The harsh backlash that Muslim Americans experienced in the aftermath of 9/11 was not an anomaly. Instead, it was a continuation of an already antagonistic climate. Well before the hijackers piloted the planes into the Twin Towers, Muslims were already living in a context where they and their faith were viewed as different, strange, foreign, violent, oppressive, and threatening. By the time Muslims saw the enormous Twin Towers come crashing down, they had already begun to brace for the backlash. In the next chapter, I draw on the voices of Muslim men and women to describe the fallout that Muslims have experienced since that ghastly September day.

4

Backlash

September 11, 2001, began like most other days for Maya, a petite nineteen-year-old Muslim American from New York City. She woke up early to pray and then showered and dressed for school. She slipped a dark jilbab, a loose-fitting ankle-length dress, over her jeans and button-up blouse and then covered her long brown hair with her favorite navy blue scarf. After gathering her books and stuffing them in her worn-out backpack, she sat down for a quick breakfast with her mother, father, and younger brother, Kamil.

All the adults were in a rush that morning. Maya's father had a meeting at his engineering firm. Her mother was trying to hurry Kamil along with eating his cereal so he would not be late for preschool and she would not be late for work. Maya was scheduled to take her first exam that Tuesday afternoon in her Introduction to Psychology course. She wanted to get to campus early so she could cram in a few more hours of studying before class.

Later, as Maya reflected back on the events of that fateful day, she wished that her family would have taken "just a little more time" to be together that morning. It was the last peaceful meal that they would share for the next several weeks.

Of course, Maya could not have known how the day would unfold, so she quickly finished her breakfast, hugged her mother and little brother goodbye, and kissed her father on the cheek on her way out the door.

Outside, the sun was shining, and the sky was a magnificent shade of blue. Maya walked five blocks to the subway station, where she caught the train to the university she attended in the middle of Manhattan. Everything was running on time, and by 8:30 A.M. Maya was sitting in the campus library reviewing her notes and readings.

Around 9:30 that morning, Maya looked up and noticed that the library was virtually empty. It struck her as odd that so few people were around, but she had no reason to be concerned. A few moments later, though, she heard a student who was sitting two seats away from her talking on a cell phone about "the terrorists, the terrorists." Maya assumed that the student must have been referring to an event in some faraway place, until she heard the young woman whisper into the phone, "Mom, I think there's going to be a war."

At that point, Maya made eye contact with the other student, and she immediately realized how serious the young woman was. Now Maya was worried. She scooped up her books and notes and decided to go find her friends at the campus Muslim Students Association (MSA). Maya reasoned that someone there could surely explain what was happening. As she stood up to leave the library, a security guard entered and announced that all classes were cancelled that day. Maya felt like the guard and the other students were staring at her as she made her way through the aisles, but she had no idea why.

It was a few minutes before 10:00 A.M. when Maya arrived at the women's MSA office (the Muslim men had a separate meeting room just down the hallway). She had just made it through the doorway when someone blurted out, "The United States is under attack!" Maya's friends hastily explained that two planes had crashed into the World Trade Center and that a third airliner had struck the Pentagon. Before the news could sink in, the chattering of the students was drowned out by the sound of people shouting on the street. They would soon learn that people were yelling because the south tower had just collapsed.

Lower Manhattan seemed to have disappeared in a giant cloud of black smoke and dust. Sirens wailed, adding to a general sense of confusion and chaos. The security guard who was in the library earlier arrived at the MSA office and told the young women that they should "stay put" and not try to venture outside the building. Shortly thereafter, a few of the Muslim men came over to talk to the women about the rumors already swirling regarding the involvement of Islamic extremists in the attacks. The men were especially concerned that people seeking revenge would target the women, almost all of whom were wearing headscarves.

Maya felt trapped. The trains had stopped running, and no automobiles were allowed in the area. She did not want to stay at the school, but she was fearful that she might be assaulted if she left the MSA office. Even worse,

Maya was overwhelmed by the thought that the terrorists could strike the city again. She decided to remain on campus until she could reach her family. For almost four hours, Maya repeatedly dialed the numbers for her home phone, her parent's cell phones, and her neighbor's phone. None of them worked. She just kept receiving busy signals and audio recordings indicating that no circuits were available.

Around 2:00 P.M., Maya's father, Adil, finally got through on her cell phone. As soon as he confirmed that Maya was still at the university and had not been hurt in the attacks, he handed the phone to Maya's mother, Jamila, who was sobbing and could barely speak. She had no idea if Maya had made it to school safely that morning, and she was terrified that something had happened to her daughter. Maya spent several minutes trying to calm her mother and to reassure her that she was okay. Adil then got back on the phone and asked Maya not to leave the campus by herself. He gave Maya the names of two Muslim males ("brothers") who were friends of the family and lived in their same neighborhood, which was located several miles from the university. Maya found the two young men and asked if they would be willing to accompany her home. They readily agreed, and soon the three set out for what Maya would later describe as the longest and most frightening walk of her life:

> That day, people didn't even wait for investigations to take place; people didn't even wait to hear more on the news. It was just hours after the attack, and there were people behind my back that spit on me, people who said, "We are going to kill them all; we are going to kill them all." This guy, he came next to me and was staring at me—the brothers thought he was going to hit me. So one brother came right next to me in the front, and the other moved by my side. They built a wall between me and the man, because he was really rude. And he was chanting, "Retaliation, retaliation, we are going to kill them all." And the brother said to me, "Don't say anything, just walk," and so we were walking. I wasn't afraid, but before we crossed the bridge, a whole group of people just stopped. And so I told the brothers, "Please do not leave me." They were like, "Don't worry." These men, they surrounded us from the back and they tried to scare us, but there were police there, so they couldn't physically attack us. But they did scare us, and they started saying things, horrible curses.

After several more hours of walking and enduring additional harassment, Maya eventually made it home and was reunited with her family. However, Maya was so scared, and her parents were so concerned for her safety, that she did not leave her house again for two weeks.

Maya's frightening encounter with the angry mob demonstrates the swiftness of the onset of anti-Muslim bias-related incidents in the aftermath of 9/11. Following the disaster, the interviewees in this study reported a significant increase in the frequency and severity of negative experiences based on their status as Muslim Americans. This increase is not surprising, given the sharp rise in hate crimes and discrimination that law enforcement agencies and minority advocacy groups nationwide have documented (see Chapter 2).

What was more striking was the broad array of discriminatory actions that the men and women described. Prior research has shown that racial or ethnic prejudice can be expressed with varying degrees of intensity, ranging from avoidance to verbal harassment to discriminatory exclusion to physical attack.[1] When I asked the participants about the differential treatment that they had personally experienced or had witnessed after 9/11, they similarly detailed a number of different actions that fell along a continuum from subtle mistreatment to overt and violent acts of aggression.

The association of Islam with the most deadly terrorist attacks in U.S. history intensified preexisting prejudices against the faith and its followers and also generated new hostilities that affected the respondents' day-to-day lives and life chances. Muslims were verbally harassed; stared at; threatened; profiled on the basis of their religion and ethnicities; and denied equal access to employment, housing, and educational opportunities following 9/11. In this chapter, I detail these different forms of discrimination, drawing on the words of Muslim men and women who endured the post-9/11 backlash.

Before proceeding, it is important to note that those persons most vulnerable to discrimination before and especially after 9/11 were those who were readily identifiable as Muslim. This confirms previous research that documents that visible membership in a marginalized group is a major determinant of racially or religiously motivated abuse.[2] Key *markers of difference* for Muslim Americans include religious symbols, cultural and physical characteristics, and organizational memberships. For example, women who wear the hijab, men with beards who wear traditional Islamic clothing, and persons with ethnic-sounding names or foreign accents were conspicuous before 9/11 and even more so in the aftermath of the attacks. In addition, Muslims with dark complexions and dark hair were more frequently targeted, because they fit the stereotypical image of what followers of Islam "look like." This conflation of physical characteristics and religious belief is problematic on multiple levels and obscures the fact that Muslims represent a transnational, multiethnic religious community. Nevertheless, in the news media and popular culture in the United States, brown skin "equals" Islam, which helps explain why dark-skinned people of different ethnicities and religious persuasions (such as Latinos, Arab Christians, and South Asian Hindus and Sikhs) were victimized after 9/11.[3] Muslims who were active in their local mosques or other religious organizations, attended Islamic schools, or worked in Muslim-owned businesses were also among the most noticeable and most frequently vilified members of their communities.

Those persons who were not as easily recognizable as Muslim also suffered from the backlash, albeit sometimes in different ways. In essence, these individuals could "pass" as non-Muslim because of their skin colors, decisions not to wear Islamic attire, or lack of formal religious affiliations. These Muslim men and women were consequently much less likely to be the primary targets of discriminatory actions. Nonetheless, they often witnessed discrimination directed toward other Muslims or Arabs. These experiences were personally painful and also confirmed the severity of Islamophobic religious prejudice and anti-Arab ethnic bias in the general public.

Verbal Harassment and Intimidation

Muslim Americans became the targets of widespread verbal abuse in the aftermath of the 9/11 attacks. Nearly 80 percent of the Muslims in this study reported that they were personally verbally harassed or in the immediate proximity of a friend or family member who was ridiculed in the weeks and months following 9/11. Participants were called vulgar names, shouted or cursed at in the street or from passing cars, and subjected to disparaging remarks in public settings. Most often, these insults came from strangers. However, neighbors, acquaintances, classmates, teachers, and co-workers were also responsible for some instances of verbal harassment.

The interviewees offered a long list of derogatory names that they or their Muslim peers or family members had been called after 9/11. "Terrorist," "dirty Muslim," "camel jockey," "rag head," "towel head," "sand roach," and "sand n-gger" were all epithets that were mumbled or yelled at males and females. As noted in the previous chapter, the participants had been called many of these names before 9/11. After the terrorist attacks, the interviewees heard these offensive slurs much more often and in a wider variety of contexts.

In addition to these more familiar anti-Muslim insults, the respondents were also referred to in new and disparaging ways that were clearly associated with the 9/11 atrocities. For example, the men reported they were called "Osama" or "Taliban," while some of the women were referred to as "Osama's goats" and were told to "take off the burqa."[4] Salman, who was born in Afghanistan, explained how he was treated by a woman whom he had just met: "I told someone that I'm from Afghanistan, an older woman. She was like, 'Oh, my God, we have bin Laden in the house.' This didn't shock me at all. Before 9/11, people hardly even knew where Afghanistan was. Now when

I tell someone I'm from Afghanistan, they'll probably treat me in a certain way, or they'll probably think about me in a different way than before."

Najah described what happened to her and her friends, all of whom were wearing headscarves, when they exited the subway in Harlem:

> Nobody abused me physically, but I got a lot of verbal slang. One time, my friends and I were coming out of the subway, and we were all hijabis [women wearing headscarves]. Two guys, when they saw us, they started joking to each other. They were saying, "Let's go kill all of Osama's goats." I looked at them and I started laughing. It was like, "What does this have to do with me?" But then I realized that they were talking about us.

Several other respondents encountered hostility as they navigated city streets. In their research on African Americans and discrimination, Joe Feagin and Melvin Sikes note that public streets represent some of the least-protected sites in our society. Consequently, racial minorities are continually at risk for verbal abuse as they move through these open places.[5] Religiously motivated harassment may follow a similar pattern, as evidenced by the numerous problems with verbal attacks that Muslims faced in public locations in the aftermath of 9/11. Badia, who lived in Colorado in the fall of 2001, talked about her experiences as she would walk near her home: "Of course, generally, Americans are really nice, very friendly people. But I was really surprised about how rude and ignorant some people were after 9/11. I remember walking down the street and people saying stuff, yelling stuff like 'terrorist, terrorist.' I really didn't think Americans would be like that."

Many other Muslim men and women indicated that they were shouted at by people in passing cars. The episodes they described involved animosity against other nations: "When I was walking down [a busy street in Denver], I saw this guy driving down the street, and this guy yelled out his window, 'F— Pakistan!'"

Sometimes people were cursed at because they were perceived to be Arab, as was the case with this South Asian man: "Once I had picked up my sister, I was walking my sister back home. This man said, 'Get out of here, you f—ing Arabs.' I'm like, 'That's funny, because nobody here is an Arab. Who's an Arab?' It's just ignorance."

And other times, the person hurling the insult drew on demeaning stereotypes, as an Arab American woman described: "I was walking down the street after work, minding my own business, and some kid stuck his head out the window of the back seat of a car and called me a terrorist. Then they turned the corner. I was expecting them to turn all the way around and come after me. I just turned around and started to run."

These hateful words not only were emotionally painful but also induced fear and served as a reminder of the risks associated with traversing public settings. As the last quote shows, Muslims were aware that at any moment these verbal confrontations could turn into physical altercations, should the harasser "turn around" and "come after" them.

Some people directed their anger at Muslims by yelling, "Go back to your country" and other taunts grounded in the misconception that Muslims cannot be native-born citizens. As discussed in the previous chapter, Muslim Americans are no strangers to this "perpetual-foreigner" stereotype. Following 9/11, however, these encounters took on a much more hostile tone. Selina, a second-generation Pakistani American who was born and raised in New York, emphasized the pain associated with verbal harassment: "It really hurts. You've been living here, and I hate it when somebody says, 'Go back to your country; go back home.' This is my home. I live here. Who the hell are you to tell me? Honestly, that's the way I feel. I'll just give them a dirty look. I try not to answer. But it really hurts. I can't see myself living anywhere else but here."

The rise in anti-immigrant and especially anti-Arab and anti-Muslim rhetoric in the aftermath of the terrorist attacks likely encouraged this particular form of verbal bigotry. Indeed, a number of media pundits and conservative political and religious figures depicted America as a country virtually overrun with hordes of violent, subversive Muslims. For instance, televangelist Pat Robertson, speaking on the Christian Broadcasting Network's 700 Club program, said, "Our immigration policies are now so skewed towards the Middle East and away from Europe that we have introduced these people into our midst and undoubtedly there are terrorist cells all over them. . . . They want to coexist until they can control, dominate, and then if need be, destroy."[6] Columnist Stanley Crouch of New York's *Daily News* wrote:

> We have had war declared on us by a spider at the center of a web of terrorist cells. Followers of that spider are hiding in the Arab American community. No one doubts this. No one. In fact, it should bother all of us that a moratorium was not declared on immigration from the Middle East after the 1993 attack on the Twin Towers, especially since most of those identified with 9/11 arrived here after that time. If more Americans are murdered by people who are part of the terrorist web from the Middle East and successfully hiding out in a certain community, the response is going to have less to do with any kind of bigotry than with the icy nature of war.[7]

Commentators also questioned the loyalty of Muslims and cast doubt on whether they could ever fully assimilate to "American" values and ideals.

In November 2001, William S. Lind, director for the Center for Cultural Conservatism at the Free Congress Foundation, argued, "There is no such thing as a peaceful Islam. . . . Islamics [*sic*] cannot fit into an America in which the first loyalty is to the American Constitution. They should be encouraged to leave. They are a fifth column in this country."[8] Lind and his colleague Paul M. Weyrich also published a pamphlet entitled "Why Islam Is a Threat to America and the West." Their pamphlet states plainly, "We do believe Islam is at war with the Christian West, and we are proud to be considered spokesmen for that view." Weyrich later warned, "They're [Muslims] going to, at some point or another, attack us. It's like having a giant fifth column in your own country."[9]

With this kind of derisive speech increasingly making its way into mainstream media, it is no wonder that a 2002 national survey found that nearly 60 percent of Americans favored reducing the number of immigrants admitted to the United States from Muslim countries.[10] Another poll, also conducted in 2002, showed that the majority of Americans believed there were "too many" immigrants from Arab countries.[11] Several surveys carried out in the days following the 9/11 attacks suggested that a significant minority of Americans felt mistrustful toward the Arabs and Muslims living in their midst: 43 percent of Americans said that 9/11 would make them more suspicious of people whom they thought were Arab; 35 percent said they had less trust in Arabs living in the United States than previously; 27 percent admitted to feeling less favorably toward Arab Americans since 9/11; and about 33 percent said they had heard friends, neighbors, or co-workers make negative comments about Arabs or Muslims.[12]

As the American public grew more wary of Arabs and Muslims, members of these communities began to receive increasingly hostile inquiries concerning everything from their religious beliefs to their perspectives on terrorism. The men and women in this study reported that they were regularly asked whether they were "glad" or "happy" that the terrorists destroyed the World Trade Center towers. The following remark sharply underscores how dehumanizing these experiences were: "Some people are like, 'Are you happy it happened?' Some people have said that to me. You're kind of like . . . what do you even say to that? It's like the mentality that people literally have is that Muslims and people from the Middle East aren't normal human beings."

The presumption of guilt by religious association was even more painful when it was friends or colleagues—people who knew the Muslim men and women prior to 9/11—who were compelled to ask how Muslims felt about the murder of nearly three thousand innocent people: "A friend of my husband, he called and said, 'How do you feel about the whole thing? Are you happy?' Then he left a message, 'God bless America.' We're like, 'Okay, now we know which way you stand.'"

The woman quoted above said her husband ultimately chose to end the relationship with the man who called and left the hostile message. She described the ordeal as "intensely stressful," because her husband had been friends with the man for many years before 9/11.

After the terrorist attacks, patriotic sentiment surged in the United States, expressed through signs and songs that represent American strength and identity. For many Americans, displaying such symbols as the American flag reaffirmed their loyalty to the nation and allowed them to show their solidarity with others. In some instances, however, patriotic displays were used to harm and to isolate Muslims. For example, Sirah, a Lebanese American woman, recounted how a man began singing "The Star Spangled Banner" when he saw her. She was certain the incident occurred because of her visibility as a Muslim: "I was wearing a hijab to school, and a big American white guy looked at me and sang the American anthem in a loud voice, in the subway. It was like he was singing it to me." As a consequence of this incident, Sirah was left feeling as though patriotism was being used as a cover for anti-Muslim bigotry.[13] She sadly commented, "Many people say, 'We love America.' But to me that means, 'We hate Muslims.'"

The 9/11 attacks introduced a new sense of vulnerability into the American psyche. Spaces that were formerly considered safe are now approached with unease. High-rise structures, once regarded as extraordinary feats of human engineering, are viewed today as potential terror targets. National monuments and government buildings are envisioned as fair game for nefarious terrorist plots. A feeling of danger is associated with activities that draw large crowds of people together, such as sporting events and music concerts. And, if aircraft are at risk in the post-9/11 era, so, too, are trains, buses, subways, bridges, ports, and dams. The list of threats is seemingly endless, and incessant warnings from government officials to "stay alert" remind Americans that another attack could happen at any time in any number of locations.

Since 9/11, Muslims have been treated with suspicion and contempt as they enter public spaces that antiterrorism experts have labeled "potential targets." In the months following 9/11, the interviewees who relied on public transportation received a slew of comments, which ranged from angry outbursts to feeble attempts at humor. The accounts below came from two young Muslim women in the fall of 2001. The first respondent was waiting to catch a train in New Jersey, and the second, a university student, was taking a bus home from Manhattan for the Thanksgiving holiday:

> I went to New Jersey. I was coming back, and I was waiting for the train. This guy, he goes to me, "Before you blow up this train station, just let me know so I can get my ass out of here." I just laughed and looked at him and said, "Okay, sure."

> Thanksgiving, I took Greyhound. I was so tired. Midterms had just finished. I was carrying all these bags. There was a huge line, because they were checking everything. Only ticketed passengers could go in the line. Usually they don't do that. By the time I actually got on the bus, I was extremely exhausted. The second I got on, the first person sitting right by the door goes, "Oh, my God, there's going to be a bomb on the bus." He said it loud enough so the whole bus heard it. I'm the kind who would stand up for myself, but I was way too tired that day.

Some of the episodes of verbal harassment were more indirect, such as when people would make comments loud enough for the Muslim men or women to hear but not explicitly to their faces. For instance, Thana, a second-generation Pakistani American, found that when she would visit restaurants or other public accommodations, fellow patrons would sometimes intentionally engage in Muslim bashing: "I have sat down, and people have come and sat down next to me. They're having a conversation loud enough so specifically I can hear them. They want me to hear them, and they'll be slamming Islam, and they'll be saying things about Muslim suicide bombers and all this. . . . It's just like, do you honestly believe the things you are saying?"

Another interviewee, Laila, also faced indirect verbal abuse. As she told her story, it was clear how hurt she was by the incident. Laila and her cousin's family, whom she lived with in lower Manhattan, were evacuated for several weeks following the collapse of the Twin Towers. When they were finally allowed to return to their ash-covered apartment, they were mistreated by another resident who had also been displaced:

> You have to give IDs in four different places just to get back to my cousin's apartment. We had our luggage, because we stayed somewhere else. So coming back, we're carrying backpacks and suitcases. We had a lot of stuff. There was this one guy who also lives in that neighborhood who was in front of us. He kept on telling all the people in the checkpoint, "You have to search their stuff. They're probably carrying bombs." He didn't say anything directly to us, but you knew he didn't want us around.

This experience was so upsetting to Laila because the man's comments essentially negated her and her family's status as victims of the terrorist attacks. They, too, had suffered losses and disruptions, but when they tried to return home, they were regarded as nothing more than potential terrorists.

In some instances, the verbal threats that were directed against Muslims and their religious institutions were serious enough that they necessitated police intervention. Two of the MSA offices I visited in Colorado summoned the campus police after they received several threatening telephone messages. After a man called in a bomb threat to a suburban Denver mosque, the local police recommended that the mosque shut down its Islamic school. Tamara, one of the teachers at the school, described what happened:

> I'm also a Sunday school teacher. We had to close down the school until late October [2001], because they knew that the Afghan community comes to the mosque. Ninety-five percent of the students are Afghan, Afghans on top of being Muslim. All these combinations led to the threats we received. We had a serious bomb scare. The next day the police came. We didn't stop Friday prayers, but the police recommended we close down the school until things settled down.

The initial and most severe wave of backlash violence that followed the terrorist attacks seriously affected Tamara and other Muslims. Then, in early October 2001, the U.S.-led invasion of Afghanistan began. This military strike resulted in another round of attacks against Muslims and led to increased scrutiny on the grounds of faith and ethnic origin.

Several interviewees reported that they had non-Muslim and non-Arab friends and acquaintances who were also verbally harassed or threatened after 9/11. Rashida noted that her roommate, who was biracial, was approached by an enraged man who screamed profanities at her: "There's so much ignorance. Nobody really knows the difference between how an Arab looks, how a Pakistani looks. One of my roommates is mixed race, half black and half white. Some guy comes running up to her and screaming, 'Look at what your f—ing people did to our country.'"

Another woman, Nadira, described what happened to her former brother-in-law a week after 9/11:

> My sister's ex-husband, he's paralyzed from the waist down, but he drives. He looks Arab; he just does, but he's not. He was in the gas station getting gas. This older, white man started screaming at him and cursing at him and saying, "I'm going to kill you. I'm going to beat you up." He said, "But I'm paralyzed, what are you doing?" He's like, "I don't care." The police had to come for this man to leave.

The man whose life was threatened was not Arab or Muslim. He was Latino and Catholic, and thus Nadira was certain that his dark complexion was the "trigger" that resulted in the confrontation outside the gas station.

This incident was particularly alarming to Nadira, as it seemed to prove that anyone who could possibly be categorized as Arab or Muslim—even a man with a serious physical disability—was vulnerable to attack.

Nonverbal Hostility

In addition to verbal harassment and threats of violence, Muslim Americans were subjected to hostile looks as they moved through public places. As one respondent remarked, "In one way or another, we all at the very least had to deal with the looks. We all get the looks." Discourteous stares may seem like a minor issue, especially when compared to the other life-threatening incidents that numerous Muslims and Arabs faced after 9/11. However, the glares and the insinuation of guilt associated with these looks made the participants feel afraid and excluded. In some cases, the stares were so menacing that the participants avoided public settings altogether. One young woman stayed home for five days because of the looks she received in the aftermath of the terrorist attacks: "Immediately when it happened, me and my dad were in the car. I had my cell phone. A white lady stopped in the middle of the street and looked at us really hard in the car. Even when I was walking around my neighborhood, I felt very terrified, because people were staring at me like I did something wrong. I didn't come out of my house for five days."

Muslim women who wear the hijab are the most recognizable representatives of their faith. In the United States, where Muslim women who cover make up only a tiny percentage of the larger population, they are especially visible. Not surprisingly, Muslim American women who wear the headscarf are used to being stared at and asked questions about their dress and Islamic faith. After 9/11, however, the looks changed from curious or confused glances to overtly hostile stares. Rajah emphasized this shift and noted that the stares also made her want to avoid venturing outside: "We're used to being stared at. But this, this was a different kind of stare, a lot of glares, suspicious looks. The first day it didn't really hit me, just the magnitude of it all. Then, all this started, and I started not wanting to go outside."

Sara, who like Rajah wore the headscarf, described a humiliating incident where she was "stared down" by a police officer just days after 9/11:

> This is a time when the patience of Muslims is being tested. We're not supposed to react how we want to. I got stared down by a cop. I've never been stared down. I don't mean to say racism or anything, maybe he's from a place where he didn't grow up with any minority people or with an ethnic background. I took that into account. He looked at me a couple of times. People had to look back to see who

> he's looking at. I was very scared, embarrassed, ashamed. I thought, "Why are these people looking at me?" I looked at him and said, "Hi, everything's okay?" He got caught by the moment that I asked him; he thought I wouldn't ask him. He said, "Hi, how are you doing?" I said, "Fine." If I would have had time, I would have shown him my ID and said, "Please don't look at us like this. I don't want to be in a situation where I'm going to be stared down and an entire block is looking at me. Look at my ID. I'm an American, just like you."

Some of the men, especially those with darker skin who "looked Muslim," also reported a dramatic change in the ways they were stared at after 9/11: "You've been living here all your life, and all of a sudden there's all this hatred. Something went wrong. Why is this person staring at me? I've stood on this corner in just the same way a billion times before, and no one ever said anything to me before or looked at me this way. We know that something has changed."

The different types of hostile looks that the men and women received represented the most consistent and unmistakable reminders that something had indeed changed for Muslims in the aftermath of the terrorist strikes on New York and Washington, D.C. Although the participants could not always know with certainty the intent of the person who was staring at them, Muslims shared a general sense that the looks were meant to intimidate and to convey hate, suspicion, and fear. I discuss these various forms of nonverbal hostility in turn below.

Hate Stares

First, there were the stares that made Muslims feel hated. These looks were penetrating and vicious, communicating anger, disgust, even loathing. The Muslims who were subjected to hate stares felt as if they were being personally blamed for destroying the Twin Towers and ending the lives of thousands of people on 9/11. These stares were so discomforting that one of the women described them as "just unbearable." Another woman experienced such a hostile look that she was brought to tears: "I remember I got on the train one time and sat next to some guy. He gave me this really, really mean look. You could just tell he was trying to . . . I started to write in my journal, because that's how I get my emotions out. I was crying when I was writing about this guy staring at me like this."

As scholars have pointed out, the hate stare is a very old racist device used against African Americans that dates back to at least the eighteenth century and still continues today.[14] John Howard Griffin, the white journalist who darkened his skin and traveled through the southern United States as a black man in the late 1950s, vividly describes this phenomenon in *Black Like Me.* Griffin's first experience with a hate stare came from a white woman selling bus tickets in New Orleans. Here he explains what the hate stare looks like: "Taking care to pitch my voice to politeness, I asked about the next bus to Hattiesburg. She answered rudely and glared at me with such loathing I knew I was receiving what Negroes call 'the hate stare.' It was my first experience with it. It is far more than the look of disapproval one occasionally gets. This was so exaggeratedly hateful I would have been amused if I had not been so surprised."

Griffin's next encounter with a hate stare came moments later, as he crossed the path of a white man sitting in the "Whites Only" section of the bus station lobby. Here he speaks of what the hate stare felt like:

> Once again a "hate stare" drew my attention like a magnet. It came from a middle-aged, heavyset, well-dressed white man. He sat a few yards away, fixing his eyes on me. Nothing can describe the withering horror of this. You feel lost, sick at heart before such unmasked hatred, not so much because it threatens you as because it shows humans in such an inhuman light. You see a kind of insanity, something so obscene the very obscenity of it (rather than its threat) terrifies you.[15]

As Griffin notes, African Americans were so accustomed to being abused with this type of hostile look that they had given it a name: the hate stare. Muslim Americans, on the other hand, do not have the same sort of lengthy history of collective suffering as do African Americans. As a consequence, Muslims in the United States have yet to develop a shared vocabulary to characterize this form of aggression. The men and women whom I interviewed used such words as "horrible," "mean," "bad," "nasty," "evil eye," and "hateful" to try to capture the essence of the looks.

> I'm just standing outside my apartment, and this couple comes out of the building. I've seen them before, but this time, they just gave me this look. I felt butterflies go in my stomach. You feel awkward, out of place. Why are they giving me this horrible look?

> Immediately after 9/11, it was hard. When walking around on the streets, it made me nervous, because people would give me the bad stares.

> One of my friends that wears the hijab, she went to Ground Zero and was helping. She was giving stuff to drink to the rescuers. She

> described how awful it was down there. She was literally going home covered in blood and mud from that place, only to receive the hateful looks from people in the train. She's down there volunteering her time and energy. She's not asking for recognition, but at least she should not be given these looks.

Intimidation Stares

Second, after 9/11, the participants were targeted much more often with stares and other nonverbal actions that they perceived as meant to intimidate and to frighten them. These forms of nonverbal hostility made the Muslim men and women feel especially vulnerable to physical attack as they navigated their neighborhoods and city streets. Jinan received looks from men in a car who repeatedly drove by her for no other apparent reason than to scare her. These actions were so menacing that she considered removing her headscarf so that she would be less identifiable as a Muslim:

> Even my neighbors, it's not the kind of neighborhood that a Muslim could feel comfortable in to begin with. It's predominantly white, Judeo-Christian. So these people have attitudes. I remember people staring at me. There were these guys who kept driving past me and giving me these looks, just for no reason, just to freak me out when I was walking in town. So I was even scared to go out of my house. I was thinking about taking off my scarf.

Suspicious Stares

Third, the interviewees noted a sudden rise in suspicious looks, double takes, and watchful stares after 9/11. Because their religion was linked to the most destructive terrorist attacks in the nation's history, the interviewees understood why those around them were monitoring their words and actions so carefully. The participants still found the prying stares bothersome, especially because they assumed that people were observing their appearance and actions because they could now see Muslims only through a lens associated with terrorism. During a focus group interview, two women described their frustration with the stares directed at them as they commuted to and from school:

> Right after 9/11, I was scared of looking into people's eyes in the subway. That's why I was always looking down. I didn't want to see that they were staring at me. Now I'll look around a little more. When I'm studying for class, I can see they try to see what I'm studying. They'll look at my books.

> I hate that, especially when I'm trying to study chemical engineering. They're probably thinking, "That's her bomb manual." They literally look and try to read. I look at their faces, and they don't feel ashamed. They just keep looking at what I'm studying.

The first speaker, Selma, responded to this form of nonverbal hostility through avoiding people's gazes. She realized that by looking down, she was feeding into the stereotype of the passive, submissive Muslim woman. She also knew that by averting her eyes, she would possibly make people more suspicious of her actions. Regardless, Selma found it too painful and too emotionally exhausting to confront the numerous people who stared at her every day.

Media and political rhetoric against Islam intensified following 9/11, which undoubtedly contributed to the cloud of suspicion hanging over the Muslim American community. In a radio appearance promoting his new novel, New York Republican Congressional Representative Peter King claimed that the vast majority of American Muslim community leaders are "an enemy living amongst us" and that "no American Muslims" have cooperated in the War on Terror. He added that "about eighty to eighty-five percent of the mosques in this country are controlled by Islamic fundamentalists."[16]

Moreover, several of the Bush administration's antiterrorism activities fueled feelings of mistrust among the general populace. One of the most notorious proposals was for the creation of the Total Information Awareness (TIA) system. The original logo for the TIA was a glowing, all-seeing eye. This image captured the intent of the program, which was to create an "ultra-large, all-source information repository" meant to track citizens' every move, from Web surfing to doctor visits, travel plans to university grades, passport applications to bank withdrawals.[17] The extensive data-mining project granted traditional law enforcement agencies as well as the Federal Bureau of Investigation (FBI) and the Central Intelligence Agency (CIA) the authority to conduct "suspicionless surveillance" of American citizens without any judicial oversight.[18]

In 2002, Attorney General John Ashcroft and the Justice Department proposed an initiative by the name of Operation TIPS (Terrorism Information and Prevention System). Under Ashcroft's plan, one million American citizens—mail carriers, meter readers, cable technicians, utility employees, and other workers with access to private homes—would be recruited as informants to report any "suspicious activities" or "unusual behaviors" to the Justice Department. Operation TIPS was not without its critics. Lee Tien, a civil-rights attorney, said that "TIPS fundamentally creates an atmosphere of community distrust and suspicion that's inimical to a free society." Tien continued, "It's reminiscent of the tactics that the Stasi [East German secret police] and the Gestapo [Nazi secret police] used."[19]

Protests by privacy rights groups, as well as apprehension by some lawmakers over what amounted to domestic spying, impelled Congress to shut down the TIA system in 2003 (although evidence suggests that President George W. Bush continued to secretly and unlawfully authorize the surveillance program).[20] Operation TIPS was stopped before it ever got off the ground. Surveys showed, however, that despite serious civil-rights concerns, many Americans were strongly in favor of initiatives such as these, especially when they were aimed at monitoring the activities of Arab and Muslim Americans.

The public unease and aura of suspicion that followed 9/11 left nearly every participant in this study feeling as though they were terror suspects. The interviewees commonly talked about how the change after 9/11 was subtle but pervasive. After the terrorist attacks, it seemed that the men and women could go nowhere without being watched:

> It's just the suspicion, the look in people's eyes. It is hurtful the way people look at you with the suspicion, the implication of . . . [w]hat are you really doing here? Are you really here to shop, or are you scouting to put a bomb here? Something like that. That has been the most negative. It is not something tangible. It is very subtle—you can feel it in the looks.

> I'm walking into some place, and people look at me and look at my hands to see if I'm holding a bomb. Seriously, this is the kind of looks I get. When I walk somewhere and they know that you're a Muslim, they look at you. They look at your hands, at your bag.

Apprehensive Looks

Fourth, the Muslims in this study indicated that they were often looked at and treated in ways that made them believe that non-Muslims were now terrified of them. Some people became visibly anxious when they came into contact with the Muslim men and women; these individuals would cast looks suggesting that they thought the Muslim in their presence would harm or even kill them. The day after the World Trade Center collapsed, Selina, a second-generation Lebanese American, ran into a friend whom she had known for years. Rather than greeting Selina with kindness or sympathy, the young woman stepped away in fear: "People were looking at me, even your friends you've known for a while, they were . . . [t]he day after, my friend Beverly, I've known her since I don't know how long. I went up to her and I was like, 'Hi, Beverly.' She got scared and moved back. I couldn't believe it."

Selina's experience demonstrates that even persons who had long-standing relationships with Muslims contributed to the backlash. The sense of fear that so many communicated was likely exacerbated by the Bush administration's liberal use of the terms "Arab terrorists" and "Muslim terrorists" in the post-9/11 rhetoric surrounding the War on Terror. Mohammed, who was born in Morocco and came to the United States as a child, articulated this point:

> When I heard President Bush give that whole long talk about how Americans should respect Muslims and respect Islam, it's a beautiful religion and stuff, I said, "Wow, I really like this guy. I'm actually growing to respect him." But then, in the next breath he says, "But we must go to war with these Muslim terrorists." On the one hand he says, "Respect the Muslims; respect the Arabs." Then out of the other side of his face he says, "We must go to war with the Arab terrorists." It's confusing to the American people. What's up with the Arabs? Should we respect them or are they Arab terrorists? How can we tell who's a regular, nice Muslim and who's a Muslim terrorist?

The horrific sights and incalculable losses associated with the 9/11 attacks struck fear in the hearts of many Americans. At the same time, the disaster aftermath opened up a space for some Americans to behave in openly prejudicial ways toward Muslim Americans. Malik described how hurt he was after a woman grabbed her child and moved away from him: "I was walking with my mother. This lady, her daughter or her son, I think it was a little boy, was walking a few feet away from her. The minute she saw me coming, she snatched him away like I was going to do something to him. The little boy, of course, children are really innocent; they're taught to be racist. He didn't want to go. He was so busy walking and she just yanked him." So, in many cases, actions really did speak louder than words. Taken together, the piercing stares and sharp movements, the vigilant looks and nervous glances intimidated Muslim Americans and made many feel like feared enemies and hated outsiders.

Access Denied: Discrimination and Profiling

The American creed, as a cultural ideal, proclaims the dignity of every individual and affirms the human right of equitable access to justice, freedom, and opportunity, irrespective of one's race, ethnic background, or religious affiliation. In reality, a gap has always existed between this American ideal and actual institutional practice.[21] Even a cursory understanding of the history of Native Americans, African Americans, Latinos, Catholics, Jews, or any number of other minority groups in the United States confirms this last point.

For Muslim Americans, the gulf between creed and conduct was never clearer than in the period following 9/11. After the terrorist attacks, Muslims were profiled on the basis of their religion or ethnicity and subjected to subtle and overt discrimination in the areas of employment, housing, and education. These experiences were personally painful and, in some instances, threatened the livelihoods of the men and women who found themselves and their families excluded from core social institutions.

Employment Discrimination

Those respondents who were seeking jobs in the aftermath of 9/11 expressed a great deal of anxiety about their ability to compete in the labor market. In particular, they feared that their Islamic names and any connection to Muslim organizations would result in rejection during the application-screening phase of the hiring process.

The nonprofit Discrimination Research Center conducted a study suggesting that the concerns of Muslims were well founded. In a 2004 study, the Center sent out six thousand fictitious resumes to employment firms throughout California. All applicants were similarly qualified, but the different resumes included twenty names identifiable as white, Latino, African American, Asian American, Arab American, or South Asian. The name Heidi McKenzie got the highest response rate (36.7 percent), and Abdul-Aziz Mansour got the lowest (23 percent).[22] Research conducted in the United Kingdom, Canada, and France yielded similar results. In each instance, candidates with Muslim- or Arabic-sounding names were much less likely to be invited for an interview than applicants whose names indicated that they were of European or African descent.[23]

Of course, Muslims who are actually searching for jobs cannot know with any degree of certainty whether their applications are summarily dismissed because of their Islamic names or other identifying features on their resumes. This sort of rejection is very difficult to document and thus represents one of the most invisible forms of employment discrimination. With that said, several of the persons I interviewed reported barriers in the hiring process that seemed to be directly related to their Muslim identities. For example, Badia, an American citizen of Cambodian descent who wore the hijab, completed her undergraduate degree in business management nine months after 9/11. She applied for several jobs in the spring and summer months of 2002, but she received very few calls for interviews. Badia recognized that the post-9/11 economic downturn and other structural changes in the economy were affecting many people's job prospects, and therefore she did not want to attribute her employment problems to discrimination. It was only after her career counselor revealed that less-qualified college graduates were securing jobs that Badia acknowledged that she may have been treated unfairly:

> When I was looking for a job, it was really hard. I didn't think it would be, because I've never had a hard time getting a job before. I know the economy is down, so I'm not saying that people are discriminating against me. I've always disliked people blaming their shortcomings on discrimination. So I really didn't like to look at that, and I didn't for months. My career counselor was the one who brought it up. She was like, "Why haven't you gotten a job yet?" I graduated with a 3.9 GPA, and I had a lot of good things on my record. She said I should have gotten a job before the other people she was helping. There were companies I think may have discriminated against me because I'm female. One was asking if I had kids. All three of the places I interviewed asked about my religion and what country I was from.

Badia's case illustrates that Muslim American women are susceptible to multiple, interactive forms of discrimination related to gender, race, nationality, and religion. Badia knew that it was illegal for employers to ask many of the questions that she received. Regardless, she answered their queries, because she feared that refusing to respond would have further damaged her already-diminished job prospects.

Ariana, who, like Badia, wore the headscarf, had a similarly difficult time as she searched for a job nearly a year after 9/11. Ariana was a stand-out student in college, had completed two marketing internships at prestigious firms in Manhattan, and was bright and articulate. With her educational and professional qualifications, she did quite well with telephone interviews. When she arrived for in-person interviews, however, she sensed that employers were taken aback by her appearance. Ariana recounted one such experience:

> I did a telephone interview, and the woman liked me very much. She asked about my resume, and she asked me to come in. She said I needed to do some tests. I came in, and I said my name. The receptionist was like, "Do you have a copy of your resume?" She was like, "Okay, we'll contact you." I said, "Can I talk with Sharon? Because on the phone she said I need to take an exam and do an interview." The receptionist said, "No, that's after you're hired." I said, "Okay, but could I talk to Sharon just to tell her I'm here?" She was like, "No, she's not available." I didn't think much of it, but there were others

> waiting for the interview, and they were kind of giving me this weird look. I think they were there for the same thing, but when they saw me, it was like, okay. . . . They never called back.

Ariana was uncertain whether this incident was the result of religious bias on the part of the receptionist or if she simply was not qualified for the position. She remarked that even if the poor treatment was not due to anti-Islamic prejudice, it still made her feel insecure.

Several other women who wore the headscarf described virtually identical experiences with being invited for job interviews and then, upon their arrival, being told that no positions were available. Husna, an Afghan American, discussed what she went through as she attempted to secure a substitute teaching job in the school district near her home:

> I talked to the head of the district on the phone, and he informed me that I needed to get a special license to work as a substitute teacher. Everything went well with our call, and so I got the money order to attain the license. When I arrived with the money at the district office, they suddenly told me that there were no placements and that I should go elsewhere in search of other districts to teach in. I was so upset, because this district has access to schools close to my home. I wore the scarf at the time of the interview, and this whole thing was immensely stressful. I am very down about this. I guess out of mere survival, I must go to the other districts with my scarf off, and then when I get out of the district, then I would wear the scarf.

Rather than challenging the discriminatory behavior, which clearly caused her much distress, Husna decided to look for another substitute teaching job in a district more than an hour from her home. She ultimately was hired before she was forced to remove her headscarf, a possibility that she contemplated only after potential employers rebuffed her on several occasions.

Stereotypes, conscious or unconscious, that associate Muslims with violent extremism caused problems for a number of men who were seeking employment after 9/11. Malik, who had lived throughout the Middle East while growing up, was aware of the many negative images associated with persons from that region of the world. Therefore, he would often withhold information about his upbringing and religious affiliation until later in conversations or job interviews, presumably in hopes that his personality and qualifications would override any preexisting stereotypes:

> In a job interview, in any encounter, why is it that I relegate saying that I'm Muslim to the end? Why is it that I don't mention it imme-

> diately? That indicates that there is definitely a problem here. I don't want people to stereotype me. It isn't like there isn't a stereotype. There's a very bad stereotype. People get scared. To give you an example, at a job interview a few days ago, they realized that I was from the Middle East. They asked me about my background, and I told them. They became visibly uncomfortable. I could tell that something was wrong. I didn't say anything. I didn't want to say anything. I was a little disappointed, but I let it go.

Because of the mistreatment that Malik experienced during this particular interview, he realized that it was highly unlikely that he was going to be hired. Thus, although he was disappointed, he made the decision to "let it go" rather than pursuing the matter further.

Those respondents who were employed in part-time or full-time positions also suffered the consequences of the post-9/11 backlash. The interviewees described numerous hurtful encounters with supervisors and colleagues who made hateful remarks or sent disparaging e-mails regarding Muslims, Islam, and Arabs. The day after the terrorist attacks, Malika, who was the only Arab Muslim in a company with roughly three hundred employees, was singled out and subjected to hostile comments:

> It was on the twelfth [of September]. I had gone downstairs, and everybody was talking about their reactions to it. That was the first time that I started hearing, "Nuke 'em, those Arabs, the Muslims. . . ." I kind of expected that, but [not] to hear it the way it was directed toward me. They know I'm Arab. I know a lot of people were talking out of anger and hurt, but this one particular guy, he looked straight at me. He was like, "We need to get rid of that entire part of the world. I know you have family living in Egypt, and I know they may get hurt or they may die, or you may get hurt as a result of it, but they all need to go."

Malika was one of the few people I spoke with who actually reported the harassment to her boss. When I asked her why she went to her supervisor, she explained: "I lost three people, three business associates who died in the collapse [of the Twin Towers]. I went into my boss's office, and I'm like, 'Listen. I need to tell you this right now, because there's no way I can deal with this. I want to grieve too, like everybody else. I can't feel like I'm being put on the defensive. Let me grieve.'"

Soon after Malika talked to her supervisor, the president of the company sent out a memo indicating that workplace harassment on the basis of gender, ethnicity, or religion would not be tolerated. According to Malika, the hostile comments subsided after the memo was distributed. She said, "I think it only stopped because I said something. Had I not, I think it would have continued."

Those who were employed in the service sector had to contend with a sharp post-9/11 rise in discrimination from co-workers and customers. Nationally, gas stations, convenience stores, and ethnic restaurants—workplaces where working-class South Asian and Middle Eastern Americans are concentrated—were especially hard hit in this regard.[24] Taxi drivers in New York City, 85 percent of whom are estimated to be Muslim, suffered a severe drop in income, increased financial worries, and more hostility from passengers after 9/11.[25] One interviewee highlighted this problem: "I know a lot of taxi drivers. They're afraid of the windows getting bashed; they have no customers. They're from the Middle East, or they're Indian or Pakistani." Another man who worked as a taxi driver in New York said:

> Ninety percent of the people who get in the cab, they just ignore you, or they're curious about where you're from, why you have the Muslim name. But then there's that 10 percent who you can just feel them tense up. You can sense that they don't like you, and they are angry about your religion, about where you come from. Those are the people I'm scared of. You just can't know what's going to happen to you, whether those angry ones are going to get violent on you.

One interviewee noted that the anti-Muslim backlash from passengers resulted in layoffs at the car company where his uncle was employed: "My uncle works in a car company. The people are calling in and saying, 'Don't send a Muslim driver.' As a consequence, the company says, 'We don't need Muslim drivers.'"

A young woman who worked with her immigrant parents at a motel stopped wearing the headscarf after 9/11. She explained that her family was fearful of how customers would react upon seeing a covered Muslim woman at the front counter: "I have been helping out my parents in running a motel business. My parents didn't want me to wear the headscarf, because they believe that when dealing with customers, you never know what type of people you will meet."

Following 9/11, participants were more hesitant to ask their employers for accommodations to fulfill their Islamic religious obligations. For example, practicing Muslims sometimes must request a private space to pray, extended lunch periods on Fridays to attend Friday prayers, time off for Islamic holidays, and modifications to wardrobe requirements to wear Islamic attire at work. Even though they have a legal right to make such requests, the men and women were fearful that they might be "looked down upon" or even fired if they asked for any type of "special treatment" on the job. Ali, who began student teaching in the fall of 2003, had a particularly difficult encounter with the principal at his new high school:

> In the situation I'm in, I have a more flexible schedule where I can sneak in the time during prep hours or during lunch hours to get my prayers done. On a daily basis, that's what I need to do to fulfill my need to pray. So on a daily basis, it's not a problem. The only concern would be the Friday prayers. That takes more than five minutes. It takes at least an hour. Depending on the location, if you have to travel there [to the mosque], it might take more. In the school where I work now, this was something I had to bring up early on. The principal had to make a schedule for me, so he deserves to know this. Before school started, before we were even in the classroom, I told my principal that I have a religious need to be fulfilled, that every Friday I have to go to the mosque. It takes an hour at most from here. He responded very unprofessionally, sucked in his breath, moaned, rolled his eyes, and said, "Oh, God," as if it was trouble for him. I knew that he was not professional about this.

After Ali described this encounter, I asked him how he responded. He replied:

> I contacted different people and heard different things. Some people said, "Schools don't have a requirement to fulfill your needs." Others said, "They have an obligation to help you practice your faith or at least make an accommodation for it." The librarian, he spoke up for me. I didn't know who he was. He came up to me and asked me how I was doing. I told him about the situation, and he spoke to the principal. He spoke up to accommodate my need. Later the principal said, "From now on you just leave at noon. We'll give you five periods of classes Friday morning and then you're gone for the day." I said, "Okay, great." I was really happy to have that happen.

Ali realized that had it not been for the intervention of the librarian, who was a highly respected senior staff member at the school, he may not have been granted this accommodation. And, in the worst-case scenario, he was fearful that he might have lost his teaching position altogether.

Housing Discrimination

Muslims also experienced discrimination in the housing sector as a consequence of the post-9/11 backlash. Among the persons whom I interviewed, non–U.S. citizens were the most likely to report being turned away or blatantly mistreated as they attempted to navigate the housing market. Khalid, a graduate student from Turkey who had moved to New York City just prior to 9/11, was unable to secure an apartment for several weeks after the disaster. He was forced to sleep in the library at his university (which fortunately was open twenty-four hours a day) and to shower at an on-campus gym. Although Khalid initially blamed his problem on the general lack of affordable housing in the city, he later revealed that several of the people he had contacted in his attempt to find an apartment had hung up on him when they heard his Islamic name and heavy Turkish accent. Khalid described one renter who was especially confrontational: "He said, 'What nation are you from?' I said, 'I am from Turkey. I am a graduate student at Columbia.' Then he said to me, 'Oh, are you working on terrorism at Columbia?' I asked his name. He told me, 'Why are you asking my name? Are you going to blow me up?' Then he starts shouting at me."

Khalid eventually found an apartment and was able to stop sleeping in the campus library. He completed his master's degree in the spring of 2003, and soon after his graduation he returned to Turkey. We spoke just before he left the United States, and he remarked:

> Before I came to the United States, I was always thinking to stay here and continue my life here, because when I moved here, I saw that you can easily live your life however you like. But after 9/11, I thought to myself that I shouldn't stay here, I should go back to my country. I really lost my motivation, and it has become very hard for me to continue here. Being a Muslim or being a foreigner in the United States is not easy.

Khalid's identity as a Muslim and a foreigner left him doubly vulnerable to discrimination following 9/11.

Those Muslims who were born and raised in the United States also experienced housing discrimination. However, the security and cultural familiarity that comes with citizenship meant that they were more likely to fight back against biased renters. An apartment manager in Brooklyn mistreated Hassan, a native of New Jersey. As he explained how he responded to the discrimination, he contrasted the reactions of native-born Muslim Americans with recently arrived Muslim immigrants:

> I'm beginning to realize through talking to people that there are two different types of reactions. There are reactions of the people who were born here, and who are American, like myself, who have been in the country and know how the system works, know a lot about

> it. And then there's the reaction of the people who are not from the country, the international students and the foreign workers, who are here on a temporary basis or just new to the country and who really are more fearful about what's going on in general. I feel like the people that are born and raised here, especially because of the language, they know how to get by; they won't really stand out as much as somebody with an accent who looks different or doesn't know how to act, hasn't melted into the melting pot that much. My reaction, when someone harassed me as I called about the apartment [in Brooklyn] was like this. First, because of my name, they know I am probably Muslim. So, when they started to get an attitude, I was able to respond and say, "Listen, what you said, you're discriminating against me. I could report you." But people from other countries, the non–U.S. citizens, they may not be as familiar with such things.

Hassan identified a number of resources that Muslim citizens were able to draw upon as they navigated a hostile post-9/11 environment. Native-born Muslims not only know the language and customs of the United States; they also "know how the system works." To Hassan, this meant confronting the apartment owner and advising him that he would report the discriminatory behavior to the local housing authority. Hassan understood that the housing discrimination that he experienced violated his civil rights and that channels were available for him to report the incident.

Government appeals for citizen vigilance in the aftermath of 9/11 may have provoked, at least in part, the hostile treatment that Khalid, Hassan, and other Muslims encountered as they searched for housing. Specifically, following the terror attacks, the FBI issued an advisory warning that terrorists might have rented apartment units with the intent of blowing up buildings from the inside. The FBI subsequently called on property owners, public housing officials, and landlords to be on the lookout for potential terrorists attempting to rent apartments.[26]

Some of the women in this study, all of whom lived in apartment complexes in New York City, were asked by their landlords to stop wearing their headscarves. The landlords made this request on the grounds that the Muslim women's visibility was making other tenants uncomfortable or suspicious. Kaori, an international student from Japan who converted to Islam, had multiple run-ins with her landlords, a married couple who lived in the same building, following 9/11:

> My landlords, they were really nice people before [9/11], but these days they are kind of mean to me and tell me to take the hijab off. They're very discriminatory people. Whenever they see me, they just

> beg me, "Please take it off. Because I don't want any Muslim woman living in my apartments." It hurts me, but they are my landlords, and they are saying these things. After 9/11, they didn't like me, and they became very mean. I'm just telling them very patiently that I can't take it off. This is my religion.

Kaori ended up staying in her apartment, even though she was very uncomfortable. Finally, months after 9/11, her landlords stopped harassing her and making comments about her headscarf. Kaori never reported the landlords for their actions.

Discrimination in Education

College campuses are often depicted as liberal bastions where tolerance and respect for diversity reign supreme. Yet considerable evidence shows that marginalized groups, including racial and ethnic minorities, gays and lesbians, women, and persons with disabilities, are often treated unfairly by their peers and professors.[27] In November 2001, the *Review of Higher Education* estimated that at least one million bias-motivated incidents—ranging from relatively minor acts of vandalism to serious episodes of violence—occur on American college and university campuses each year, the vast majority of which are never reported to school or law enforcement authorities.[28]

In the year following the 9/11 attacks, the American-Arab Anti-Discrimination Committee (ADC) and the Council on American-Islamic Relations (CAIR) documented more than two hundred cases of physical violence, threats, and harassment against Arab American and Muslim American students.[29] The incidents began to accumulate almost immediately after the collapse of the Twin Towers. A Muslim student at Arizona State University was pelted with eggs. Muslim and Arab students at the University of California at Berkeley received death threats and hate mail. Anti-Muslim signs were posted at Indiana University in Bloomington. Vandals smashed the windows of the MSA office at Wayne State University in Detroit. Two men beat a Lebanese student on the campus of the University of North Carolina at Greensboro. The men yelled, "Go home terrorist!" as they repeatedly punched the victim in the face. Arab and Muslim children in elementary and secondary schools faced similar problems, and Muslim teachers and professors were harassed and, in some cases, unlawfully dismissed from their jobs.

The undergraduate and graduate students who participated in this study recounted a number of incidents of discrimination on their college campuses. At one of the universities in Manhattan, an angry mob gathered outside the student center and began chanting, "I hate Muslims." They stopped only after someone called building security. One of the Muslims at the school described the scene: "A big group of students were all gathered around shouting, 'I hate Muslims; I hate Muslims.' Those people around them are laughing at that. Nobody said anything to them. It is really the worst I have seen. They only wanted to stop after the security guards arrived."

Some college professors singled out Muslim students and subjected them to hostile comments. The Muslim men and women who suffered from bias in the classroom felt mostly powerless to respond, in part because they believed their course grades depended on their relationships with the teachers. Therefore, victims of this form of hostility usually chose to remain silent in the face of verbal slights. Shafana described what happened to her friend, a young woman who had the unfortunate distinction of sharing the same last name as Ramzi Yousef, the terrorist convicted of planning the 1993 bombing of the World Trade Center: "One of my friends is in law school. Her last name is Yousef. When she was in class, the professor talked about history. Somehow they got onto the topic of the World Trade Center. And because the man in the last bombing, his last name is Yousef, the professor said, 'Well, Miss Yousef, what do you think about this?' She felt so pinpointed." I asked Shafana if her friend said anything in response to the teacher. She laughed and said, "No way! Are you kidding? This guy would have failed her."

A few of the interviewees believed that professors had given them lower grades on assignments as a result of anti-Muslim prejudice. One young woman, Neva, noted that her political science instructor had made several negative comments about Islam in class in the weeks following the 9/11 attacks. When she received her first assignment back, the teacher had given her a low grade but offered no clear explanation for why the paper had been marked down:

> My teacher gave me a C– on an assignment. There were no marks on it, nothing. The only comment is "This isn't at all what I expected." I could not understand what she meant. So I am trying to decide whether I should talk to her about it. This teacher has been making negative comments all semester about Islam. I think this grade must be religiously motivated. Or maybe she is racist? But then I blame myself, maybe if I would have gone to the writing lab and had it checked first.

Even though her professor had made hateful remarks about Muslims and Islam on numerous occasions, Neva still felt self-doubt and self-blame regarding the low grade that she received.

In the aftermath of the terrorist attacks, educators, many of whom were struggling with their own feelings of loss and anger and fear, were confronted with difficult student questions about the causes and consequences of 9/11. The students in this study reported that many of their professors avoided the subject altogether. Other professors acknowledged their own limited understanding about Arabs, Muslims, and Middle East politics but attempted to provide their students with credible scholarly sources on these subjects. In some instances, professors created classroom environments where Muslim students felt that their faith was inaccurately portrayed or even discredited altogether.

Several students reported that their professors misrepresented the concept of jihad, a word that has appeared frequently since 9/11 in the Western media and is most often translated as "holy war." However, the word "jihad" actually has many different meanings and may be used in various contexts. According to religious studies scholar Frederick Denny, "jihad" means "exertion" or "struggle for a better way of life." In its spiritual sense, it is an inner striving to rid the self from debased ideas, inclinations, and actions and to exercise constancy and perseverance in achieving a higher moral standard. Jihad can involve, if necessary, armed struggle against the enemies of Islam, but only in self-defense.[30]

Rania, a second-generation Indian American, was distressed by the way her professor described Muslims and depicted jihad: "In one of his lectures after 9/11, my history professor added a section on Islam and terrorism. As he was lecturing, he puts up these pictures and says, 'These are Muslims. They believe in something called jihad, and the women carry bombs in the clothes that they wear; that's why they wear this attire.' I felt terrible about this, sitting in this class as the only Muslim woman covered." Rania decided to drop the class rather than to challenge her professor.

Basem, who was working on a master's degree in Colorado, had a similar experience with a professor who portrayed jihad as a form of violent holy war. Basem spoke to the professor after class and explained that jihad has multiple meanings and that many Muslims view jihad as a personal inner struggle to adhere to their Islamic faith. Basem asserted that various misperceptions about Muslims and Islam emerge from questionable sources that students and faculty read in our nation's universities: "Most of the books we are reading, they are not written by Muslim people. They don't know anything about Islam. They write wrong stuff about jihad. They don't know anything. The students need to know that we are not terrorists, and this is not jihad."

Non-Muslim students were the source of many of the hostile comments that the participants reported post-9/11. Even in classes where the professors attempted to approach the subject of violent extremism from a more global and historically informed perspective, some of the students seemed capable of viewing terrorism only in relation to Islam:

> In one class, we're learning about terrorism right now. We were going to learn about it later on, but she [the professor] moved it up so we can learn about it right now and follow things. You can tell the professor's trying to explain that terrorism is everywhere and provoked by many different factors, not just Islam, but it is clear from the students' reactions that they don't really understand that terrorism is everywhere and it's not just Muslims.

In other cases, students were overtly hostile toward Islam and the Muslim students in the classroom:

> This guy in my class, he blurts out, "Muslim parents teach their children to become terrorists." Another guy piles on and says, "Yeah, we should kill all the Muslim children now, because when they grow up, they're going to be terrorists. They're brainwashing the kids." The sad thing is it is clear that I am Muslim. I am sitting in there, and they know this is my faith, but they say it anyway.
>
> Last week we had our student-teaching seminar. It was on a different topic, but the professor shifted it to making groups to discuss what happened on 9/11. There was one woman in my group who was talking about how Muslims and Arabs should be shipped back to where they came from. I'm listening to her, and she's looking at me. I said, "Where are you going to send me? I'm from this country." And she's an educator and still saying these things. I said to her, "You have to take ignorance out of your mind, step out of it." She didn't want to hear it. She just got up and walked away.

Tahira, who was pursuing a doctoral degree in English and was employed as a graduate teaching assistant, encountered problems with one of the students enrolled in her class in the spring of 2002. The student, whom Tahira described as a "very liberal, progressive, feminist woman," complained to the professor about Tahira's religious attire and refused to interact with her in the classroom: "This student, she went up to the professor and said, 'I don't feel comfortable having this woman for my TA, because she's oppressed. Look at what she's wearing.' She went to the professor twice and said that. I went up to her and said, 'Look, I chose to do this [wear the hijab] when I was nineteen years old. I am not oppressed. No one is forcing me to do this.' But she really didn't accept it."

Although Tahira attempted to dispel the negative stereotype of her status as a Muslim woman, the student was unwilling to listen. The professor for the course eventually offered to talk with the student, but Tahira asked the professor to "just leave it alone."

Because several of the 9/11 hijackers entered the United States on student visas, the attacks brought new scrutiny to immigration regulations and to international students and foreign-born professors on college and university campuses. In 2003, the Department of Homeland Security implemented a vast electronic tracking system in an effort to monitor the activities of nearly a million foreign scholars in the United States. The Student and Exchange Visitor Information System (SEVIS) requires that institutions of higher learning send the federal government the names, addresses, course schedules, and majors of foreign students, as well as information on any disciplinary actions against them.[31] Under this program, if a student changed apartments or majors without informing the government, or if the student's grade-point average dropped below a certain level, he or she could be immediately deported. Also after 9/11, federal authorities began enlisting campus police officers in the domestic War on Terror, in part to gain better access to communities of Middle Eastern students.[32] About two hundred colleges and universities eventually acknowledged that they had turned over personal information about foreign students and faculty members to the FBI, most of the time without a subpoena or a court order.[33]

The security changes and delays that tightened visa regulations caused apparently deterred young people from predominantly Arab and Muslim countries from studying in the United States following 9/11. Some students were so intimidated in the aftermath of the terror attacks that they returned home in the middle of the school year. By the fall of 2002, the number of Middle Eastern students attending American universities had fallen by 10 percent. In addition, numerous educational institutions reported significant declines in new student enrollment from Muslim-majority countries, such as Saudi Arabia, Pakistan, the United Arab Emirates, and Indonesia.[34] Arab companies and organizations run by elites with a strong preference for American higher education sponsored fewer than half the average number of scholarships for students to study in the United States in the year after 9/11.[35]

The sharp drop-off in foreign-student enrollment was a concern to many observers. Foreign students contribute an estimated $15 billion to the U.S. economy each year, and the nation has benefited significantly from the skills of foreign-born doctors, scientists, teachers, and others who have stayed after completing their degrees. After 9/11, these contributions were largely overshadowed in a climate marked by suspicion and fear.

Religious and Ethnic Profiling

After 9/11, the executive, legislative, and judicial branches of the federal government implemented a number of antiterrorism policies and programs that explicitly targeted Muslim and Arab communities in the United States. These initiatives—warrantless surveillance and wiretapping, secret searches and seizures, detentions and deportations, special security checks, "voluntary" FBI interviews, raids on homes and businesses, and special registration programs—singled out entire groups on the basis of their religion, countries of birth, or ethnicities in response to the actions of a small number of people who shared their ascribed characteristics.[36] These policies have most directly affected immigrants and visitors from Arab and Muslim countries. However, Arabs and Muslims who are citizens have also been subject to blanket suspicion and racial profiling.

A growing body of empirical research demonstrates that when law enforcement officers rely on broad, generalized categories, such as race or religion, they are distracted from using more refined and effective investigative techniques, such as behavioral cues and suspect- or crime-specific descriptions.[37] Put more simply: Racial profiling is an ineffective law enforcement strategy. It casts too wide of a net that depends on police officers drawing on stereotypes in determining whom to target, which often results in missed opportunities to apprehend criminals who do not fit the prescribed profile. Moreover, profiling may alienate already marginalized groups and can evoke feelings of resentment and distrust among community members toward the police.

In February 2001, seven months before the 9/11 attacks, President Bush gave a speech in which he unequivocally stated that racial profiling is "wrong, and we will end it in America." He continued, "Racial profiling in law enforcement is not merely wrong but also ineffective. Race-based assumptions in law enforcement perpetuate negative racial stereotypes that are harmful to our rich and diverse democracy and materially impair our efforts to maintain a fair and just society."[38] In June of the same year, the End Racial Profiling Act of 2001 was introduced with bipartisan support in the U.S. Senate. Polls showed that the vast majority of Americans—more than 80 percent—disapproved of the practice of racial profiling and believed that it was inappropriate for law enforcement to single out minorities for special interrogation or searches.[39] The dubious practice of racial profiling seemed to be on its way out in the United States.

But everything changed after nineteen Arab Muslim men perpetrated the most deadly terror attacks in American history. A shocked and fearful nation expressed newfound levels of support for ethnic and religious profiling. A poll conducted days after 9/11 revealed that nearly 60 percent of Americans were in favor of profiling when directed at Arabs and Muslims, including those who are U.S. citizens. Almost half favored special identification cards for such people, and 32 percent backed "special surveillance" for them.[40] More than three years after 9/11, 44 percent of Americans said they believed that some curtailment of civil liberties was necessary for Muslim Americans, 26 percent said they thought that U.S. law enforcement agencies should closely monitor mosques, and 29 percent agreed that undercover law enforcement agents should infiltrate Muslim civic and volunteer organizations.[41]

During a U.S. Civil Rights Commission hearing in 2002, President Bush's appointee, Peter Kirsanow, raised the possibility of prolonged detentions for Arab Americans in the event of future terrorist attacks. In response to reports of widespread civil-rights violations against Arabs and Muslims, Kirsanow stated, "If there's another terrorist attack, and if it's from a certain ethnic community or certain ethnicities that the terrorists are from, you can forget about civil rights in this country." He went on to suggest that U.S. internment camps may return, like those used for Japanese and Japanese Americans during World War II. When pressed to clarify his remarks, Kirsanow simply responded, "Not too many people will be crying in their beer if there are more detentions, more stops, more profiling."[42]

After the 9/11 hijackers turned commercial airliners into weapons of mass destruction, airports became one of the most common settings in which those perceived to be Middle Eastern or Muslim were targeted. Several of the persons I interviewed, including men and women, reported that they were subjected to lengthy security checks when they attempted to fly. Even though these checks were inconvenient, and sometimes humiliating, most of the participants said they understood why they were being scrutinized. Others seemed resigned to the fact that their travel would be delayed. Jamil, a Pakistani American man, described his experience flying from New York to Louisiana to see his family soon after the terrorist attacks:

> I was going on an airplane. When I was going up with my boarding pass, there were two people taking boarding passes. Then there was a guy behind them waiting for me. He searched and did everything. You always want to feel angry, but he's just doing his job. Somebody's telling him to do it. You can never actually get to the core of the issue, like who's responsible. So you just let it go. It happened to my brother, too. He just let it go. What can you do?

Another young Pakistani American male explained the length of time it typically takes him to get through airport security: "I understand how people feel about this, about being targeted. It takes me seven hours, literally, this is no joke, to get from the ground to a plane. On my passport, my name is identical to that of a wanted terrorist. I know the frustration that goes along with being Muslim."

After the passage of the Aviation and Transportation Security Act in 2002, the federal government assumed direct responsibility for airport security. As complaints of discriminatory passenger removal and abusive treatment on the part of airport security personnel mounted, the Federal Aviation Administration implemented the Computer Assisted Passenger Screening (CAPS) system, which purportedly standardized the criteria for deciding which passengers to scrutinize closely.[43] Knowledge of these new criteria did little to assuage the concerns of Arab and Muslim Americans. The Arab American Institute Foundation commissioned a May 2002 poll that found that 78 percent of Arab Americans believed that profiling of Arabs and Muslims had increased after 9/11. After taking a flight from Denver to San Francisco, one interviewee in this study said, "I can tell you, I have never had to go through so many checkpoints. Being pulled out of a screening line and forced to go through three 'random' searches on one trip."

Participants were also subjected to additional security checks in other public settings and at special events that drew large crowds of people. As with other forms of discrimination, the visibility of the individual played a major part in whether law enforcement or security personnel scrutinized him or her. This topic came up when I interviewed a second-generation Pakistani American woman, Rashida, and her friend Katie, a white convert to Islam. Rashida did not cover her hair and wore typical American clothing. Katie, on the other hand, wore the hijab and more traditional Islamic dress. Rashida described two instances in which security checked Katie's bags, and she was certain it was because of Katie's attire: "When I'm with Katie, I notice things like . . . [m]e and her were out last week, and we went into a building downtown. We both had bags with us, but they only checked her bags. They called her back to look into her bags. To me, they were like, 'Oh, you're fine; go ahead.' It's because she wears the head cover. Even at the Mets game, they checked Katie's bag and not my bag."

Almost every Muslim I spoke to knew someone—a family member, an acquaintance, a friend of a friend—whom law enforcement authorities had questioned after 9/11. Interviews with FBI agents and other officers were frightening, stressful, and demeaning and made Muslims feel like suspects. Salih was friends with several people who were subject to FBI interviews in the months following the 9/11 attacks. Because he knew these people were in no way involved with terrorism, he expressed doubts regarding the methods and motives of the FBI:

> I know several people who were questioned after 9/11. It's sad. The fact that the FBI is questioning people who are your friends means that they have no idea what they're doing. Because your friends are completely innocent, and you know that. So if they're coming to question your friends, you kind of wonder if they have their act together. But also, it really concerns people. Even if you haven't done anything, it can make your life difficult. I'm concerned about that. I'm more careful about what I say and where I say it.

In reflecting on the profiling initiatives that targeted the Muslim and Arab communities, one woman said, "I think the most negative thing that came out of 9/11 was the laws being passed. It's not only about people, about singling you out—it's about the government actually passing laws to single you out. It's very scary."

The tapping of telephones and monitoring of e-mail correspondence was yet another civil-rights concern that the respondents identified. Parents and other family members had asked some of the participants to avoid speaking on the telephone about 9/11, the wars in Afghanistan and Iraq, Islam, and any number of other "suspicious" topics. Several of the interviewees were personally convinced that their phones were indeed tapped and that the federal government was spying on them. Abdul, who had come to the United States as a refugee from Afghanistan as a very young child, discussed what happened to him:

> I was talking to my cousin. He lives in California. He told me that FBI agents would come through Afghans' homes. They'd come to their houses and say, "Why did you talk to Pakistan three times last month?" Because they were talking to their family. They came to one of his uncles on his mother's side and asked questions for about forty-five minutes. He was saying this on the phone. All of a sudden we heard something in the phone. The phone was tapped. He said, "If anyone's on the other side listening to this conversation, I just want them to know that we're not for terrorism; we're just talking about our families." We were talking, and we heard people from the other side talking, and he said that so they would not come and ask him questions.

Another man, Marwan, nodded as Abdul spoke and then said, "I'm sure our phones are tapped. I'm sure we're being watched. You've got to be careful about what you say. There's always that possibility that they could do anything they want at any time, which I really do believe."

The possibility exists that Marwan was indeed "being watched" after 9/11. Several provisions in the USA PATRIOT Act introduced controversial tactics that expanded the ability of the government to conduct secret searches of private property, seizures of assets, and surveillance of electronic communications with reduced standards of cause and levels of judicial review.[44] Years after the 9/11 attacks, the Bush administration acknowledged that intelligence agencies conducted warrantless eavesdropping on Americans with the help of several large telecom companies. Although these revelations came as a shock to some citizens, the news of government spying simply confirmed what Muslim Americans already knew.

Violent Confrontations

The 9/11 atrocities provoked a nationwide surge of retaliatory attacks against Muslim and Arab people and their property. ADC and CAIR received a combined total of more than 2,400 reports of violent incidents in the wake of the terrorist attacks, and the FBI tallied 481 hate crimes in the last three months of 2001 (see Chapter 2 for a more thorough description of post-9/11 hate-crime statistics). Some of these incidents caused tens of thousands of dollars worth of damage to mosques, Arab- and Muslim-owned businesses, and homes. Others involved grievous bodily harm that resulted in hospitalization and permanent physical damage to the victims.[45]

Ten of the people whom I interviewed, three men and seven women, were physically assaulted after 9/11. These individuals reported being spit on, shoved in the subway, and having things thrown at them while walking down the street. Some of the women had their headscarves yanked or pulled off. Although less than 10 percent of the participants reported that they had been personally physically assaulted, all the interviewees had learned about violent attacks and other anti-Islamic crimes through family, friends, media coverage, or e-mail messages. This knowledge sent shockwaves of fear through the Muslim American community.

Nine of the ten interviewees who were physically victimized did not report the incident to law enforcement authorities. These individuals offered different reasons for why they did not go to the police, including their beliefs that the incidents were not serious enough to warrant investigation, uncertainty about whether the perpetrator(s) would or could be punished for the assaults, and unease with going to the authorities due to fears of hostile repercussions. Only one of the respondents, Shaheen, went to the police after an incident that involved her and her mother. If it had not been for the encouragement of a neighbor and a security guard, Shaheen may not have reported the confrontation either. She said:

> What happened to me personally with my mother was we went for a walk. We both wear the scarf. There was this punk little kid, maybe

> fourteen or fifteen [years old], mouthing off. My mother went to talk to him and said, "You need to go home." He spit right in front of us, on our shoes. It was horrible. I said, "You know, I feel sorry for you, because your mother didn't teach you any manners." That irritated him, and he started yelling, threatening us. A friend of ours had also been harassed by the same boy. She called the apartment security. They came and talked to us, and my mother told them what had happened. He said, "Go to the police station and file a report." We went there and filed a report. The police officers were very supportive. They said, "Next time this happens, call 9-1-1, and he will be arrested." He was just a kid. We don't mean any harm to him, but they need to be reprimanded for what they're doing. They've probably been influenced by adults around them who have the same opinions. The police officers took us in their car, and we showed them the location. They drove us up and down in the neighborhood to see if the kid was still anywhere around. They were like, "It's okay, you don't need to be afraid. If anything happens, just come to the precinct." They were very supportive.

Some of the interviewees talked about friends or family members who had been physically assaulted in retaliation for the 9/11 attacks. Muslims would often share these stories with one another, and the backlash was a central topic of conversation and concern among peer groups and families for many months after 9/11. A young woman from New Jersey explained what happened to her best friend, who had immigrated to the United States several years before the 9/11 attacks:

> I remember my best friend came home. She was waiting for the bus to come and drop off her daughter. On the opposite side of the street, there was another bus. He [the bus driver] stopped the bus, came across the street, spit in her face, and told her to go back to her country. She told her husband she wants to go back home [to Syria]. Now she's going back in three weeks. It's hard for her. . . . But she can't stay here. She says, "I can't stay in a country where they don't want me. He came and spit in my face and said they don't want me here. I can't do it."

In Colorado, two men described a physical altercation that happened between their friend and two police officers. The incident, which occurred in early November 2001, ended in the arrest and detention of the young Muslim man:

MARWAN: One of our [friends] got stopped by a policeman [in Denver] just because he had a turban on. They pulled it over his head and beat him up so he wouldn't know who did it. He's in jail right now.

BAKIR: He was driving home one night. He had a turban on his head. Cops pulled him over and said something like, "Do you know how to fly a plane?" They proceeded to beat him up.

MARWAN: He didn't hold back on his verbal insults towards the police officers who were beating him up, so they put him in jail on some charge. He's been in jail for a month now. They're holding him for another month.

Many law enforcement officers responded to the post-9/11 backlash in a swift and professional manner, as illustrated by Shaheen's story detailed above. Yet, in some instances, prejudice on the part of police officers led to anti-Muslim verbal and physical assaults. The potential for police misconduct generated an added layer of fear among Muslim Americans, as they recognized that officers had the power to arrest, to detain, and to physically harm members of their community.

In addition to these more personal incidents, respondents often spoke of physical attacks that they had learned about through the media or e-mails. These included stories of murders, shootings, stabbings, rapes, and mob beatings. Sometimes these accounts had been substantiated; for example, several retaliatory murders were committed after 9/11, and the FBI prosecuted a number of these cases. Regardless of whether the information came from a "reliable" source, the stories of violent assaults were pervasive, especially in the weeks and months immediately following 9/11.

Muslims came to understand the seriousness of the post-9/11 backlash through personal experiences, the accounts of friends and family members, and the media. Because these stories were so common and were shared so frequently, many of the men and women I spoke with believed that federal hate-crime statistics grossly underrepresented the actual number of anti-Islamic assaults perpetrated after 9/11. Jafar emphasized this point: "Everyone has been closing their eyes and ears to people who have been attacked after 9/11 because they're Muslims. In the news they say, 'There have been 150 cases; the FBI is investigating 40 of them.' Come on. Just by myself, I know more than 40 people who have been harassed, discriminated against. There are thousands of these cases."

In addition to targeting individuals directly, property may be damaged or destroyed to frighten and to intimidate members of minority groups. Some of the participants in this study attended mosques or lived in homes that vandals struck after 9/11. Others had personal property that was ruined, although many attempted to avert this form of backlash by removing Islamic or Arabic symbols from their homes and cars.

Mosques and Islamic schools have become common targets for bias-motivated property crimes, largely because of their visibility and accessibility within communities. In the wake of the 9/11 attacks, a sniper shot out a stained-glass window in the dome of the Islamic center of Greater Toledo; vandals lobbed bricks through seven windows at the Islamic center in Norfolk, Virginia; and someone painted obscene graffiti on a mosque in Louisville, Kentucky. Dozens of similar incidents were reported from Tacoma to Tallahassee.[46] Laila, who was originally from Georgia, recounted what happened to the only mosque in her hometown: "Our local mosque was vandalized. Someone came in and spray-painted 'USA' and a couple of expletives. The whole community was scared. Our mosque has been doing a lot of interfaith work. By afternoon, there was a local rabbi who organized all the religious leaders to come in to clean the signs that were vandalized."

The interfaith community in this Georgia town came together to respond quickly and proactively to the attack on the mosque. What is less clear is whether this act of solidarity was enough to counterbalance the fear and isolation caused by the vandalism.

One of the interviewees from a midsize city in Colorado reported that a vandal scrawled swastikas on the door of the Islamic center in his community. A woman, originally from Michigan, described what happened to the mosque in her city. As she talked, there was a strong sense of resignation in her voice: "We've had a couple instances where somebody calls the mosque with threatening things, or somebody leaves tacks out, or nails out, hoping to puncture some tires. I suppose it's no more than what any ethnic group has to go through."

Natasha, who was a graduate student in journalism in the fall of 2001, was assigned by her professor to write reaction stories following 9/11. Two days after the attacks, she traveled to Brooklyn to visit an Islamic school that had been targeted. She described the scene: "They had that day, during the attacks, or shortly after, someone had thrown pork chops at their school, bloody pork chops and rocks." Natasha noted that the vandals obviously had enough knowledge to understand that pork is forbidden in Islam. Yet the perpetrators used this information to harm an entire community of Muslim youth and their families.

Beyond directing hatred at Islamic institutions, bigots also damaged the personal property of the Muslim respondents and their friends or family. One interviewee believed that her car windows were "smashed out" because she had an Arabic symbol on the dashboard. Another participant said someone had thrown rocks at his car, and he assumed the person did it because he "looked Muslim." A third respondent said that her Afghan Muslim neighbor had her door kicked in and graffiti painted on her home.

At times it was difficult for those who had been victimized to know with any certainty whether the crime was the result of bad luck or bias. For example, two weeks after 9/11, Roshan was visiting a friend at the hospital. When he returned to his car, he found that the tires had been slashed. When he told his parents about the incident, he said that his father "was upset because he thought it was because I had a slight beard growing." After this incident, Roshan's parents insisted that he shave his facial hair so that he would be less recognizable as a Muslim. Thus, even though no evidence proved conclusively that Roshan's tires were slashed because of his Muslim identity, he still suffered the consequences.

A number of men and women who were students offered examples of anti-Islamic and anti-Arab vandalism that had occurred on their university campuses in the days and weeks after 9/11. At one of the universities in Colorado, vandals scrawled, "Go home, Arabs," "Bomb Afghanistan," and "Go home, Sand N-ggers" on the pillars of the library. The graffiti on the outside of the building was removed the morning that it was discovered. Inside the same library, in one of the stairwells, someone had spray painted, "Stop Muslim World Takeover." This graffiti was not painted over for several months.

Sanae, an undergraduate student at a university in Manhattan, said that when Muslim students would put up fliers for their Islamic Association, other students would "pull them down, write negative stuff on them, or just throw them in the trash." Another student, Habeel, spoke of what happened at his university:

> We couldn't unite with others, because when we came back to school the day afterwards, we had boards in the hallway with condolences [for the victims of the 9/11 attacks]. But then somebody took it a step further and said, "Let's nuke the Middle East. Kill all the Muslims." It became violated. They started writing things like, "Get them all. Throw them out of the country. Kill all the Muslims. Deport the Muslims."

University officials eventually took the condolence boards down, but only after members of the MSA and Arab club complained about the derogatory comments scrawled across the board.

Witnessing Discrimination

The cases described above, almost without exception, involved men and women who were visibly Muslim. Their religious dress, dark complexions, or associations with Islamic organizations allowed bigots to identify and then to subject them to hateful treatment. Indeed, those who were recognizable as Muslim were more likely to be verbally abused, stared down, discriminated against, profiled by police, or physically attacked. The visibility factor also helps explain why other minorities who fit the stereotypical image of "what a Muslim looks like" were targeted after 9/11.[47]

Those Muslims whose faith was not as readily apparent were less likely to experience anti-Islamic bias at work, in the street, or in myriad other public spaces. This does not mean, however, that those who could pass as non-Muslim were left unscathed by the backlash. By virtue of their faith alone, these individuals felt vulnerable to being swept up in the Bush administration's terrorism investigations and were fearful of additional hostile repercussions against the entire Muslim American community. In addition, less-visible women and men became *witnesses to discrimination* as they observed overtly biased acts waged against other Muslims.

In the aftermath of 9/11, prejudiced individuals felt free to communicate their anti-Muslim perspectives in front of others whom they imagined would share their views. Kamilah, a university student from New York, described her confrontation with a classmate:

> When I came back to school, I was going to class. There was an African American female commenting about Muslim women. She said something completely disgusting. She turned to me and said, "Don't you think? Don't you think they should all just die?" I laughed and said, "That's funny." She said, "Yeah, you know, they should just all die." And I said, "You know, then I'll have to die." I looked at her and said, "I'm Muslim. You need to choose your words wisely." I got up and left. I haven't been back to that seminar. I couldn't believe something like that could be told to my face. You automatically assume because I don't cover, that you would think that I would be one of those ignorant people who think all Muslims should die?

Kamilah was aware that, because she was indistinguishable as a Muslim, the young woman felt comfortable making hateful comments in front of her. Kamilah verbally confronted this woman and revealed her faith identity. Although she felt good about responding proactively to the situation, Kamilah was so demoralized by the confrontation that she dropped the class so she would not have to "deal with" a similar situation again.

Many Americans have proven amazingly resistant to understanding that Muslims can be of any race, ethnicity, or nationality. This confusion is likely a consequence of pop-culture representations that conflate brown skin, Arab ethnicity, and Muslim religiosity. Such misperceptions prompted some people to say biased things in front of persons whom they assumed, because of their racial identity, would not be Muslim. Jinan recounted one such experience that happened to her father, an African American convert to Islam:

> My father was telling me about one time he was with one of his co-workers. They were driving past a mosque. The co-worker said something like, "I wonder why someone hasn't gone and blown that up yet?" He had no idea that my father was Muslim. My father was like, "Yeah, you know, I'm a Muslim." But when people do that, when these kinds of things come out, you start to wonder. You don't want to do that, but you wonder, what are they really thinking?

The uncertainty that Jinan expressed as she questioned, "what are they really thinking?" was quite common. When bigots made vicious remarks, unaware that a Muslim was in their presence, it left Muslims feeling that the prejudice against them may have been even more widespread than what they had initially imagined.

Some Muslims chose to remain silent after they witnessed anti-Muslim acts or overheard hostile comments. Jasmir, who had been hired at an investment firm just prior to the 9/11 attacks, wanted to confront the Muslim-bashers at his work and tell them that it was his religion that they were degrading. Yet he feared that if he spoke up, he would be ostracized and might even lose his job:

> I work as a consultant at a pretty high-profile investment firm. Listening to very educated people with master's degrees from Ivy League schools stereotyping, it just really made me feel very sick that people could be educated yet ignorant. It made me feel like I'm going to have a very hard time, even though I'm trying to stay away from all the negativity and just be very optimistic. I want to tell them I'm a Muslim, just throw it out there, just so they know, but I'm scared to do so. I'm sick and tired of hiding to go to prayer every day. At lunchtime—I'm fasting right now—I don't make plans to go out for lunch. I'm a very social person, too, but I just can't let these people know. I'm sick and tired of keeping it down. It's blatant in the workplace. People talk about Islam in such a negative manner.

The people that Jasmir worked with were highly educated and held degrees from some of the most prestigious universities in the nation. In light of their background, Jasmir was especially disappointed that they acted in such overtly prejudicial ways. The stress that Jasmir felt emerged from overhearing hateful comments and from having to hide a core aspect of his identity from his co-workers. Four months after 9/11, Jasmir began searching for another job, and he eventually left the investment firm. His new job paid less, but the environment was less stressful. Jasmir told me that although he had to struggle a bit more financially, the emotional trade-off was "definitely worth it."

The women who did not cover their hair were particularly attuned to the hostility that their Muslim sisters who wore the hijab faced after 9/11. Ni'ja was one of the few women among her peer group who chose not to wear the headscarf. As she traveled around New York City with her friends, she saw how often they were subjected to hateful stares. She explained one such incident that happened to her best friend, Tisha:

> Things didn't happen to me, because I don't cover. But my friends who wear veils, every day I would see them getting glared at. Just to give you an example: The other day, I saw this woman smiling at her little girl. Tisha walks by, and she was wearing a full veil. This woman, one minute she was beaming at her child with so much love, and the next minute she turns to Tisha and glares at her with so much hate. I feel so bad for the girls who are getting glared at. It has just been so disturbing.

Ni'ja was so upset about the hateful treatment that she witnessed repeatedly after 9/11, she seriously contemplated beginning to wear the headscarf. She ultimately decided not to do so, as she felt that she needed to make the choice "for the right reasons."

In sum, in the wake of 9/11, Muslims personally experienced, heard about from others, or observed first-hand several different types of discrimination, which ranged from hostile stares to physical attacks. The severity and duration of the backlash exacted a heavy emotional and physical toll on Muslim men and women. The next chapter takes up this issue and explores the many costs of discrimination.

5

Repercussions

The day after the most deadly terrorist attacks in the nation's history, the *New York Times* attempted to capture the collective mood and communal response in the city at the epicenter of the disaster:

> A sense of shock, grief, and solidarity spread rapidly through the city. There was the expectation that friends and relatives would be revealed among the victims. Schools prepared to let students stay overnight if they could not get home, or if it emerged that there was no one to go home to.
>
> There was also the fear that it was not over: Stores reported a run on basic goods. And there was the urge to help. Thousands of New Yorkers lined up outside hospitals to donate blood.
>
> As in great crises past, people exchanged stories of where they were when they heard the news.
>
> "There is a controlled professionalism, but also a sense of shock," said Mark G. Ackerman, an official at the St. Vincent Medical Center. "Obviously New York and all of us have experienced a trauma that is unparalleled."
>
> "I invite New Yorkers to join in prayer," said Cardinal Edward M. Egan as he emerged from the emergency room of St. Vincent's in blue hospital garb. "This is a tragedy that this great city can

handle. I am amazed at the goodness of our police and our firefighters and our hospital people."[1]

The newspaper report depicted a number of fundamentally human responses—the solidarity, a sense of collective suffering, the sharing of personal stories, the desire to help, and the strength and kindness of people on the ground—that have been replicated time and time again after disasters have struck small towns and large cities across the United States. Indeed, the creation of a "community of sufferers" is a phenomenon that has been repeatedly observed in the aftermath of natural disasters and other extreme events that have caused widespread social disruption.[2]

Charles Fritz, a pioneer of disaster research, contends that the community of sufferers develops in three distinct stages.[3] First, the emergent community begins to take form after the survivors experience firsthand or learn of the disaster and begin to communicate about it. Neighbors and strangers describe to one another where they were when the disaster struck, what happened to them and their family members, the feelings they experienced, and what they lost.

Second, the integrative stage emerges from the widespread sharing of danger, loss, and deprivation that accompanies all disasters. Survivors of these events subsequently experience a strong sense of mutual suffering and an intimate, primary-group solidarity that occurs as a result of "having been there." The emotional climate of the postdisaster community, which Fritz refers to as a therapeutic social system, elicits selflessness, generosity, friendliness, cooperation, and consideration. Information about the needs of community members is widely shared, and consensus is rapidly reached regarding actions to be taken to meet those needs.[4] In large-scale disasters, the therapeutic community response may persist for several weeks or even months, and one's personal identification as a disaster survivor may continue for much longer.[5]

The third and final stage marks the disintegration of the therapeutic community. This stage occurs as people return to everyday life and is evidenced by a growing concern with private interests. As the disaster-stricken community begins to feel "normal" again, the system swings back toward more common self-oriented behaviors.

When considering prospects for postdisaster recovery and healing, it is important to acknowledge that the types of interaction that the community of sufferers adopts offer a number of social and psychological benefits to the survivors. A sense of common danger draws people together and allows them, even if only temporarily, to resolve past conflicts and to work together for the common good. In essence, the shock of the disaster serves to shake people loose from ordinary concerns. "In everyday life many human problems stem from people's preoccupation with the past and the future, rather than the present," Fritz argues. "Disasters provide a temporary liberation from the worries, inhibitions, and anxieties associated with the past and the future because they force people to concentrate their full attention on immediate moment-to-moment, day-to-day needs."[6] This shift in awareness, Fritz adds, speeds the process of decision making, facilitates the acceptance of change, and motivates individuals to take action to begin the long process of restoration in the disaster aftermath.

The therapeutic community response also leads to a breakdown of barriers to intimate communication and interaction and subsequently opens up opportunities for collective grieving. When norms that typically discourage emotional expression are lifted, members of the disaster-affected community have the opportunity to publicly mourn, to weep, and to comfort one another. Rather than suffering privately and in silence, as so often happens to individuals in our society, the postdisaster context actually encourages survivors to share their stressful experiences.

Enhanced social cohesiveness and emergent norms that promote positive coping behaviors offer much-needed sources of physical and emotional support for disaster survivors. Yet in their quest to emphasize "the good news about disasters," researchers have too often overlooked the fact that social divisions and patterns of unequal treatment persist alongside altruism and heroism.[7] Consequently, we know very little about the social forces that might prevent interaction among those most affected by disaster. We know even less about what happens to individuals or entire groups of people who identify as disaster victims but are excluded from the emergent community of sufferers.

What is clear is that the "city of comrades" did not open its arms to the men and women who shared the same faith as those who brought down the Twin Towers and punched a hole in the Pentagon on 9/11.[8] In this chapter, I argue that the sudden and severe onset of the post-9/11 anti-Islamic backlash—the hate crimes, discrimination, and civil-rights violations—set Muslim Americans on a fundamentally different *emotional and behavioral response trajectory* than the wider U.S. population. This particular trajectory has been marked by a gamut of stressful responses, which, in turn, manifested themselves in ways that inhibited the ability of Muslims to collectively grieve, restricted their freedom of movement and speech, and resulted in conflict and other forms of distress within Muslim households.

The Initial Impact

As Muslim Americans received news of the hijackings and the explosions at the World Trade Center and the Pentagon, they, like most other Americans, reacted with some combination of shock, disbelief, confusion, anger, and fear. Selma, a twenty-six-year-old Yemeni American who witnessed the second plane crash on television, described the emotions she felt that morning as she watched the disaster unfold a thousand feet above ground: "I was definitely in shock. Sometimes it just takes you a little while to digest something. My mind just couldn't take it the first few minutes. It really was like I was in denial. I was thinking it was a movie. I must have just watched something out of a movie. I was definitely shocked."

When comparing the destruction to something out of a movie, Selma was searching for a frame of reference to help make sense of the horrific spectacle in lower Manhattan. Hamad, who lived in Colorado in the fall of 2001, learned of the attacks while listening to the radio. He reacted with a sense of disbelief and therefore initially assumed that what he had heard over the airwaves must have been a fake news broadcast:

> I woke up that morning, and I began ironing my shirt and pants for work. I turned on the radio, and the radio announcer said, "Please send your prayers out. There has been an attack on the World Trade Center." I said to myself, "Really? Is this serious?" I just couldn't . . . do you remember that story where, over the radio, where the guy said that there was an alien invasion, and everybody went nuts? You know, "War of the Worlds?" That is what I was thinking to myself: "This is a joke. Nah, they are just playin' around. This cannot be real." But then I remembered that they made a law that you can't do that, you can't make stuff up and put it on the radio. It was then that I realized that they were not playin' around. I ran downstairs and turned on the TV. That's when I saw the towers burning.

For many who were watching news coverage at the time of the second collision, it was apparent that what had transpired in the financial district of lower Manhattan was no accident. Khadija, who lived and worked in Brooklyn, saw the commercial airliner hit the south tower on live television. She immediately realized that a terrorist attack was underway:

> That morning, I was watching TV with my mom while we were eating breakfast. I saw the first building burning and I said, "Oh, this is a big accident!" I really thought it was just an accident. While I was looking at the TV, the second plane hit. I turned to my mom and said, "Oh God, this is a terrorist act." I just sat there in front of the TV. It was like I couldn't move. I'm like, "No, no. This can't be happening."

Although Khadija knew that an act of terrorism had just occurred, she had an incredibly difficult time coming to terms with the frightening reality that New York City was under assault. Noreen, who lived in the middle of Manhattan, noted that the sense of disbelief didn't wear off for days: "I was absolutely in shock at first. It didn't sink in. The calamity of it didn't sink in. I'd wake up each morning and I'd have to think, 'Did it really happen? Is the World Trade Center really not there? Did so many people really die?' It was just this overwhelming sadness, trying to understand why this happened."

Rawan, whose family immigrated to the United States from Saudi Arabia, was at school in Brooklyn on 9/11. Her older brother, who had recently graduated from college, had a job interview at the World Trade Center that morning. Because the phone lines were jammed after the attacks, Rawan was unable to reach him to find out if he was okay. She was terrified that she had lost her only sibling when the Twin Towers collapsed. Weeks later, when she told me her story, she still appeared traumatized:

> At first, I didn't even understand. Okay, there was an accident at the World Trade Center. A couple of planes crashed. Then I remembered that my brother had a job interview that morning at the World Trade Center. I knew he was supposed to be there at about 10:30. I thought to myself, "What if he was a little early?" I went to the phone. The line at the phone was so long. I kept hearing people talking about it. I started crying. A couple of people said, "We'll take you home. Everything will be okay." They had cell phones. I tried calling him with their cell phones. I couldn't get through, all the lines were busy. Finally I got home, and he answered the door. I was so happy. I looked at his face, and it was so pale. He kept saying, "Thank God I wasn't there." It was unbelievable. Even now when I think about it, anybody could have been in that building. I cannot really explain how sad and scared I felt that day.

Anger was another common emotional response reported by the interviewees. Shada, a Lebanese American woman, shared how she responded to the terrorist attacks: "How did I feel after this? Angry. Angry at the people who did this. Look at what they did. For the first few days, I was trying to just sit in front of the TV. I didn't know what to do. Looking at the families of the victims, it hurts."

The confusion, the paralyzing uncertainty, and the overwhelming emotions that Muslim Americans felt mirrored the sentiments that many non-Muslims across the nation expressed. However, the tragic events resulted in additional negative consequences for the Muslim American community, consequences not experienced among the general population. These added impacts set Muslim Americans on a divergent response trajectory and ultimately led to their exclusion from the community of sufferers.

Bracing for the Backlash

As Muslim Americans struggled to come to terms with the shocking reality of the attacks, they simultaneously began to worry that members of their community would be held responsible for what had happened. Malika, an Egyptian American investment banker, knew that if she immediately assumed that Muslims or Arabs were somehow involved in the explosions at the World Trade Center, then surely others were thinking the same thing:

> That morning, one of the offices at work had a radio going. That's when we found out that another plane had hit. Then you start hearing "terrorism." I was like, oh, no, please do not let it be terrorism; please do not let it be the Muslims again. I am sorry to say it, but that's the first thing that ran through my head . . . Muslim terrorists, Arab terrorists. If it ran through my head, then it was running through everybody else's head, too.

It is not shocking that Malika, as well as many other Muslims and non-Muslims alike, would guess that Arabs or Muslims were responsible for the assaults on New York City and Washington, D.C. Muslim Americans are painfully aware of the negative views that many people hold of their faith. Journalists were writing about "Muslim terrorists" and "Arab terrorists" long before 9/11. "Radical Islam" attracted widespread media attention when the 1979 Islamic revolution occurred in Iran, and American fears were further heightened with the seizure of the U.S. embassy in Tehran in November of that year. Bombings, hijackings, armed conflicts, and other political crises that took place in the Middle East in the 1980s and 1990s provided continuous fodder for an increasingly Islamophobic and anti-Arab Western press.[9] Thus, by the fall of 2001, the association of violence with the Middle East, Muslims, and Arabs was firmly entrenched in the public imagination.

Yet, contrary to the images cemented in the minds of so many, the Middle East is not the most terror-prone place in the world. This status was especially true before the 9/11 attacks and the ensuing "War on Terror," which inflamed tensions and sparked increasing bloodshed throughout the region.[10] According to U.S. State Department data on international terrorist attacks perpetrated between the years 1995 and 2000, Latin America experienced the most incidents, with 729 recorded acts of violence. For this same time period, Western Europe was second with 608 attacks, and Asia was third with a total of 267 attacks. The Middle East ranked fourth with 199 incidents, followed by Africa with 160 attacks and Eurasia with 151. North America had the lowest concentration of terrorist attacks, with only 15 incidents from 1995 to 2000.[11] In the year 2000, 86 percent of all anti-U.S. attacks occurred in Latin America. The rest of the recorded anti-U.S. attacks were in Asia (4.5 percent), Western Europe (3.5 percent), Africa (3 percent), Eurasia (2 percent), and the Middle East (1 percent).[12] These figures include attacks against U.S. facilities and attacks where American citizens were killed or injured. Regardless of the story these numbers tell, selective reporting on violence in the Middle East has contributed to a distorted and harmful perception of Muslims and Arabs living in the United States and abroad.

Given this preexisting context, and as the scale and ferocity of the 9/11 terrorist attacks became clear, Muslim Americans began bracing for the backlash. Even before a number of Arab Muslim men were officially identified as the perpetrators, Muslims recognized that they were likely going to become the targets of a shocked and angry public that had witnessed an unimaginable catastrophe unfold in real time.[13] During a focus-group session, several participants discussed their initial reactions to 9/11. For these women, the terror of learning of the physical destruction and loss of life coincided with their recognition that the entire Muslim American community would be blamed.

> SADAF: The first thing I thought was there are a lot of people who may be dead. This is so horrible. Right after that, it was we're going to get blamed. [*Everyone nods in agreement.*] We've always been blamed, so this time obviously we're going to be blamed too.
>
> IFFAT: This was such a big thing, the Twin Towers. It was the biggest thing we had seen on American soil.
>
> ANNA: We have this feel for it. We are American. I was born here. The Twin Towers meant a lot to me. They represented New York.
>
> SARA: I was just as surprised and saddened as anyone else. I was angry at the fact that people could do such a thing, angry that so many people were killed, and I was hurt and frustrated that people were blaming us. You feel so bad about what happened, but you're pinpointed as the evil one.

Wali, who immigrated to the United States from Morocco when he was five years old, indicated that he and his family were fearful that Muslims would be identified as the perpetrators and that a serious backlash would ensue. Wali's mother and sisters, in particular, were frightened that the backlash would be so violent that they would be trapped inside their home.

Therefore, on the day of the attacks, they sent Wali to the grocery store to buy vital supplies. He said, "I'm the oldest son, so after 9/11, I had to take care of everything. It was really hard. Right off, we were scared that the public was going to turn against us, that there was going to be this backlash like we had never seen. We had to stockpile everything, a week of food and other supplies. We had our supply of food for a week."

The sentiments expressed above and the precautionary measures that many Muslim families took do not represent a paranoid response. Quite the opposite: Knowledge of the bigotry that Muslims and Arabs have endured in the aftermath of other crises shaped, at least to a certain extent, apprehension on the part of Muslims. Another interviewee, Amani, remembered hoping that an American anarchist group would claim responsibility for the assaults on the World Trade Center and Pentagon. She felt this was the only way that Muslims and Arabs would not be victimized: "When I heard there was an attack, when I turned on the television and saw the plane hit the building, the first thing I said was 'I hope it's not a Muslim.' I just remember, I had this mental thing going. I kept thinking, 'I hope this is an American anarchist group. I hope this is an American anarchist group.'"

I asked Amani why she was thinking that. She replied: "A lot of it was that I was remembering the Oklahoma City bombings. I was hoping there wouldn't be that violence toward Arabs and Muslims before anyone knew who had done it. And I was hoping it hadn't been a Muslim group, because I knew it would come back on the community, and lots more people would be hurt."

Amani, a second-generation Pakistani American who was raised in Colorado, was only thirteen years old when Timothy McVeigh and his accomplice, Terry Nichols, destroyed the Alfred P. Murrah Federal Building, killing 168 people and injuring more than 800 others. Despite the fact that McVeigh and Nichols—both white, Christian men—were soon identified as the prime suspects, the 1995 Oklahoma City bombing led to a rash of hate crimes against Arabs, Muslims, and mosques across the nation (see Chapter 2). Amani and many others recalled the dread that they and their families felt during that time. They knew that the backlash would likely be much worse if Muslims were, in fact, found to be responsible for destroying the World Trade Center and attacking the Pentagon.

On the morning of 9/11, it was not yet clear who had carried out the hijackings. Nevertheless, speculation quickly began building in the media that Arab or Islamic extremists were behind the deadly attacks. Soon after the Twin Towers collapsed, Agence France-Presse reported that a group with the word "Palestinian" in their name had claimed responsibility. Video footage of a group of Palestinian children cheering in the streets, reportedly after they had learned of the terrorist attacks, accompanied this news.[14] The Taliban in Afghanistan were also identified as possible suspects, although they condemned the suicide mission and emphatically denied any involvement.[15] Several high-ranking military officers asserted that the only group in the world that had the ability and resources to carry out such a sophisticated attack was Osama bin Laden's terror network, al Qaeda.[16] On September 12, 2001, bin Laden met with Arab reporters to deny that he was behind the aerial assaults, although he offered praise for the hijackers.[17]

Rumors were also spreading on the ground about the source of the attacks. Several respondents—all of whom lived, worked, or went to school in one of the five boroughs of New York City—described encounters they had on the morning of 9/11. In most cases, the speculation focused on Muslims or Arabs as the likely perpetrators. Roughly an hour after the initial explosions in lower Manhattan, Bushra, a native of Bangladesh, had an uncomfortable exchange with a subway toll-booth attendant who asserted that Palestinian militants had piloted the planes into the Twin Towers:

> That day I went down to the train. I get down there, and there's no service. I asked the toll guy, "What time is it going to start again?" He was like, "Maybe tomorrow." I was like, "What?" People were trying to get into the trains, just trying to get home. Then the guy says, "Don't blame me; blame the Palestinians." At that time, I didn't even know why he was saying that. It was only an hour after it happened. I said, "Do you even know for sure that they did this?" He said, "Yeah, it's all over the news."

Nabiha, who wore the hijab, began receiving accusatory stares almost immediately after the planes hit the north and south towers: "An hour after it happened, just the way I was dressed, automatically everybody was staring. That fact that automatically people registered in their minds . . . Muslims, bombing, terrorism. That means it's really ingrained, and that's very scary."

Habeel, a Bangladeshi American whose dark complexion marked him as an ethnic outsider, recalled how a bus driver accused his "people" of instigating the attacks:

> I heard it from the bus operator. The first thing he told me was "Your people have done this thing." I was like, "What?" I didn't even know anything at that point. I could see the clouds of dust. He said, "They took the planes and hit the World Trade Center and the Pentagon. Your people did that. The president is going to attack." I thought he was just making fun of me. Then I went home and saw the TV.

Andrea lived in Denver, which is two time zones behind the East Coast, on September 11. Therefore, by the time she found out about the events that had transpired that morning, suspicion had already been cast on Muslims in general and on bin Laden in particular. As a result, her sadness of learning of the lives lost coincided with her recognition that a backlash against Muslims was likely inevitable:

> That morning, my mom told me there was some kind of bombing or some kind of attack. She said people were automatically saying, "It's the Muslims; it is probably the Muslims; it is probably bin Laden." And I was like, "Oh great." I knew, because every single time one of these things happens, the Muslim community, we react almost the same way every single time. We just hold our heads in this dread, because we know what is going to happen, because it has happened over and over and over in Western society, all around the world. The second a bomb goes off anywhere, "Oh it must be Muslim fundamentalists." So that is what we were mostly fearing, and I just knew it was going to be bad. Later on that day, I saw the clips of what happened and heard everybody talking about it, and it just put me to tears, just tears. On the one hand, I am crying for all the thousands and thousands of people who died. At first, they were saying there were probably thirty thousand people who died in the attacks. You just can't even imagine those types of numbers, and so it is like, I am crying just out of shock and grief from that. At the same time, I am crying because I just knew exactly what was going to happen to the Muslim community.

Andrea's quote serves as a reminder of the dreadful uncertainty that accompanied the 9/11 attacks. That day, reports were made, all of which were later determined false, of a third airliner heading for Manhattan; of a car bomb outside the Capitol Building in Washington, D.C.; of dozens of hijacked planes in the sky; and of airplanes being shot down over major American cities. In the face of this misinformation, the media was unusually circumspect in issuing potential fatality counts.[18] However, several newspaper and television outlets indicated that tens of thousands of people may have perished when the huge buildings came crashing down in lower Manhattan. These estimates most likely emerged from the knowledge that as many as fifty thousand people worked in the Twin Towers on a typical weekday, with another two hundred thousand passing through as visitors.[19]

On September 13, 2001, Secretary of State Colin Powell became the first Bush administration official to declare that the FBI's most-wanted man, bin Laden, was indeed the prime suspect in masterminding the attacks on

New York and Washington, D.C. Already linked to the 1993 explosion at the World Trade Center as well as the bombings of American embassies in Africa, bin Laden had long declared himself an enemy of the United States. Even before Powell's announcement, the media had widely broadcast images of bin Laden. For instance, just hours after the attacks, the Fox News Web site featured a depiction of a turbaned, bearded, bin Laden next to a burning World Trade Center tower. Similar photos of bin Laden were ubiquitous following Powell's press conference.

Three days after the terrorist attacks, the FBI released the names of the nineteen hijackers aboard the four airliners that crashed on 9/11. It was now official. A group of men, all of whom the government and the press identified as Arab Muslims (none were U.S. citizens), was responsible for coordinating and carrying out the most deadly terrorist assaults in the nation's history. The revelation confirmed the initial worries of Muslim Americans and contributed to what was already shaping up to be the most severe wave of anti-Islamic backlash in recent experience.

Compounded Fear and Avoidance

The 9/11 attacks heightened fears of international terrorism and altered many Americans' sense of security. Muslim Americans were no different in this regard. However, Muslim Americans also experienced *compounded fear*—that is, additional fears beyond those that the wider disaster-affected population most commonly expressed. Table 5.1 illustrates this concept. The list on the left side of the table depicts some of the terror-induced fears that were reported nationally in the aftermath of 9/11.[20] Persistent worries regarding future terrorist attacks, which government antiterrorism initiatives and frequent terror alerts reinforced, shaped many of the fears that Americans experienced, such as the fear of attending events that attract large crowds of people.[21] Other serious concerns, including the fear of economic collapse and the fear of war, were in response to the immense fallout caused by the 9/11 attacks. The right side of the table lists the additional fears that the Muslim Americans whom I interviewed expressed after 9/11. Research shows that other targeted communities, such as Arab Americans and South Asian Americans, struggled with similar fears and consequently experienced a number of adverse psychological reactions.[22] The lists below are not meant to be exhaustive but instead are intended to demonstrate some of the added repercussions of 9/11 for Muslim Americans.

Each of the backlash-related fears that the interviewees reported translated into other specific anxieties. For example, when participants indicated that they were scared of hate crimes, they also expressed fear of bodily harm (against themselves, their loved ones, or members of their community) and

TABLE 5.1 FEAR IN THE AFTERMATH OF 9/11

Commonly Expressed Fears among the General Public	*Compounded Fear Experienced by Muslim Americans*
• Future terrorist attacks • Flying • Traveling on buses, commuter trains, subways, or other public transportation • Visiting government office buildings • Attending public events (e.g., sporting events and music concerts) • Going to malls, movie theaters, or other crowded locations • Working in high-rise office buildings • Economic collapse • War	• Hate crimes • Hate speech in the media • Stereotyping and prejudice • Discrimination • Religious/ethnic profiling • Heightened surveillance, mandatory interviews, home and business raids • Arrests, detentions, deportations • Mass internment • Future status of Muslims in the United States

fear that Islamic institutions would be attacked or destroyed. When the respondents spoke of fears of being stereotyped or discriminated against, their apprehension was rooted in the related possibility of being verbally harassed, rejected, excluded, or denied basic opportunities. Government policies and law enforcement tactics that singled out members of the Muslim community prompted additional fears of public humiliation, police brutality, unlawful arrest, and myriad other civil-rights concerns. The cascading nature of the fears that Muslim Americans experienced after 9/11 caused emotional turmoil and resulted in the respondents' altering many of their day-to-day activities as they attempted to avert hostile reactions. The emotional and behavioral repercussions of the backlash were inextricably linked and permeated nearly every aspect of the interviewees' lives for months after 9/11.

The majority of the men and women who participated in this study reported that their primary concern in the immediate aftermath of the terrorist attacks was that the Muslim community would be subjected to a wave of violent hate crimes. Islamic leaders clearly shared these concerns, as mosques and Islamic schools across the nation suspended worship services and classes for days, and in some cases weeks, following 9/11.[23] Hafeez, a Pakistani American man, said that the Muslim community was "driven into a state of fear." He continued, "Immediately, it started from day one. All the mosques, all the leaders from the mosques, they were saying, 'We are not going to have prayer at the mosque. It is just too dangerous; we're not going to take this risk.'"

Over the past two decades, civil-rights organizations have documented a pattern of increased attacks on Arab and Islamic institutions during times of conflict and national crisis. The American-Arab Anti-Discrimination Committee (ADC) reported a dramatic spike in arson attacks, property damage, and bomb threats against Arab and Muslim homes, businesses, community centers, and places of worship after the start of the first Gulf War.[24] At least seven mosques were burned down or seriously vandalized after the Oklahoma City bombing.[25] Islamic institutions are typically visible and accessible within communities, and events held in these structures draw large numbers of Muslims together at one time. Muslim Americans understand that these factors make mosques and other Islamic organizations easy targets for hate-crime perpetrators, and this knowledge deepened their post-9/11 anxieties. Abdul, an Afghan refugee who lived in Colorado, underscored this point: "Immediately after, when I would think about going for my Friday prayers . . . I would think to myself, 'There are so many Muslims. What if somebody were to bomb this place if they're really angry? They'll kill a lot of Muslims, wipe out the entire population.' It does scare me, and so I just wanted to stay home, just do my prayers at home rather than take the risk."

As the above quote suggests, staying home was a common response among Muslims in the initial aftermath of the 9/11 attacks.[26] A Muslim engineer in Colorado described the reaction as follows: "Everybody just basically locked themselves inside their homes. There was fear all around. Not just fear because of the terrorist attacks, but fear because Muslims were being attacked." Manal, an Iraqi American undergraduate student in New York City, discussed this climate of fear: "For a lot of people, there was a lot of fear. I did go in to school on Thursday [two days after 9/11], and I've never been so scared in my life. After that day, I was not about to go in. It's your surrounding climate. When I came in here, I was so terrified, and I was not going to come back."

Manal, who wore the hijab and thus was easily identifiable as Muslim, received hateful looks in the subway and was verbally harassed on the street after the terrorist attacks. She was so frightened that she contemplated dropping out of school for the semester. After Manal spent two weeks at home, her Muslim friends eventually convinced her to return to her classes.

The length of time that Manal stayed home was not unusual, especially among the women who wore headscarves. Halima, who immigrated to the United States from Egypt as a teenager and who wore the hijab, was one of several female respondents who stayed home for more than a week after the terrorist attacks. The experience was emotionally exhausting, but Halima believed that her life might be at risk if she left her house: "I knew that a lot of people were very angry about what had happened. I stayed home for just over a week. When I was stuck at home, when I actually didn't physically go outside, that was the worst. You feel like you're being caged in. You can't even go outside. I literally felt like I had a target on my back, that I could die at any moment."

Stories of personal victimization spread rapidly through Muslim familial and friendship networks after 9/11. The information that Muslims relayed to one another intensified fears among the interviewees and shaped many of their behaviors in the disaster aftermath. Some participants who were at school or at work on the morning of 9/11 had traumatic experiences as they attempted to make their way home after the attacks. Women were spit on. Men were called vulgar names and threatened. Those who were victimized shared their experiences and, in many cases, actively discouraged other Muslims from returning to their normal routines. Sabiha, who worked as a teller at a bank in Manhattan, described the character of a telephone-call chain that developed among a wide network of Muslims—which grew to include family members, friends, acquaintances, co-workers, and strangers—after 9/11: "I got fifty million phone calls. 'Be careful.' 'Don't go outside.' Everybody was like, 'Oh, God!' We would call each other and ask, 'Are you okay?' We had people being harassed. I was verbally assaulted. I was scared. I got a call from this woman on the network. I had never spoken to this woman ever. She said, 'We heard you were harassed.'" This network allowed Muslims to openly convey their fears and to share their problems, but it also created what race-relations scholars refer to as a "domino effect" of anguish and anger rippling across the extended group.[27]

Given their increased sense of vulnerability, Muslim Americans were especially likely to seek out and to read news reports that focused on the nature and scope of the backlash. In their attempt to understand the risks that religious and ethnic minorities faced after 9/11, Muslims were exposed to numerous unsettling accounts of profiling, discrimination, and hate-related incidents. As one man remarked, "You listen to the media, and it makes you crazy. You think there's a war against Muslims out there."

How widespread was media reporting on the backlash? One study found that in the first week after the terrorist attacks, newspapers and other media serving major cities across the United States published 645 separate accounts of bias incidents directed toward those perceived to be Muslim or of South Asian or Middle Eastern descent.[28] These stories were picked up by the Council on American-Islamic Relations (CAIR) and posted on the organization's Web site. CAIR also sent out frequent alerts to thousands of individuals who subscribe to its e-mail list. The national media dedicated a considerable amount of attention to the most vicious crimes, such as the hate-motivated shootings that occurred just days after 9/11.[29] The fact that the backlash had escalated to murder in different regions of the country sent additional shockwaves of terror through the Muslim American community. A woman in Colorado described how she reacted to news of hate crimes in the week following 9/11: "The whole week I was home. I couldn't go anywhere, not even to the store. My mind was so closed from watching the television. After the Sikh guy [Balbir Singh Sodhi, who was shot to death in Arizona on September 15, 2001] was killed, I felt like if I would step outside, everything would stop, and everyone would look at me, and someone would try to kill me too."

Although some of the post-9/11 media coverage was sympathetic to the plight of Muslim Americans, much of it was not. Highly negative and inflammatory portraits of Islam and calls for retaliation against Arabs and Muslims overseas and in the United States abounded after the attacks. This type of reporting further reinforced fears and safety concerns among the interviewees. Even before 9/11, Arabs and Muslims were frequently vilified in contemporary American popular culture. After terrorists attacked the United States, inhibitions against open verbal attacks on Arabs and Muslims in the media were significantly lowered, and the rate of defamation and its intensity steadily worsened.[30]

Just two days after 9/11, conservative commentator Ann Coulter penned a column entitled "This Is War." In the piece, Coulter suggests that the United States has been infiltrated by a cult of Muslim fanatics, promotes racial and religious profiling, advocates for the assassination of international leaders, and champions the invasion of foreign countries and the indiscriminate bombing of civilians. An excerpt follows:

> This is no time to be precious about locating the exact individuals directly involved in this particular terrorist attack. Those responsible include anyone anywhere in the world who smiled in response to the annihilation of patriots. . . .
>
> The nation has been invaded by a fanatical, murderous cult. And we welcomed them. We are so good and so pure we would never engage in discriminatory racial or "religious" profiling.
>
> People who want our country destroyed live here, work for our airlines, and are submitted to the exact same airport shakedown as a lumberman from Idaho. . . . Airports scrupulously apply the same laughably ineffective airport harassment to Suzy Chapstick as to Muslim hijackers. It is preposterous to assume every passenger is a potential crazed homicidal maniac. We know who the homicidal maniacs are. They are the ones cheering and dancing right now.
>
> We should invade their countries, kill their leaders, and convert them to Christianity. We weren't punctilious about locating and punishing only Hitler and his top officers. We carpet-bombed German cities; we killed civilians. That's war. And this is war.[31]

A week later, Coulter published another column endorsing racial profiling and the deportation of Arab noncitizens. In the article, she argues that

"Congress could pass a law tomorrow requiring that all aliens from Arabic [*sic*] countries leave. . . . We should require passports to fly domestically. Passports can be forged, but they can also be checked with the home country in case of any suspicious-looking swarthy males."[32]

The increasing prevalence of malicious anti-Arab and anti-Muslim commentary—on talk radio, over the Internet, and in the mainstream media—took a significant physical and emotional toll on Muslim Americans. Najah, a first-generation immigrant from Trinidad, remarked, "It ruins my day. Sometimes it ruins my week. I got extremely, extremely depressed. When I hear the stuff on the news, the portrayal that the media is giving of Muslims, I wish I could have a microphone and tell people that we're not like that. It would really, really aggravate me. I was so tired, I was having headaches every day. It definitely hurts." Shadi, who was born in Yemen but raised in the United States, described how hopeless he felt after 9/11. As a growing chorus of hysterical commentators demanded that all Arabs and Muslims be deported, Shadi and his family actually began travel preparations in anticipation of being forced to leave the country:

> I really did go through a depression. I had no goals. I thought there is nothing worth going for. I had no hope. I thought I might have to drop out of school. This is a setback. I might have to move back to the Middle East. That week I got a passport ready; my whole family did. We originally came from Yemen. I came here when I was four years old. We were afraid. People on the radio were saying that we were all going to be deported—every Arab, every Muslim shipped away. You don't know what's going to happen. Something like 9/11 happens, and you don't know what's going to happen in the future.

It is important to note that Shadi and his family members were all of legal status. This status did not allay their fears, however, as they assumed that at any moment the government could arbitrarily choose to deport them.

Jinan, the daughter of a West African immigrant and an African American convert to Islam, became extremely scared after receiving e-mails about the backlash and listening to a pundit call for the mass internment of Muslims. Jinan, like so many others, reacted by locking herself inside her house for days after 9/11:

> I was getting a lot of e-mails that were saying, "Stay in the house. Don't go out if you don't have to." It was freaking me out. I remember somebody was on the news talking about how they should put all the Muslims in concentration camps. When people are saying stuff like that, they were talking about it like it was a valid viewpoint; when

> people are talking about things like that, you're like . . . "How can I leave the house? How can I go anywhere? I'm scared out of my wits."

Another interviewee, Sahar, explained why she found the derogatory representations of Muslims so harmful:

> No matter where you go, the depiction of the Muslims is in the media. It's a weight on our shoulders. We feel it. The media makes others think, "Attack the Muslims." They say, "These Muslims walk around as law-abiding citizens. They go to our schools. It could be your neighbor next door. You never know." That's what they're making it feel like. Across my hallway, there's a Vietnam veteran. They're making him think, this Muslim lady across the hall from you, she could have bombs in her house.

In voicing her concern, Sahar was making the case that a direct connection exists between a media culture that promotes bigotry and suspicion and violent attacks that are perpetrated against Muslims.

The fear of attack was especially acute for those who relied on public transportation to travel to and from work or school. Halah, a young woman who was identifiable as Muslim because of her clothing and headscarf, described the situation as follows: "I felt very safe [at the university], but the commute was another thing. However you came, it was dangerous. There are a lot of ignorant people out there." Countless Muslims were harassed and intimidated as they traveled on subways and buses after 9/11, and, as a consequence, many of the participants came to view taking public transport as a particularly dangerous act. For weeks following the terrorist attacks, a number of the interviewees altered their normal schedules so that they could travel together in groups to school, to work, or while running errands. All the Muslim Students Association (MSA) offices that I visited in New York City established "buddy systems" so that those who feared for their safety would not have to travel alone. Rajah, an undergraduate student in Queens, described how she and several of her Muslim friends worked together to try to ensure their mutual security:

> We set up a buddy system. A lot of [Muslim] brothers and sisters were in need of help. They were scared of traveling alone. Either that or their parents wouldn't let them travel alone. I know one sister who didn't come into campus for a week, because her parents wouldn't let her. She started classes a week after. We did try to set something up for her; brothers who were commuting from the same area met up with her, and she traveled with them.

Shaheen, who grew up in the Bronx, explained that her friends began traveling in groups to support one another: "We went out in groups, not alone. We didn't even cross the street. Emotional support to each other was the key." Tarah, who lived in Colorado, stopped going out alone in the evening for several months after 9/11. She also began thinking more frequently about ways to defend herself in case of physical attack: "Well, I no longer walk around in the evening alone. I didn't go to the grocery store for a while, because I was like, 'I only need to do necessary things.' I don't go anywhere without a bottle of pepper spray, whereas before 9/11 that idea was completely foreign to me. I learned tae kwon do for fun, whereas now I think of it as a form of defense. I have changed the way I interact with society now."

Although the women expressed more concern about traveling alone, most of the men acknowledged that they were fearful of being harassed or physically attacked as well. Salih, who worked in international relations and lived in Manhattan, explained the system that he and his male friends developed after 9/11: "I used to go out without my friends in the evening. We stopped and said nobody can go out alone. We have to go out in the full group, six people. We can only go out in groups and come back in groups. That's it. No single person can go out."

As the respondents became more cautious regarding their daily routines and travel habits, many also began to self-monitor their communications to try to reduce the likelihood that they would be "swept up" in the post-9/11 investigative dragnet. Bushra, who had lived in New York City for years but still frequently communicated with her family members in Bangladesh, described the "constant fear" that she felt and the ways that she altered her behavior: "It has made me more alert all the time. Like even now [seven months after 9/11], when we are talking on the phone to our family, we know that the phones are bugged. I'm sure this place [the mosque] is bugged, too. It's like this constant fear. Sometimes when you're walking down the street, you don't want to talk too loud about anything. I can't discuss my feelings. You're scared."

Mohammed, who was born in New Jersey and worked in Brooklyn, expressed related concerns: "I'm always going to be careful about what I say or do, just because you can get in trouble for what you say or do. You hear about all these people who have been arrested for no reason. You have to be careful about that."

The level of hostility that was directed against "foreigners" after 9/11 led some Muslim Americans to conceal certain aspects of their identity. Tayeb, whose parents were from Syria, reacted to the backlash by suppressing information regarding his ethnic background. He said, "I'm hesitant to say where I'm from now. People ask me if my name is an Arab name, and I say, 'No, it's an international name.' This is not ideal, but it's what I need to do for now." Sabah graduated from college in December 2001. She spent the next several months unsuccessfully searching for a job. Out of fear that she was being discriminated against, she eventually removed all the information from her resume that indicated that she had been involved as a leader in her campus MSA: "Any mention that depicted that I was active in the Muslim community, I took it off my resume completely. I don't bring that up on my resume, and I won't bring it up in job interviews."

The interviewees also talked about Muslims they knew who had altered their names after 9/11. One man told me about his friend "Mustafa, who now calls himself Matt." Another interviewee, Leila, described how her sixteen-year-old cousin, Kashif, had been teased mercilessly by his high school classmates after the terrorist attacks. When the other students began calling him "Ka-shit," Leila said that he "changed his name from Kashif to Steve." She explained that it was "the prejudice that was everywhere after 9/11" that made Kashif stop using his given name. She later casually remarked that she planned to give her future children "American-sounding names," presumably so that they would not have to suffer the same mistreatment.

In the weeks and months after 9/11, as anti-immigrant sentiment reached an alarming crescendo, many of the bilingual men and women in this study were hesitant, frightened even, to converse in a foreign language in public. For example, Deena and Ahmad, siblings who were born in the United States to Palestinian parents, spoke Arabic fluently. As soon as the backlash started, they began to limit their conversations to English when other people were around:

> DEENA: On the train, while my brother and I are speaking to each other, we'll use half Arabic and half American and make our own little language. But lately it's been, stay on the American. If I notice people, we'll talk American. English. New Yorker.
>
> AHMAD: Before you would say things, and it would be a joke. Now you have to be so careful of what you're saying. Anything and everything. Maybe that's paranoia, but you don't want to get in trouble.

The pervasive sense of insecurity and vulnerability made some of the participants feel as though they had to be constantly "on alert." It was as if the world had become a place of constant peril, and every unfamiliar person was now a potential assailant. Leena, a New Yorker, was unusually anxious and vigilant for months after 9/11:

> When I go outside now, I'm walking outside, and in my head I'm like . . . "Please don't let anybody touch me. Please don't let anybody

> touch me." It's so weird. It's all the time. Why is this person looking at me? All day when I'm walking, part of me is saying, "I don't want to be like that; I don't want to think about it." But everybody's talking about 9/11, about the Muslims. I'm walking down the street, and somebody's talking about it.

Asma, who lived in Colorado, described how she had also become more wary of strangers:

> I just look more. People look at me. I'm more aware of what's around me, trying to stay away from people who I see looking at me weird. Let's say I needed directions, and I wanted to ask somebody. That's what I usually do. I couldn't find somebody with a friendly-looking face. Somebody could have spit at me and said, "Get out of here. I'll give you directions back to your country." Something like that.

Some of the women and men became intensely concerned about how others would perceive them and react to their physical presence after 9/11. These concerns grew out of their perceptions of the horrific images of Islam and Muslims that they assumed were now solidified in the minds of many Americans. Leila, who wore the headscarf and lived in New York City, described some of the things that she stopped doing in the months after the terrorists brought down the Twin Towers:

> We were waiting for my friend in Starbucks. This was by Trump Towers, Trump Plaza. I've been there before. I was telling all these girls, "Let's just go and see inside." Then I was like, "Wait a second. We can't go inside. We're wearing headscarves. They'll think we're terrorists. We'll make them uncomfortable." Maybe it's my thinking, but sometimes I feel uncomfortable to go to certain places. I'm like, "This is not good. I don't want to cause any trouble." After 9/11, I haven't traveled on a plane. Before that I was on a plane; in one year I would go back and forth to Florida so many times. Things like that have really changed.

In their book *Backlash 9/11,* Anny Bakalian and Mehdi Bozorgmehr argue that "fear" is the one word that best describes the post-9/11 atmosphere in Middle Eastern and Muslim communities across the United States.[33] My data support this proposition and also demonstrate that avoidance was the most common behavioral response to the overwhelming fears that Muslim Americans experienced in the immediate aftermath of the terrorist attacks.

Isolation and Exclusion

Muslim Americans had a strong desire to interact in meaningful ways and to share their grief with other survivors after 9/11. This type of reaction to such a tragic event is understandable and represents a "normal" response to traumatic loss. Unfortunately, however, the participants in this study reported that they felt mostly unwelcome and unable to join together with the community of sufferers.

Physical Isolation

In the first place, many Muslim Americans were physically unavailable to participate in various aspects of the collective grieving process. Muslims were simultaneously overwhelmed with shock and sadness (due to the tremendous losses incurred from the attacks) and widespread compounded fear (because the anti-Islamic backlash was so severe). A number of the respondents subsequently isolated themselves inside their homes for days or even weeks after 9/11, because they were scared of what would happen if they tried to venture outside. One interviewee described the reaction among Muslims as follows: "Everyone was depressed. I had a headache. The Muslims couldn't even come out. They were scared of going to their jobs. As a community, Muslims were not even coming out of the house, so how could they participate? How could they join together? How could we join together with others to show our sorrow?"

The many safety concerns that emerged as a result of the backlash made the respondents apprehensive about participating in events or visiting places where they assumed that their presence would arouse suspicion or hostility. Because of their fears of being hurt or ostracized, the majority of the interviewees avoided public memorial services and other communal rituals designed to provide an avenue for collective displays of grief. Muslims were therefore unable to come together with other affected members of the community and to share in important mourning rituals. Iffat, a native of New York City, explained why very few Muslims attended an interfaith service that was held the day after the terrorist attacks:

> We were supposed to have a Jewish speaker, a Christian speaker, and a Muslim speaker so that we could show that we don't accept this violence. But there weren't a lot of Muslims there, because we were scared. We couldn't go there. It was the day after and at nighttime. I felt bad, because they were thinking, "The Muslims aren't here because they don't care." We do, too, care, but we don't feel safe to go there at night. So I felt like we couldn't show how we really felt. That means people will think we're less humane and that we don't care.

This quote underscores the added burdens that Muslims experienced after 9/11. In this particular case, most of Iffat's Muslim friends were too fearful to attend the nighttime service and thus decided to stay away. This decision left them without an outlet for publicly expressing and sharing their grief. In addition, because so few Muslims attended the service, Iffat understood that many of the attendees may have assumed that Muslims did not care about the losses sustained from the terrorist attacks. Another respondent made a similar point as he described the reactions of Muslims after 9/11:

> Among Muslims, the reactions are mostly the same: Stay quiet and not say anything. But that means that people don't understand that we sympathize with them. We do care about what has happened. We are grieving, too. My mom's been here for twenty or thirty years. When she saw the attacks on TV, she was crying. The first thing she said was "So many innocent people died." She was totally hysterical.

The perceived need to keep a low profile also meant that many Muslims stayed away from important memorial sites associated with 9/11. Spontaneous makeshift memorials sprang up in locations across the United States after the attacks. Most were temporary shrines where people left candles, flowers, and other meaningful memorabilia, such as firefighter hats and American flags. Official memorials were eventually established in Manhattan; Arlington; and Lower Makefield Township, Pennsylvania. Each day, thousands of people from around the world visit Ground Zero, but many Muslims came to view this site as "off limits" for people of their faith. In fact, two years after the attacks, most of the respondents living in New York told me that they had not yet visited Ground Zero. One man explained that it was fear that kept Muslims, as well as some other religious and ethnic minority group members, away from the memorial: "I haven't gone down there yet. I've wanted to go to Ground Zero, and a lot of my friends have wanted to go there, even some of my Indian friends. But we haven't, because we're still scared." Those few who had visited Ground Zero uniformly reported that they felt "strange," "peculiar," and "out of place," and thus they decided not to return.

Many of the interviewees, just like other Americans, were compelled to help after 9/11. Yet the fear that they experienced deterred most of the participants from joining the emergency response. Muslims had much to contribute to the relief efforts, however, which sadly went mostly unrecognized. For example, more than 70 percent of the persons in this study spoke an additional language besides English. Several of the participants who lived in New York City said that they wanted to volunteer at the Victim Assistance Center near Ground Zero, where the demand for foreign-language translators was significant. But they ultimately chose not to go, because they felt "self-conscious" or "threatened." Of the individuals in this study, only one woman reported that she volunteered at Ground Zero; seven others donated blood at their local American Red Cross shelters. Randa, a graduate student in New York whose educational background and language skills qualified her to help at the World Trade Center site, described her longing to be involved in the disaster response. She did not end up volunteering, though, because she was concerned for her own physical safety:

> When everything happened with the World Trade Center, my first instinct was to try to do something to help. I wanted to join those people who were volunteering downtown and do stuff. My undergraduate degree was in engineering, and they needed engineers there to help with excavation at the site. They also needed people who could translate. To me, that was the American community coming together and trying to do what they can. But I didn't feel like I could, for my own safety. I wear a headscarf. I wanted to be a part of that community, but I'm not really.

Perceived Exclusion

In the second place, Muslim Americans believed that their religious identity alone would disqualify them from membership in the community of sufferers. Amani, a second-generation Pakistani American, emphasized the desire among Muslims to unite with other Americans: "We felt ourselves in general to be a part of the grieving and the need to pull together and unite and be strong." At the same time, Amani recognized that Muslims would be vulnerable to harm due to their religious affiliation:

> We were aware that people of our faith were responsible [for the terrorist attacks], and therefore our brothers and sisters were going to be hurt—if not personally hurt, then others within the community could be. In many places, uniting and standing together was uniting if you [were] white. Christian. American. It wasn't the unity of the melting pot. It was the unity of mainstream America. And I think that was something a lot of us felt in many ways.

The collective solidarity that Amani described was delineated along the lines of race, religion, and citizenship. From her perspective, entry into the community of sufferers was restricted to those dominant group members associated with "mainstream America." Hassan, a second-generation Egyptian American, expressed a similar view:

> Muslims were victims of what happened. We had loved ones stuck in the World Trade Center. We couldn't get in contact with our loved ones, and we were scared and upset as well. And on top of that, we felt accused. So we were doubly traumatized. When they say, "America unites," they did not mean us. They did not mean Muslims. At every moment when they said, "America must unite," I know that they did not mean us.

Muslims obviously recognized that those who perpetrated the 9/11 attacks had done so in the name of Islam. It was this knowledge—and the associated feelings of defensiveness, guilt, self-blame, and even shame—that contributed to their perceived exclusion. The perceived exclusion, in turn, had powerful emotional effects for the respondents. Rather than mourning the losses that had occurred, Muslims moved into what one man described as "defensive mode." This mindset left many of the interviewees without an adequate opportunity to grieve. Basma, who was a second-grade teacher in Brooklyn, described her feelings after 9/11: "I didn't have time to grieve. It hit me ten days after. I was watching a telethon. I started crying. I felt so bad. I felt so bad when the buildings came down, but then they said, 'It's Osama bin Laden.' I was like, 'Oh my God.' I went from grief to feeling like I had to have guards around me, and I have to have all the answers."

Arwa, who was from Colorado, felt the same way: "After I realized what happened, I felt so scared. There must have been thousands of people there [at the World Trade Center]. I felt so sad. But at the same time, I wasn't given time to grieve. I had to get my act together and be on the defensive. I had to be strong and hard."

Maen, who had lived in New York City his entire life, emphasized how sad, defensive, and excluded he felt after the terrorists attacked the Twin Towers: "I'm so sad about it, but you can't really show that you're sad, because you have to be more defensive. We can't express how we were just as sad as anyone else. I don't think I felt included as one of them who were affected by it. I felt I had to defend myself and defend my religion, more than being a New Yorker who was affected by it."

A few of the interviewees reported that they were racked with guilt after learning that the hijackers were Muslim. Leila, whose family moved to the United States from Pakistan when she was a teenager, talked at length about how guilty she felt and how scared she was of upsetting others. Because she wore the headscarf, she was aware that she was a walking representation of Islam. This situation made her want to avoid the fire station in her neighborhood, which was the site of a makeshift memorial for one of the firefighters who perished when the World Trade Center collapsed. She said:

> I had a lot of guilt inside of me. Some Muslims who have done these horrible things are now representing you. Then, with my headscarf, I'm representing Muslims. So in a way, I would feel guilty. . . . In my neighborhood, there's a fire station, and every time I would pass by it, there was a picture of one of the firefighters who passed away. It was so sad. All I wanted to do was go inside and hug every firefighter and tell them, "You guys are wow, amazing. I'm supporting and praying for you." But then I was like, if I do that . . . every time they see me, I probably remind them of 9/11. Every time. Even every time I pass by, I'm like, "Oh God, I hope I don't remind them." But I know I do with my headscarf. Sometimes I feel ashamed. I really do.

Pervez, who worked as a computer technician in Denver, also experienced guilt after 9/11. Unlike Leila, however, he quickly dismissed his emotions as an irrational response to events that were clearly out of his control. Nevertheless, he, too, missed out on opportunities to collectively grieve and to support other survivors:

> I will be honest with you. I did feel guilty for a few days. Then I started thinking about it. Why am I feeling guilty? If these hijackers really were Muslims, they could not have been good Muslims. Muslims are not supposed to do this. I thought to myself, "Why are you feeling guilty? I'm like everybody here." Finally, I got out of that state of mind, but this still affected all of us significantly. I stayed away from the [memorial] services downtown. I stayed away from those who were crying and did not try to comfort anyone. I just figured that no one would want to share their grief with me, and I should not share my grief with them.

Because Pervez perceived that others would not want to "share their grief" with him, a Muslim man, he withheld his own feelings of sorrow from others.

Active Exclusion

In the third place, the respondents were treated in ways after 9/11 that led to their active exclusion from the community of sufferers. Almost every person in this study was subjected to some form of anti-Muslim bias after the terrorist attacks. The experience of being harassed or discriminated against, combined with the knowledge that the larger Muslim American community was under siege, made the men and women feel especially unwanted. In addition to more direct instances of hostility, Muslims also encountered subtle forms of exclusion that left them cut off from the collective grieving process.

Immediately following the 9/11 attacks, Muslim Americans could see how other survivors were joining together and sharing their stories of loss. Yet when the participants were in the presence of non-Muslims, they were not, in their words, "allowed" to communicate about the events of 9/11 as "normal" people but rather had to provide an "Islamic perspective" on seemingly everything. Indeed, the respondents had to answer a barrage of questions about topics ranging from their religious beliefs and practices to their personal views on violence. Regardless of whether the questions were asked out of anger or genuine curiosity, the end result was the same: Muslim Americans were forced to respond to 9/11 as outsiders rather than as mutually affected survivors. Yasmin, a native of Great Britain who came to the United States as an adolescent, described the inability to engage in what she deemed "regular conversations" in the weeks following 9/11:

> One thing that hurts is the lack of regular conversations with people. A lot of other people I could see were having conversations with each other about what happened and how it happened and where they were. I'll have a conversation like that with my Muslim friends that know me, but with other people that I don't necessarily know that well, the only conversation we'll have is something about Muslims. We can't have a normal conversation about "Yeah, this is where I was when it happened. . . ." It's always about "How do you feel about this? How do you feel about that?" Because we have to look at it differently. We can't just sit there and go, "Oh my God, this happened, it's so sad." Instead, all of a sudden, we're called to duty. Muslims are crazy lunatics, so we have to go do something about it. No, no, we're not. I just want to sit here and mourn what happened.

Marta, a Puerto Rican convert to Islam, also noted that the way people talked to her made her feel as if the danger and suffering that Muslims experienced after 9/11 went unacknowledged: "It is as if people think that Muslims are immune from getting hurt by this. We're not. We're just as much a target as anyone else. Those terrorists didn't say, 'Wait, there might be Muslims. Let's make them aware that we're going to bomb the U.S.' They said, 'We don't care.' I'm just as much a target as anybody else. But people don't talk to me like that. I'm not an exception to the suffering."

Hadeel was in the middle of Manhattan on the morning of the attacks. Later, she described how scared and alone she felt that day: "When it happened, I felt like it was the end of the world, because the U.S. is supposed to be this great big superpower. I was all by myself, and I was scared. Everybody in the street was bonding, like, 'Oh, my God, look what happened to us.' We were totally excluded from bonding. This happened to the country where we live, too, but no one acted like that to us."

The exclusion from "normal" or "ordinary" interactions was clearly hurtful to the Muslims who participated in this study. The additional overt mistreatment that so many of them were subjected to made them feel even more like outsiders. Amer emphasized that being stared at was enough to make him feel rejected from the entire American community. For him, grief was reduced to an individual rather than a collective experience: "I definitely didn't feel like I was part of the American community. One or two stares, but that was enough. I figure, I'm not like you, that's it. The grief I felt, it was more like my own individual thing."

Jameela, a stay-at-home mother of two young children, also received hostile looks after 9/11. Even more troublesome, however, were the accusatory comments that she received. These encounters made Jameela believe that others could not understand, and were unwilling to acknowledge, the pain that she experienced:

> The first time I went to the store after 9/11, I could tell that people were looking at me differently. It made me feel like I don't belong here. When people would make comments to me, it was the worst. The fact that this woman yelled at me, "Do you like living here?" Then people would say to me, "Go back to your country." I've been living here my whole life. This is my home. I'm just as mad, sad, and upset about what happened as anyone else. Just because I'm Muslim doesn't mean I'm happy about it. Yet somehow people look at me as if I'm a part of what happened.

Muslims clearly experienced a series of barriers to joining the community of sufferers in the aftermath of 9/11. Physical isolation and perceived exclusion shaped the ability and willingness of Muslims to engage with other non-Muslims after the attacks. In addition, the individual acts of hostility that Muslims were subjected to—the persistent questions regarding their national loyalty and their faith, the angry stares, the verbal harassment—had a powerful cumulative effect in lowering the probability that they would participate in rituals of solidarity and collective grief after the terrorist attacks.

Home as Haven?

In their book *Living with Racism,* Joe Feagin and Melvin Sikes argue that "to black families, the home represents one of the few anchors available to them in an often hostile white-dominated world." They continue, "Home is for African Americans the one place that is theirs to control and that can give them refuge from racial maltreatment in the outside world."[34] Elsewhere, other social scientists have described the home as a "protected site," a "sacred space," and a "haven" for racial minorities and women.[35] A home is clearly more than just a physical dwelling that people inhabit. For marginalized groups, in particular, the home is also a place where family members can retreat from outsiders; put their guards down; and find comfort, support, love, and acceptance.

Following the events of 9/11, the home became an especially important anchor for Muslim Americans. The perceived danger and the actual hostility that Muslims faced at work, at school, in the street, and in myriad other locations left the respondents longing for home. As one man explained, "Most Muslims were so afraid [after 9/11] because of the insults we faced all the time, we didn't even want to go outside. We just wanted to be at home with our families." Another interviewee described his home as "the only safe space" where he could relax and not worry about being mistreated. A third participant remarked that her apartment was the one location where she "didn't feel out of place all the time."

The home certainly offered some protection from harsh mistreatment. The privacy and security that Muslim Americans hoped to attain, however, proved elusive. In the weeks and months following the terrorist attacks, federal immigration officials and law enforcement agents conducted raids on Muslim residences and businesses in Virginia, Georgia, New York, and other locations along the East Coast.[36] Vivid accounts of dozens of armed men searching homes and seizing possessions while frightened mothers and daughters were handcuffed on the floor spread like wildfire through the Muslim community, as did news that the government was now engaged in the wholesale monitoring of telephone conversations and e-mail messages.[37]

As concerns about government surveillance mounted, so, too, did other anxieties within Muslim households. The respondents reported that one of the most significant tensions that erupted between family members after 9/11 was related to their dress and other aspects of their physical appearance. Religious visibility was a key predictor of who was, and was not, discriminated against after 9/11. Because visibility was so important in determining the likelihood of being harmed, it is understandable that much discussion and debate ensued within Muslim homes and the larger faith community regarding acceptable norms of dress in the disaster aftermath.

Among the participants in this study, more than half the men said that their mothers or fathers asked that they change some aspect of their physical appearance after 9/11 so they would look "less Arab" or "less Muslim." Most often, the men's family members wanted them to trim or shave their beards. Other times, the men faced opposition when they attempted to wear Islamic attire outside the home. Farook, who lived in Colorado, wore a kufi, which is a brimless, rounded cap donned by some Muslim men. The day after the terrorist attacks, Farook and his parents, who lived in New Mexico, got into an argument over the telephone regarding his decision to keep his kufi on:

> My parents wanted me to take it off. The day after, I was fighting with my parents on the phone about it. They wanted me to take it off—they ordered that I stop wearing it. I took it off, and I sat it on my knee. But then I thought about how the [Muslim] sisters would be treated, because you can see them even more than you can see a Muslim man. So I felt like I had an ethical responsibility to leave it on. I took it off for about twenty minutes, but then I put it back on.

Nearly three-fourths of the women who covered reported that their parents told them to wear the hijab in a "less Muslim way" (i.e., instead of letting the headscarf drape around their shoulders and bosom, tying the headscarf back tightly around their heads) or they insisted that their daughters quit wearing the headscarf altogether. Leila described what happened to her after 9/11:

> When the whole thing happened, after two hours I'm getting phone calls from my relatives saying that I should take off my headscarf, saying, "No way in hell. You shouldn't even go out. Take off your headscarf. You're going to get yourself killed." I'm like, "What are you talking about?" My relatives were giving lectures to my parents and telling them, "You should stop your daughter from wearing a headscarf." I'm the only child living with my mom and dad right now. They were like, "No way. No headscarf."

Leila quit wearing her headscarf to appease her parents. She was distressed, however, that she was unable to express herself or display her identity as a Muslim. When I interviewed her four weeks after 9/11, she was wearing the headscarf again, unbeknownst to her parents. She said, "I go to school, I put it on, and then I take it off when I leave." This was far from an ideal solution. Leila felt extremely guilty about doing something against her parents' wishes and without their knowledge. At the same time, she was unwilling to stop wearing the hijab.

Women in New York and Colorado experienced similar challenges as they attempted to balance the demands of their family members and the practices of their faith. Several college-age women who participated in a focus group in Brooklyn described how adamant their mothers and fathers were that they take off their headscarves following 9/11:

> SARAH: My family was like, "I knew you shouldn't have covered." My mom used to cover, and now she doesn't. She and my father are like, "Why are you punishing yourself? You're not going out like that. You're going to wear a hat."
>
> MINA: My father literally stood in front of me. . . .
>
> RAINA: My family doesn't cover. [*Everyone talks at once.*]
>
> MINA: My dad said to stay home for a couple of days until everything calms down. He said, "You're going to get really bad reactions if you go out that way." But after the first week, he let go. He trusted that we know what we're going to do. No way am I going to take it off. [*Everyone talks at once.*]
>
> DARIA: My dad was yelling at me, "You take that off your head." He actually said to me, "It's for safety purposes." In our religion, you are allowed to take off the headscarf if you are in danger. He was so angry at me, because I wasn't obeying him. I said, "No, I'm not taking it off." Right now—thank God, I don't want to jinx myself—ever since this has happened, nobody has really come up to me or said anything or physically tried to do anything to me. It's all about how you feel inside. If you know what kind of person you are, and if you carry yourself . . . [w]hen people stare at me on the train, I stare right back at them. I'm not going to put my head down.

The respondents quoted above, as well as many others who had similar confrontations with their family members, understood that their parents asked (or demanded) that they stop wearing Islamic attire because they were truly worried about their physical and mental well-being. Nonetheless, some of the participants were hurt that their mothers and fathers would make requests that violated their religious beliefs. Habeeba, a native of India, shared what happened with her family:

> My mom wants me to take my headscarf off, because she's terrified that somebody is going to hurt me. This is my religion. I can override whatever my parents want. I have to do what the religion says. I told them, "Leave me alone. I want to wear it. You can't tell me to take it off." But it's very hurtful, growing up in an Islamic home and then

> having your parents say this to you because they're scared. It makes me feel very sad. I lock my door and think about how they're so religious and they pray all the time. What is going through their minds? How do they feel when I leave the house in the morning? They know that they can't stop me. If I want to do something, I'm just going to do it. It's hard that this happened and the situation that it puts us all in as Muslim women.

Many of the women in the study were quick to point out that their decisions to wear the headscarf had provoked conflict long before the post-9/11 backlash began. The headscarf is one of the most contested symbols in Islam, and an array of complex cultural, historical, political, socioeconomic, and religious factors influence whether women in nations around the world accept this form of dress. For example, in some of the respondents' or their parents' countries of origin, women who wear the headscarf represent the most poor, uneducated, or stigmatized members of society. Moreover, a number of the participants' parents had immigrated to the United States to escape repressive social conditions that required all Muslim women to cover. Some of the mothers and fathers viewed wearing the hijab as strictly a cultural practice—not mandated by God and certainly not required for girls or young women. Given these varied perspectives, it is not surprising that the women described many different familial reactions to their choices to wear the hijab, reactions that ranged from happiness to shock and even anger. Hiba, who began covering five years before the 9/11 attacks, recounted her family members' initial response to her decision:

> For my dad, after I put on the headscarf, it was "Why are you wearing that?" Then when I started wearing the jilbab, it's like, "Oh my God, those are Arab clothes. Why are you wearing Arab clothes?" The way we were raised, women don't wear this. If you see the Muslim women who are on television, the majority don't even cover. So for them, it's not even an issue. But the fact that our generation wants to cover—my relatives are so Westernized, you can't even tell they're Arab, let alone Muslim. They have blonde hair, [light-colored] contact lenses, tight clothes. They're like, "Why are you wearing that?" I'm like, "Why not? Why aren't *you* wearing it? I should be asking you that question." They're like, "You're young; you shouldn't do that to yourself." They think that I shouldn't wear my headscarf until after I get married. And even if I wear it now, I should wear more tight clothes and be more Westernized. I think they want that. If I tell them something, they're like, "Oh my God, are you the priest or what?"

Randa described similar opposition from her family after she decided to cover:

> On 9/11, they were worried about me, but even before that. . . . There are all these sentiments about religion that result from being from a colonized country, like insecurity about their religion. Especially educated middle-class and upper-class people tend to think that if someone wears a scarf, that means that they're ignorant and uneducated, poor, lower class, backward. Educated people don't do that. My parents tend to have that feeling. They also think that it's not necessary. You can be Muslim and not wear a scarf, but I wanted to move to another level. They still have a hard time with it. I'm working on trying to explain things. It's hard when it's your family, when you'd think they would understand.

Those women who had encountered familial resistance to wearing the hijab *before* 9/11 were especially likely to describe elevated tensions within their households *after* the terrorist attacks. Semira's experience underscores this point. She started covering when she was a teenager. Her actions were met with disapproval by her parents, who were natives of Egypt and who wanted their daughter to have "every opportunity" in the United States. Thus, Semira's Islamic dress had been debated in the household for years. After 9/11, Semira received angry stares and verbal insults from strangers, but she decided not to tell her family members, because she assumed that they would advise her to stop wearing the hijab. The struggle between Semira and her parents intensified after her father witnessed her being harassed a few weeks after 9/11. She described what happened:

> My father had come to pick me up after work, because they weren't allowing me to take the train again yet. They were too scared something was going to happen to me, so my dad was driving me everywhere. He came to pick me up one day, and I was just sitting on the bench in front of the office building. As my dad pulled up, this gentleman and his wife, they were in the next car over. The man raised the middle finger to me and started cursing. My father saw this happen, and he started yelling at the couple in the car, "Why are you doing this? Why are you looking at her?" He was so mad to see me, his only daughter, treated this way. But at the same time, he was so angry at me. We went home, and my mother, father, and I had this huge fight. It was all "We told you that you shouldn't cover. We told you that you are going to get hurt. What if I wouldn't have been there to protect you? What if you get yourself killed?" It was absolutely

> terrible. I know that they love me very much. I know that they want me to be safe, but it was a very difficult time.

Beyond the conflicts with their parents regarding their clothing and appearance, many of the younger respondents, and especially the women, who still lived at home were required to adhere to stricter curfews after 9/11. Some parents also asked their children to "report in" and let them know where they would be and whom they would be with during all evening and weekend outings. The interviewees with the most protective mothers and fathers described how their parents began checking up on them constantly. For instance, Iffat, who was twenty-two years old, detailed the lengths her parents had gone to after 9/11: "My parents got me a cell phone. Yesterday I went to the library to study in school. I checked my voicemail, and there were nine messages from my parents at two-minute intervals! I turned it off after a while. [*The rest of the women in the focus group laugh and nod.*]"

Even though the interviewees sometimes joked about their highly cautious parents, they understood their apprehension and obviously shared many of their parents' concerns. At the same time, it was difficult for the interviewees to relinquish freedoms that they had taken for granted before the terrorist attacks.

As the participants began returning to other normal activities in the weeks following 9/11, their family members encouraged them to take special precautions to try to reduce their vulnerability. Specifically, parents urged their children to keep a low profile and to try to avoid drawing attention to their religious or ethnic identities. Some of the interviewees' parents insisted that they stop attending activities associated with Arab or Islamic organizations. Kamilah, a second-generation American of Egyptian descent, noted that her mother no longer wanted her taking part in events associated with the Women in Islam club at her college, even though Kamilah was the president of the group: "My mom has always been supportive. They have always let me do whatever I want to do with my life. They've never butted in—except for now. My mom won't let me go to food sales, fundraisers for Women in Islam. She's like, 'No. People would know. They'll follow you around.' She's not scared of me getting killed. I'm not scared of getting killed. But I'm scared of getting harassed."

Hamad, who was active in the MSA and a Palestinian human-rights organization on his university campus, similarly noted that his parents told him to "stay away from politics, to stay away from everything" after 9/11. Despite their warnings, Hamad said, "I just couldn't stop, though, because I've always been involved in certain things." Hamad continued his association with these student groups, but he was forced to hide his actions from his parents, which left him feeling guilty and unsettled.

The men in this study also described how worried their parents were about their participation in activities at their local mosques. Immediately after the terrorist attacks, law enforcement officers interrogated and arrested thousands of Muslim men across the nation. In the ensuing years, the FBI sent undercover agents posing as worshippers into mosques and allegedly pressured Muslim men to become government informants.[38] Ali, whose parents were Indonesian, said that the public and governmental backlash that followed 9/11 "posed big challenges for me personally." He elaborated: "I know that my parents have not been happy that I go to the mosque to pray in the morning. They have never been very happy, but now they really don't want me to go to the mosque in the morning. They are worried I could be attacked there or that the government will follow me and accuse me of being an extremist."

Faraaz, whose family was originally from Yemen, had a cousin arrive for a visit to the United States the day before the terrorist attacks. Even though the cousin, Amin, was in the United States legally, his presence in the household caused "a lot of tension" within the family. In particular, the fact that Amin had a beard and insisted on visiting the mosque for his daily prayers made Faraaz's father worry that the entire family would be scrutinized. Faraaz explained the situation:

> It was kind of crazy. Amin got here on Monday [September 10], and September 11 happened on Tuesday. He was like, "What do I do now?" He has a beard. Lately, with Ramadan and the last ten days, which are the holiest days of Ramadan, he's been going back and forth to the mosque for prayers. He's let his beard grow a little. It's something he says he does every Ramadan—he gets a little bit more into it than normal. So my dad's freaking out about that, about him going back and forth to the mosque, somebody seeing that, tracing that back to us. So he's really worried about that. There's been a lot of tension as a result of my cousin's presence in our house.

Converts to Islam faced a distinct set of challenges after the 9/11 attacks. These individuals—like many persons who adopt a different religion—had struggled to explain their conversion to their family members before 9/11. After the terrorist assaults on the World Trade Center and the Pentagon, converts experienced even more opposition in their households, which led to many hurtful exchanges. Eric, a white man originally from Minnesota, described his mother as "very loving" but "never accepting" of his decision to convert to Islam. Eric recalled the painful questions that his mother asked him following 9/11:

> My mom, she's just like a normal American mother. She's not Muslim. After all this, she actually asked me if I believed in flying a plane into a building. I don't think she really thought that I would do something like that, but the fact that she asked me, that was really . . . I am not sure I can even express how painful that was. I think she was kind of scared. She was scared about me being beat up because I'm Muslim, but I think she also was scared that I was some kind of fanatic. We had a lot of disagreements for weeks after the attacks; then we just stopped talking about anything related to 9/11.

Tim, also a white convert to Islam, experienced similar issues with his family after 9/11. Although he described his family as "liberal and open-minded," Tim acknowledged that the terrorist attacks deeply unnerved him and his relatives:

> When you convert, it's like your family tries to accept it, because they love you, even if they don't fully understand it. But then they see these Muslims who supposedly represent Islam doing these horrible actions like this. . . . It is just really hard for them to see you and know that you are a part of the faith that is being put on trial for these attacks. When you aren't Muslim, I understand that it is really hard to differentiate between the good and the bad. When they show Osama bin Laden on the news every night, saying crazy stuff, my family has a really hard time knowing what I believe. My grandfather has asked me some questions. He's said some pretty mean things to me, but I understand it's hard for them.

The home certainly offered some protection from the hostility and suspicion that pressed in on Muslim Americans from all sides after 9/11. Ultimately, however, the home did not function as the haven that Muslims so desperately needed. Instead, the effects of the backlash disrupted even the most private spaces and intimate relationships, intensifying old conflicts and adding new stresses to the lives of Muslim Americans.

Aftershocks

For most Americans, the feelings of crisis surrounding 9/11 eventually began to recede.[39] For Muslim Americans, the fallout caused by the terrorist attacks has been painful and enduring. Although the most violent backlash against Muslims, Arabs, and those who were mistakenly perceived to be Muslim or Arab subsided in the months following 9/11, covert and overt forms of discrimination; anti-Muslim and anti-Arab defamation in the media; and government surveillance of mosques, Muslim homes, and Islamic businesses have continued to cast a cloud of suspicion over the entire community. Hafeez, who lived in New York City on 9/11, described the context as follows: "We were all attacked once on American soil. We all felt the pain and the loss and the fear. But Islam is under continuous attack. For us, this disaster has had no end."

This sense of being under "continuous attack" was pervasive among the Muslim community in the aftermath of 9/11. On the five-year anniversary of the terrorist strikes, Salma, a second-generation American of Indian descent, reflected on the long-term consequences of 9/11 for Muslim Americans:

> It's never been as bad as it was the couple of weeks after the actual event on our soil. That was the worst and most frightening time for all Muslim Americans. But now, every time something happens that's on the news—the wars, suicide bombings, whatever is going on in the Middle East—it comes back a little bit. We still get aftershocks. Muslims still feel it when something happens. Those events are what remind us of our place in American society.

The unprecedented severity of the backlash that followed the 9/11 attacks and the persistent rise in anti-Islamic incidents linked to political turmoil in the Middle East shaped the lingering atmosphere of fear within the Muslim community. CAIR and ADC documented surges in hate crimes following the U.S.-led invasions of Afghanistan and Iraq.[40] Vandals set fire to an Iraqi-owned automotive garage and scrawled the words "We Hate" across the front of the building just days after the United States began military strikes in Afghanistan in October 2001.[41] In the subsequent weeks, mosques from California to Connecticut were seriously damaged, and Muslim- and Arab-owned businesses and homes were attacked. A similar pattern followed the start of the Persian Gulf War in March 2003. Muslim women were physically assaulted, rocks were thrown through the windows of Islamic centers, and vile graffiti was painted on MSA offices on several college campuses.[42] Bias crimes jumped again following the beheading atrocities that terrorists committed in the Middle East, the 2004 Madrid bombings, the 2005 London bombings, and other instances of mass violence that produced a direct sense of outrage among many Americans.[43]

The aforementioned events, as well as many others, provoked recurrent waves of anxiety that spread across the Muslim American community. As one participant commented, "Now, every time a bomb goes off anywhere in the world, it's the Muslims who need to duck and cover. . . . One way or the other, it will come back on us, and there is always that chance that someone we love could be hurt." Miriam, a native New Yorker, noted that she had tried to stop thinking so much about the 9/11 attacks and other global events, as all the worrying was "taking too big of an emotional toll" and was making her feel "a little bit crazy." Yet she explained that the "sense of fear comes back from time to time." When I asked Miriam to elaborate, she offered the following example:

> A month or so ago [in March 2002], there was the woman suicide bomber in Israel. They were showing her picture all over the news. That day, I got really worried, because I saw men on the train reading the *Daily News,* and the front page said, "She-Devil," in really big letters. I thought, "Oh no, here we go again." It is just that every time something happens that is connected to Muslims, I start getting that anxious feeling again.

Some of the participants in this study wondered whether things would ever "return to normal" for the Muslim community or if their lives, relationships, and futures in America would forever be altered for the worse. Ahmad, a second-generation American of Palestinian descent, worried not only about his future but also about the prospects for his children:

> Our main concern here is what is our future? That's what it comes down to. You get these new history books [that will say]: "Muslims attack America." What's going to happen when kids in school read them? Your people attacked my culture. How do you raise children in such an environment? It all comes into effect in the long run. You've really got to look into the future perspective rather than what's just now, about what's going to happen a month, a year, ten years, a few generations from now. What is this country going to fall back on?

6

Adaptations

The post-9/11 backlash clearly set Muslim Americans on an emotional and behavioral response trajectory that deviated significantly from the reactions observed among the wider U.S. population. Muslims experienced heightened fears stemming from the backlash, and the interviewees in this study were subsequently left feeling isolated and depressed. The stress of responding to the backlash spilled over into the participants' homes and generated conflict within their families. Muslim men and women altered their daily routines for weeks (and, in some cases, for months) after 9/11 as they attempted to avoid hostile confrontations with non-Muslims. Because Muslim Americans stayed away from locations and activities that they viewed as unsafe for members of their faith, they were denied the opportunity to participate fully in rituals of national solidarity and were unable to collectively mourn the losses that the terrorist attacks caused.

The violent and discriminatory backlash deeply wounded Muslim Americans. They also recognized, however, that many of the protective strategies that they relied upon in the immediate aftermath of the terrorist attacks—locking themselves inside their homes, keeping low profiles when forced to return to school or to work, avoiding mosques and other Islamic institutions, concealing certain aspects of their identities—were simply not emotionally, financially, or physically sustainable. Amana, a native New Yorker, captured the pain and the gradual shift in perspective that many Muslims experienced after 9/11:

> Muslims couldn't even come out of their houses. I stayed home for six days after the towers came down. I had a constant headache. I couldn't focus. I barely ate anything. Everyone, every Muslim I knew, was depressed and scared. We were all filled with so much uncertainty. But then, after a while, my dad was like, "We can't live like this. We can't be hiding all the time." I guess we understood that everything changed for the worse for Muslims, but we also knew that we had to go out and educate and inform others.

Based on religious affiliation alone, the entire Islamic community had become associated with the perpetrators of the terrorist assaults. Muslims were subsequently discriminated against by other Americans, maligned by the media, selectively targeted by law enforcement officials, and portrayed as the ultimate enemy by some outspoken political and religious leaders.

This chapter focuses on how Muslim Americans have adapted to this new and often frightening post-9/11 reality. As the data presented below illustrate, Muslims attempted to defend themselves and their religion through forging a stronger sense of group solidarity; they turned to their faith and to other Muslims for comfort and support after they were shut out from the national community of sufferers; and, rather than downplaying their Islamic identity, Muslims began to more prominently display symbols of their faith in an effort to actively combat negative stereotypes.

Solidarity and Strength

After 9/11, one of the themes that the interviewees conveyed was that their isolation from the larger U.S. community led to an increased sense of solidarity among Muslims. As one participant declared, "It always happens that when you attack some group, they are going to try to reaffirm who they are. If you cast them out, they're going to come together to try to prevent themselves from being attacked. The more people attack Muslims, the more we're going to come together."

This reaction is not unique. Decades of social science research have established that groups that feel ostracized or threatened are likely to experience a wave of collective solidarity.[1] The perception among marginalized group members that they are *all* being targeted based on one specific identity—racial, ethnic, religious, or cultural, for instance—lies at the core of this response.[2] In the aftermath of the 9/11 attacks, fears were widespread within the Muslim American community that *all* Muslims were at significant risk for being publicly harassed, discriminated against, or profiled by government authorities.

Of course, the millions of Muslims living in the United States represent a broad range of people from different places with varied perspectives and values. Muslim Americans are the most ethnically diverse religious group in the United States. The population includes newly arrived immigrants, later-generation descendants of immigrants, and converts to the faith. Muslims' political beliefs range from ultraconservative to ultraliberal. And the community consists of devout, practicing believers at one end of the continuum and secular, nonpracticing Muslims at the other end. Yet following the terrorist attacks, the countless ways of situating Muslims in the complex American social landscape paled in significance when compared to the master status of "being Muslim."[3]

One young woman summed up the exclusion that Muslims experienced after 9/11 as follows: "Muslims weren't treated as Americans. We were hardly Americans at that time. We were just Muslims, just enemies, definitely outsiders." Pervez, a Pakistani American from Colorado, claimed that the backlash impacted every Muslim, at least to some extent: "In one way or another, the backlash had an effect on all of our daily lives, whether it's the negative images of Islam they are showing on the TV or whatever. As a Muslim, you can't sit back and say it doesn't have an effect on you. Now, whether you like it or not, if you're a Muslim in America, you're targeted somewhat."

The unprecedented severity of the backlash and the harsh rhetoric directed against Islam and Muslims made many of the participants feel like social outcasts. Rais, a native New Yorker, explained that Muslims developed a heightened sense of collective identification not by choice but rather in direct response to this extreme marginalization: "Muslims haven't come together by our own will. We've been alienated. People have been concentrating on the Muslim part and totally disregarding the American part. They've alienated us from society, made us feel like we're not welcome. That's what brought us together. That's the only cohesion."

Malik, who was raised in Saudi Arabia and moved to the United States for college, asserted that it was "only natural" that this sense of alienation would draw Muslims together: "You can see that it's only natural that something like this would foster group cohesion. You're being identified in a particular way. When that is the case, in order to feel stronger, you'll identify with that group. You want to get closer to that group. It's a natural urge." As this quote suggests, many Muslims experienced a powerful impulse to join together in the weeks and months after 9/11. These individuals believed that the only way the community could "stand strong" was for Muslims to collectively organize and to establish a united front.

In her book *Islam in America,* which was published two years before the 9/11 attacks, author Jane Smith wondered "what, if anything, unifies all Muslims in America."[4] Smith noted that "immigrants have squabbled over differences in culture and custom," while a "distinct division" developed between the Pakistani, Indian, Arab, and African American Muslim communities in the United States.[5] In the early 1990s, Earle Waugh, a professor of religious studies, chronicled the many factors that distinguish indigenous and immigrant Muslims in the North American context. He concluded that Muslims "may have as much separating them from each other as divides them from the host societies of Canada and the United States."[6]

The sharp lines that separated Muslims before 9/11 began to blur considerably after the terrorist attacks. Muslims of different ethnicities, nationalities, and social-class backgrounds established new alliances and identified with one another more closely and purposefully than ever before.[7] This coalition building occurred in part because the U.S. government used Islam as a major classification category for policy initiatives that involved such activities as singling out Muslims for special scrutiny and investigating Islamic charities. In addition, many citizens treated Muslims as a more or less homogenous group.[8] Badia, who was from Colorado, argued that the media's portrayal of Muslims as an undifferentiated mass of threatening outsiders also helped forge a stronger overarching group consciousness among followers of the faith:

> I think that the way that things were handled after 9/11 made the vast majority of Muslims identify more strongly with their religious community, because it was Muslims that were being hated. The media reported on everything as "Muslim terrorists" and "Islamic terrorists." It was always the word "Muslim" being thrown everywhere, with absolutely no regard for how different we all are. Because the media grouped us all together under the religious aspect, then Islam was what we were identifying with and trying to defend.

Kamila, who was close friends with Badia, listened intently and then said:

> I agree. The media failed to make the point that a few crazy individuals cannot represent over a billion people. Reporters started reciting verses from the Qur'an, taking them out of context and misrepresenting Islam. Then some of the politicians were making negative comments about the Prophet Muhammad, peace be upon him. All of this woke up the Muslims. The one thing we have in common was under attack. We started identifying more with Islam, because we shared the goal of protecting our religion.

Christopher, a white convert to Islam, described the post-9/11 social solidarity as an "us-ness" among Muslims. From his point of view, the common desire among Muslims to help one another resulted in members of the community putting aside past differences and suspending, even if only temporarily, conflicts over other matters: "I definitely felt like there was an 'us-ness' among Muslims. There's a lot of history and politics among Muslims. But when 9/11 happened, a lot of people felt like we have to help each other. Muslims became closer, because we were sharing the same concerns and worries. We wanted to be there to support one another, and the only way we could do that is if we were all united."

Farook, a second-generation Pakistani American, associated the heightened solidarity among Muslims with the need to "defend something." He said, "After 9/11, there really was a coming together, because we knew we had to defend something. We knew we were in this together. The community has gotten a lot closer together, more tight-knit." When I asked Farook what Muslims needed to defend, he paused and then replied, "Our faith, our community, ourselves. When you are threatened, I guess it feels like you have to come together to protect pretty much everything."

Muslims experienced individual and collective vulnerability after 9/11. One survey of 946 Muslim Americans found that a majority of the respondents (57 percent) had personally experienced bias or discrimination in the year following the terrorist attacks.[9] An even higher number (87 percent) said that they knew of a fellow Muslim who had been discriminated against.[10] When a minority group is subjected to such pervasive mistreatment, members of the community will often search for, or attempt to create, stronger collective bonds to protect one another. Shada, a second-generation Moroccan American, articulated this point: "I think what brought us together was the need to stand up for the group instead of just letting individuals get treated this way. We want to have a unified group so that people don't feel like they can just be rude to an individual Muslim."

Many participants also believed that unity was the key to having a voice in American public and political spheres. Munirah, who came to the United States from Kuwait as a young child, said, "One of the most important things is just ensuring that we as Muslims are unified and that we have a voice. A lot of problems in the past have come from the lack of unity amongst the Muslim community. Now we have an opportunity to work collectively, to be more active in politics, and to come together to inform people about who we are, what our religion is all about."

Bakir, a soft-spoken Lebanese American man, added, "I think one of the positive outcomes from [9/11], the only positive thing I've seen so far, is that we have this opening, this chance to educate people and remove ignorance. But it is only going to work if Muslims keep working together."[11]

Keeping the Faith

In the wake of 9/11, a great deal of public discourse emerged concerning the effects of the terrorist attacks on Americans' attitudes and beliefs. Journalists depicted the United States as a "nation transformed" and declared its citizens "forever changed." In response to these claims, Yvonne Haddad, a distinguished scholar of Islam and the Arab world, asserted that "whether or not such hyperbole is completely justified, there can be little doubt of the reverberations of the event in all spheres of American life in general and the lives of Muslims and Arabs living in the United States in particular."[12]

The dramatic fallout that the attacks caused forced the men and women in this study to carefully assess what it means to be a Muslim in post-9/11 America. Zoya, who worked in a building located just a few blocks from Ground Zero, was regularly reminded of the terrible losses that occurred on September 11, 2001. Although her close proximity to the epicenter of the tragedy was unusual, the concerns that she expressed were common among Muslims:

> I work in lower Manhattan, where you could smell it every day. Every time you go down there, every time you see what happened, you can't forget. Every day you're constantly reminded that Islamic people, supposedly in the name of God, crashed airplanes and killed people. This made me ask a lot of questions about myself and my religion. I just don't understand how something that has been so meaningful in my life could be used in such a terrible way.

The overwhelming magnitude of the terrorist attacks increased the interviewees' need for a spiritual anchor, just as the trauma of the events did for millions of other Americans of different faiths.[13] Although most participants self-identified as practicing Muslims before 9/11, these individuals reported that they became even more reliant on God as they struggled to make sense of such senseless acts. This struggle led the majority of the respondents to pray more frequently and to focus more intently on their religious traditions. Kaori, a Muslim convert originally from Japan, remarked, "I think prayers are much more serious than before. We are supposed to pray seriously every time. Usually we pray five times [a day], but we want to do more and more. When you have free time, maybe you do one more. It's like more sincere." Kaori's friend Sadiya agreed: "We're definitely more focused now."

Some of the interviewees emphasized that they had been praying not only to cope with the sadness and uncertainty caused by the attacks but also to handle their fears of hostile repercussions against Muslims at home and abroad. Sabeen, a second-generation Syrian American, indicated that she had prayed specifically for the protection of Muslims after 9/11: "When this happened, it was so scary that I was praying for my people who were Muslim, because I knew they were going to be the target." Eric, who converted to Islam as a teenager, offered a similar perspective: "I developed a deeper passion for Islamic knowledge. You know how they're talking about people running back to religion, how all the churches are full. I was never running from my religion, but I have been praying more, more into the faith. I think we felt more religious and more galvanized as Muslims, because we had to protect ourselves."

Whether Muslim Americans as a whole ultimately became more "religious" after 9/11 is an empirical question that has yet to be fully addressed.[14] What is clear, however, is that members of the community became a good deal more self-conscious as a result of the anger and abuse that Muslims endured. Hafeez, a second-generation Pakistani American, underscored this point: "Every Muslim I've met became a lot more conscious of their religion after 9/11. I don't know if that's meaningful for the sake of Islam, since it didn't always correlate to the sense of being more practicing or devout; 9/11 made us all more aware of our faith, but did that make us truly closer to God? I really cannot say."

For many Muslims, the increased focus on their religion translated into a strong desire to embrace that aspect of self. Take Noreen for example. When I asked her how 9/11 had affected her daily life, she responded: "Just the need to assert my religious identity. For me, religion was always at the front part of my life. But now that Islam is on the forefront of everything, it seems there's the need to use that as my defining characteristic, a greater need to do that, now more than ever." Jeena shared Noreen's sense of obligation to defend her religion:

> I think my religious identity became stronger. I became more like, "Don't say anything against Islam." Giving an analogy, especially being female, in college or high school, if I saw someone being picked on, I would become her friend. Seeing Islam go through that, being so different from what it was portrayed to be by the media or just by assumption, I became more strong in needing to speak out against that and change that. This is not what it is. This is Islam. This is reality.

Muslims moved into an unwelcome and harsh spotlight after terrorists used Islam to justify the attacks on New York City and Washington, D.C. Headlines screamed, "Why do they hate us?" Newspapers and magazines printed an unending stream of images of nameless, gun-toting, bearded Muslim men and of faceless, burqa-clad women. Despite the fact that every major Muslim organization in the United States, without exception, condemned the terrorist attacks, talk radio hosts continued to angrily ask, "Why haven't Muslims spoken out against terrorism?"

Just over a week after the 9/11 attacks, President George W. Bush delivered a much-anticipated speech to a joint session of the U.S. Congress in which he solemnly declared, "Every nation in every region now has a decision to make: Either you are with us, or you are with the terrorists."[15] Other politicians and media pundits picked up on this dictum as they challenged Muslims and Arabs living in the United States to "demonstrate their allegiance," to "show their loyalty," and to "decide which side they are on." This overtly hostile rhetoric played out in very real ways in the everyday lives of Muslim Americans, as men and women of the Islamic faith felt compelled to choose between their American and Muslim identities. Natasha, a second-generation Egyptian American, talked about this issue:

> I think 9/11 made me feel forced to choose between identities. It was big. You've got to choose one or the other, and they're [still] not going to accept you at all. At first people weren't going to accept us. I was like, if they're not going to accept me as an American, meaning that I'm going to have to choose one or the other, then I'm going to have to choose Islam. If they're not going to accept me as an American, if they're going to tell me I don't deserve to be here, when I am an American, if they're going to try to make me feel that way, then, hey, I'm going to be a Muslim. No one's going to ever tell me, "You can't be a Muslim. You're not a Muslim. Go back to some other planet where there isn't Islam." I felt like I had to choose then. I don't think I felt like I had to choose before then. But after [9/11] it was like, well, fine. If I have to choose, I choose to be Muslim.

Amani, who was born and raised in the United States, also described a remarkable change in identification in the post-9/11 period. She indicated that she used to self-identify as an unhyphenated "American," but once the backlash started, she began thinking of herself as "Muslim only":

> If you asked me about how I define myself before 9/11, I would have said I was an American, plain and simple. Now I would tell you I am a Muslim only. I am an American, and that is definitely a large part of who I am, but it is hard to identify yourself as something when you don't feel accepted or respected. I guess when people hate you for a certain part of yourself, you end up making that part who you are. People hate me because I am Muslim; therefore, I am Muslim and that is all.

Many people in the United States were unaware of the Islamic faith and of the Muslims living in their midst before 9/11 (in 1993, when the *Los Angeles Times* asked Americans about their impression of Islam, more than half of those surveyed said that they did not know enough to even have an opinion).[16] After the attacks, ordinary Americans were scared and confused, and they had many questions that they wanted—indeed, needed—to have answered.

Muslims consequently received a barrage of inquiries from friends, strangers, teachers, co-workers, and journalists. Some of these individuals wanted to understand relatively straightforward facts about the faith (Do Muslims believe in God? Who is Muhammad? Why do Muslims pray five times a day?), while others demanded responses to more complicated questions (Does the Qur'an condone violence? What is jihad? Why are so many countries in the Middle East undemocratic? How are women viewed in Islam?).

To reply to the numerous questions that they received, Muslims began to carefully read the Qur'an and other religious and historical documents. Across the nation, mosques established formal study groups for their congregants, and Muslim Students Association (MSA) offices sponsored educational lectures for their members. Some Muslims set up their own informal study sessions. For example, I interviewed six women in New York City who met every Thursday evening for nearly a year after 9/11. Arsheen, who was one of the regular attendees, explained why she and her peers had come together in this way:

> We're Muslims, but some of us don't have enough knowledge. It's like if all of the sudden you asked Christians to know every passage in the Bible. We were all really stressed and wondering how we were supposed to talk to people about Islam. Of course, people are going to ask us questions; it's understandable. We knew we needed to be prepared so we can provide them with the correct information.

As they searched for answers, many of those whom I spoke to said that they were becoming "better Muslims" and drawing even closer to their faith. Thus, the 9/11 tragedy and the backlash that followed inadvertently caused many Muslims to learn more about Islam. Over time, these investments strengthened their religious identities. Hassan, who was born in the United States and had lived in several different Arab nations while growing up, described how he had become more religious since the attacks:

> For me, since 9/11, I do feel more obligated to know my religion more, for the reasons that I gave before: to better communicate who

> Muslims are, to understand for myself what are the problems within the community, to be able to evaluate the Muslim identity, and to be able to say, "These are the flaws and these are the strengths, and we should fix the flaws and build the strengths further." I have become more religious, and it's a daily struggle. I wanted to become more religious. I feel comfortable with who I am when I'm more religious.

Sanae reacted similarly: "After 9/11, Muslims were so criticized for it, we all turned in. We were like, 'What's happening? Let's read up.' After 9/11, when we were subjected to the questions, like, 'Tell us, what the hell is jihad?' then we started reading more. We turned in and came together and started attending more meetings. We read up more and more and became stronger Muslims."

Muslims in the United States generally kept a low profile for the first few weeks after 9/11. As the most violent acts of backlash subsided, Muslims expressed a growing desire to become more active. With the passage of time, Muslim involvement in mosques and other Islamic institutions actually surpassed pre-9/11 levels.[17] One study found that attendance at New York City mosques doubled during the twelve-month period following the 9/11 attacks.[18] MSA leaders on university campuses across the nation documented a similar rise in student participation in weekly meetings, Friday prayers, and other special events. As a case in point, the New York University newspaper reported that the Islamic center on its campus went from accommodating about 20 Muslim students to more than 250 Muslim students in the three years following 9/11.[19]

A personal need for inner solace and a broader search for community undoubtedly shaped this movement toward religious affiliation. Mosques, MSA offices, and Islamic centers offered *physical spaces* where Muslims could practice their faith as well as *emotional spaces* where they could find comfort and a sense of belonging. In light of the devastating exclusion that Muslims experienced after 9/11, these institutions also served especially important functions in terms of mental-health care. According to the Arab Muslim American Federation of New York and the Imam's Council of New York, the number of Muslims seeking mental-health counseling at New York City mosques quadrupled after September 11. Many Muslims sought help to deal with heightened safety concerns, anxiety, emotional problems, and depression.[20]

Most of the participants in this study said that they prayed daily and attended worship services on a weekly basis before 9/11. Although their religious participation increased after the attacks, the most striking change that I witnessed was among those persons who were not involved in mosques or other Islamic organizations prior to 9/11 (religious studies scholars often refer to these individuals as the "unmosqued"). For instance, Ilias, who was born in Morocco but was raised in the United States, discussed how he and his family had altered their religious practices since the terrorist attacks:

> I wasn't really a good practicing Muslim before 9/11, but that changed. I changed. Now I am more aware of my religion. . . . Actually, nobody in my family prayed the required five times a day before [9/11]. We did occasionally, but mostly we just prayed any time we wanted. Now we started to become more regular in our prayers, the whole family. My parents, my younger sister, and me, we all pray together.

Ilias also began to regularly attend Friday prayers at his neighborhood mosque in Brooklyn and joined the MSA at his university. Likewise, Saba, who was a self-described "marginal Muslim" prior to 9/11, explained how after the attacks she had become significantly more active in the Women in Islam club on her college campus:

> I'm much more involved in the Muslim community now. Initially, I wasn't. I'd go to lectures, to Islamic club once in a while. But now I'm the vice president, trying to get involved more, trying to establish a citywide MSA. There are times when you need to get active, and right now is the best time for Muslims. I think that every community in the U.S. has had to fight for their rights. Look at the women. The females had to fight for their rights, the African American community, too. Now it's the Muslim community's turn to fight for their rights.

In the year following 9/11, more than three-fourths of the respondents indicated that they had either helped organize or had participated in efforts meant to combat misconceptions about Islam or Muslims. These men and women wrote statements and newspaper editorials condemning terrorism, delivered guest lectures at churches and synagogues, offered tours of their mosques, and sat on interfaith panels aimed at promoting dialogue and educating non-Muslims about Islamic beliefs and practices. Amer, who became a regular mosque attendee after 9/11, highlighted the increased participation among fellow Muslims: "I'd say that after 9/11 was the first time that so many of us got involved in activities related to Islam and to Muslims. We were drawn in. We needed to attend events and share our views about what was going on, how we felt about all this, and show that we do not support terrorism."

Building Relationships

The interviewees turned to prayer as they searched for consolation after 9/11. However, the most immediate and tangible support that they received came from other Muslims. I found that the respondents began to prioritize their relationships with their Muslim peers and family members for a number of different reasons.

In the first place, the backlash-related fears that Muslims experienced after 9/11 required an outlet. When surrounded by non-Muslims, Muslims often felt "judged," "defensive," "misrepresented," or "misunderstood." Given this context, it is not surprising that Muslim women and men discovered that they were able to best express themselves—to share their deepest concerns, their sorrow, and their frustrations—when they were surrounded by other Muslims. This realization also helps explain why so many of the interviewees reported that they felt "closer" and "more connected" to their Muslim friends and family members after 9/11. Before the terrorist attacks, Hassan saw his family "only about once every two months or so." But after 9/11, he began driving to his old home, which was nearly two hours away from his apartment in New York City, every weekend to visit his parents and siblings. Hassan emphasized that he "needed" to be around people with whom he could "talk openly" regarding the issues facing the Muslim community:

> I definitely got closer to my family, although the relationship has always been close. You cherish your family a lot more and want to be with them. After 9/11, after all the hate crimes started, I wanted to be at my family's house and just talk openly about things that were going on. It wasn't just that I wanted to go, but I really needed to go. I had this urge to go home and just be with my family. The backlash has been a topic of conversation at every dinner since the attacks. Every time we're together, we're talking about what's going on with the Muslims in the United States. My family and my Muslim friends are the only ones I can really talk to about this, about how I really feel about everything.

A number of interviewees described similar changes with their relationships after 9/11. Alisha, a second-generation Syrian American, depicted how the hostile post-9/11 climate shaped the differences within her own family: "When you feel like you are under siege, which we felt like we were, we really came together. So in that sense, my relationship with my family grew much stronger." Asma explained that her family had come together, because they were experiencing the same backlash-related anxieties:

> My family, we're really, really close. The whole family is really close, and after 9/11, we got closer. As soon as the World Trade Center was hit, my mom and dad called me and my sisters. From the beginning, they were giving us the support we needed, because it was very scary; the backlash was very scary. We would all come together on the weekends and be like, "How are you doing?" We knew what one another were going through, our fears, our stress, because we were all going through the same thing. So within the family, there was this mutual understanding, like, "If you need help with anything, I am here."

Other respondents turned to their Muslim friends for support because of the conflicts that had erupted within their own households. As I describe in the previous chapter, many of the participants were pressured by their mothers or fathers to change their appearance and behaviors following the terrorist attacks. Disagreements over how to best respond to the backlash led to heightened tensions among family members, and especially between parents and their sons and daughters. The young adults in this study had friends of similar ages who were often confronting the same challenges in their homes. Hanan, who spent the first two weeks after 9/11 arguing with her father about whether she should continue to wear the hijab, explained why she had grown closer to her Muslim friends: "Everyone was so concerned and so understanding, especially my Muslim friends. They were going through the exact same thing, in public with the backlash and at home with the tense atmosphere. That made me realize that they're really there for me."

Because Muslims shared similar fears after 9/11, they were able to actively respond to each other's needs. This included providing various forms of assistance. First, they offered emotional support: "A lot of us were terrified to go outside. It was horrible. We were calling each other and trying to give each other moral support. We connected a lot during those first few weeks after 9/11." Second, they shared knowledge and information: "It wasn't just emotional support. We also helped one another to learn more about Islam so we could answer all these questions. [Muslim] sisters who weren't knowledgeable about a particular subject could come to one of the other sisters and ask." Third, Muslims encouraged one another in the face of opposition to their religious practices: "Most of the people told me to take off my headscarf, to hide my identity. My Muslim friends were the ones who encouraged me." And, fourth, they provided physical protection: "The subways were closed for weeks. We had a [Muslim] brother who drove us home each evening. People were pointing at the car, trying to scare us. But I felt like he would protect us."

As Muslims strived to support one another, they began spending more time together—on the telephone, over e-mail, at meetings, and in mosques.

Muslims spent countless hours talking about what one young woman referred to as "things that a non-Muslim might not understand." I asked her to elaborate, and she replied, "Well, for example, most of my Muslim friends stayed home for about a week after the backlash started. When we decided to go back out with the hijab on, we were so scared. So we were always calling each other, asking about how we should act or what we should do. It was just that we were going through the same thing, sharing the same concerns and worries. That's what brought us closer."

The number of educational and community outreach activities that Muslims organized after 9/11 also brought members of the community together. One man in Colorado described how much more connected he was to his friends as a result of the work they had been doing: "We're planning all these events, working together to try to raise funds for a new Islamic center. Now I see my Muslim friends a lot more than I used to. Because of that, I feel a lot closer to them than I did before."

Another participant, Rashida, explained that she had started to actively cultivate friendships with other Muslims. Prior to 9/11, she was fine with more casual "mosque friendships." But this feeling changed in the aftermath of the attacks:

> I see it more as a priority to establish better friendships with them. Before I was fine with just having a mosque friendship with them, like, I see you in the mosque a lot and chitchat with you, and maybe once in a while we go out for tea. Now it's more a priority to make them part of my circle of friends. I do have a lot in common with them. For example, the fact that we put spirituality as the number-one priority in our life is really important. But I guess it is more than that. We also seem to connect, to understand each other more now, after everything we've been going through.

Before the terrorist attacks, Hamad acknowledged that he was "more into the American culture" and noted that his closest friends were predominantly non-Muslim. After 9/11, Hamad began to pull away from some of his old friends, who "could be a bad influence," and became better friends with the men he knew through his mosque:

> It was a big change for me. I wanted to get to know my Muslim identity, hang out with Muslim friends. A lot of times, people don't realize that the people around you make you who you are. If I want to pray and everyone around me doesn't need to pray, I likely will not go. If everyone around me is going to pray, I probably will go with them. My need to hang out with Muslim friends happened. There was a

> shift to wanting to be active with the community. Nowadays all of my community work is towards Muslim groups, and it's because of 9/11.

In a few cases, the post-9/11 climate of fear, and the protective response that it generated, led individuals to develop entirely new relationships with Muslims. Nadira smiled broadly as she recounted how a Muslim woman who was a "complete stranger" had called to check up on her after 9/11. Nadira recalled how they had later become friends:

> That's the day I realized that people love me. Muslims you didn't know, those kinds of people who called and said, "I heard something happened. Are you okay? Do you want any help from anybody?" Things like that really made a difference. . . . I stopped and thought to myself, this is the type of person that I should be friends with. Someone who cares and understands. It was then that I made the decision to build the relationship with her.

Some participants developed stronger bonds with fellow Muslims, because they felt isolated and even fearful of non-Muslims. A mother of two young boys clarified how this happened: "The news of unexplained arrests and hateful attacks were reaching all of the Muslim homes in the community. We felt like we would be better protected by those in our own community, because we didn't know if others were planning to hurt us." For others, the hatefulness connected to the backlash led them to distance themselves from non-Muslims. Janan discussed how her outlook had changed since 9/11:

> I hate to say that it has changed more for the bad—the kind of attitudes that I saw, the kind of behavior. . . . The same people who would have smiled to my face a week before were basically calling all of us terrorists and saying that we should be killed. It made it more difficult for me to trust them. I had a lot of non-Muslim friends, really good friends, before 9/11. . . . Now, they're still my friends, but I feel that there's a little bit of . . . like, I couldn't run to them at this time. I don't know how to explain it. There's a little bit of a distance there. It's really unfortunate. I don't know if it's going to continue. Right now it's like, the Muslims, they are my shelter. They were who I needed at this time. There were a lot of non-Muslims who were saying all kinds of [negative] things, and it made me question, are they sincere, or do they really feel these things about us?

Like Janan, Mina encountered some problems with her non-Muslim friends in the aftermath of 9/11. Although Mina was quick to emphasize that she was still friends with these young women, she also sadly observed that sometimes they just "don't understand":

> I was talking with some friends from high school. I had just started wearing my hijab two months ago, right before I started college, just after I graduated from high school. My friends, four Hindu friends, were really good friends of mine. They still are. Regardless of their religion, they're still good friends to me. They were talking to me [soon after 9/11], and one of them said, "Why don't you just take it off?" They don't understand the importance of it—why I started it, why I need to keep wearing it now more than ever. My Muslim friends just understand and right now, I don't want to have to be explaining myself all of the time.

Abdul described the first six months or so after 9/11 as a "high-connectivity" period among Muslims. He noted that during those months "you hung out with Muslim people even if you didn't have many shared interests. It was because we were going through the same thing." Over time, Muslims began to "settle in" to relationships with those with whom they had the most in common. Some of the friendships that grew out of the response to the backlash persisted, but others did not. What clearly remained, however, was the lingering sense among Muslims that the community was "under siege." The most blatant acts of hatred may have decreased in the months after 9/11, but the War on Terror—and the associated government surveillance programs and inflammatory media coverage of Islam—kept Muslims in a heightened state of insecurity.[21] Muslims thus continued to cling tightly to other Muslims as they attempted to navigate the post-9/11 social environment together.

Representing Islam

Journalist Geneive Abdo, in her book *Mecca and Main Street,* vividly depicts the numerous ways that life changed for the nation's Muslims after 9/11. "For more than a century, Muslims had lived in America in peace, blending into the ethnically diverse landscape," Abdo argues. "But suddenly, they were no longer in the shadows as an all but invisible minority. From now on, their every word would be noted, their every action seized upon by a nation gripped with fear and inflamed by political manipulation."[22]

Muslim Americans were well aware of the heavy cloud of suspicion hanging over their community after 9/11. "We're all suspects, every one of us" is how one man described it. Another respondent captured the all-encompassing nature of the backlash: "Your neighbors are watching you. Strangers are staring at you on the street. Police are shaking you down at the airport. The FBI is spying on you at the mosque." And another participant said, "It's like living your life under a microscope. Everything you do is magnified."

After the World Trade Center crumbled, many Americans started to view Islam through a lens that allowed them to see only the pain, violence, and terror now associated with the faith. Malika, a Muslim who lived and worked in New York City, stated bluntly, "Look, we get it that these stereotypes weren't created out of nothing. Obviously they've been around for a long time; 9/11 unfortunately served as proof to a lot of people that Muslims really are terrorists and as evidence that every bad thing they thought about our religion was actually correct. The only way to combat these negative ideas is from our side."

So Muslims also turned the microscope on themselves. The participants in this study were virtually unanimous in reporting that they had grown more mindful of their words and behaviors in the wake of 9/11. Muslims described themselves as "cautious" and "careful," and, in some cases, they were unwilling to confront non-Muslims for fear that the entire Islamic community would be cast in a negative light. One woman put it this way:

> I don't want to do anything even remotely questionable. If I'm about to get into an argument with someone about something stupid, like they sold me something defective, I'm thinking, "Oh my God, if I start arguing with this guy, he's going to think that all Muslim people are argumentative." If I'm driving and I happen to run a red light and a cop pulls me over, he's going to think that all Muslim people are law-breaking citizens. It's like you can't do anything wrong, because you're there for your whole community, and everyone's going to be branded in the mind of this person.

Other respondents expressed the same general sentiment:

> It's really hard, but I know I have to be more careful in how I conduct myself. Like even something as simple as riding the subway. If somebody shoves you out of the way, you should be able to glare at that person. But since I feel like I have to represent all Muslims everywhere now, I feel like I have to smile at the person and say, "Oh, I'm sorry, I must have been in your way." Instead of, "Hey! Why'd you shove me?" Because I have to constantly be the sunny, shiny picture of friendly Islam.

> You have to be cautious. I'm beginning to realize that I have to be aware of how I represent myself, because people are going to infer

> from how I act what a typical Muslim is like. If I do something wrong, they'll say, "Oh, that's because he's Muslim." If I do something right, hopefully they'll think it's because I'm Muslim and representing the culture. I've been more aware of how I act in situations, of who I am and what I represent.

In 2002, while speaking to a large gathering of Muslim Americans, former Democratic Congressional Representative Jim Moody reminded the crowd that most Americans had never met a Muslim before and had never thought about Islam at all until 9/11. He encouraged the audience to show Americans the "true nature of Islam," with its focus on respect for neighbors, hospitality, compassion, truth, generosity, justice, and tolerance.[23]

Moody picked up on a refrain that was already common among Muslims. As the post-9/11 backlash grew in intensity, many Muslims came to believe that if they could just show people what a "good Muslim" and the "true Islam" were all about, then some of the stereotyping and antipathy would end. (This feeling was widespread among the Muslims that I interviewed in New York and Colorado.[24] Jennifer Bryan found the same thing within the Arab Muslim community that she studied in Jersey City,[25] as did Louise Cainkar in her research with Muslims in Chicago.[26])

Muslims used such words as "responsibility" and "duty" when they described the pressing need to positively represent their faith. This sense of obligation was especially salient among second-generation Muslim Americans. Their status as Muslims *and* Americans provided these individuals with a number of resources that they drew on as they attempted to defend their faith. Because they were born and raised in the United States, these men and women were intimately familiar with American culture, customs, and values. They had grown up in communities where non-Muslim neighbors, teachers, and peers surrounded them. In addition, they were college educated, and they spoke the English language without an accent. Marwan emphasized how important having an "American identity" became after 9/11: "We're like a fresh generation. We don't have a foreign accent. People listen to us differently. They react differently to us. They don't shut their ears, because we sound American, we look American, we act more American. We've grown up in this culture."

Similarly, Kamila emphasized how her background and her knowledge of Islam had shaped her desire to "teach others" about the faith:

> I want to teach others about my religion, more than before 9/11, because now people are hearing a lot of lies and stereotypes and stuff like that. So I take it more upon myself that it is my duty, especially since I grew up in America and I have the language. . . . I have some

> of the knowledge of Islam, too, because some people grew up here, but they don't really know that much about Islam, so it is harder for them to speak about it. So since I have some knowledge, too, I think it is my responsibility to be talking about it and letting people know how my religion is.

Symbols and Stereotypes

After 9/11, some observers questioned how Muslims would respond to the fallout that the attacks caused.[27] Would the sharpness of the rejection that Muslims felt cause them to shed their most visible signifiers of difference? Or would they more prominently display their faith? Would Muslims attempt to "melt" into mainstream culture? Or would they rise up and attempt to reclaim their religion and culture in more public ways than ever before?

Although some women responded to the backlash by removing their headscarves, and some men shaved their beards, these reactions tended to be fleeting and were largely induced by profound feelings of fear and/or intense pressure from family members (see Chapter 5). Most Muslims who wore religious attire before 9/11 continued to do so in the aftermath of the terrorist attacks. And, in the months following the attacks, more, rather than fewer, Muslims began to adopt noticeable symbols of their faith. Several factors help explain these trends.

As the data presented above suggest, Muslims experienced a powerful sense of responsibility to "reach out" and to "educate others" after 9/11. For this information sharing to occur, Muslims either had to approach or be approached by non-Muslims. A few particularly bold interviewees said that if they saw someone giving them "looks," they would walk directly up to that person, introduce themselves, and ask if the individual had any questions. This gave Muslims the opportunity to actively engage with others outside their faith. This strategy was atypical, however, especially in the first several months after 9/11. Given the extreme tension that marked that time period, the thought of confronting strangers in such a manner simply seemed too risky to the majority of Muslims.

Therefore, more often than not, Muslims would either use formal mechanisms to try to educate people about their faith (e.g., hosting mosque visit days, sitting on interfaith panels, giving media interviews), or they would wait for non-Muslims to approach them. It was the women wearing headscarves and the men with brown skin and beards (in other words, those who fit the stereotypical image of "what a Muslim looks like") who most commonly received questions from strangers about their religion. Because this opened up a window of opportunity to dispel harmful misconceptions, a significant number of Muslims began to frame being visible in a positive light. Ameena said the following in reference to wearing the hijab, which she believed enhanced her ability to "attract" non-Muslims who might want to ask her questions about her faith and identity as a Muslim: "This is a gateway for me to introduce who I am. I can attract more people. They can ask me questions and find out what Muslims are really all about. I hope they can learn that we're not out there to kill and be violent."

Ali, who had a beard and often wore a kufi, was also normally happy when people would ask him questions: "Yes, I get some hostile questions. But I also get some very educated and polite questions, like 'May I know what religion you are from? Why are you wearing this?' I like it when people ask, so that I can make things clear for them."

And a female respondent observed, "I know a lot of women who started wearing the headscarf after 9/11. If you're not covered, nobody can tell if you're Muslim or not, so they can't talk to you about your religion. You lose that opportunity to share with others."

Of course, wearing the hijab or any other symbol of Islam came with certain costs. As I describe in the previous chapters, those Muslims—and other religious and ethnic minorities—who were highly visible were most at risk for physical or verbal attacks after 9/11. Maria depicted the double-edged sword of being easily identifiable as Muslim:

> What's good about wearing the headscarf? People look at me and think, oh, that's a Muslim girl. That's a good thing, I'm identified for who I am. They look at me, and instantly they know, she's Muslim.

Maria paused for a moment; then she continued:

> What's difficult about wearing the headscarf? The same thing. People look at me and they instantly know I'm Muslim. [*Laughs.*]

Even though standing out as a Muslim was difficult—and potentially dangerous—after 9/11, some of the participants were unwilling to stop wearing what they considered to be religiously mandated clothing. Amani, who was from Colorado, explained, "Personally, my understanding of Islam is that the veil is an integral part of the faith. To dress modestly is mandated for both women and men. I know that many people will contest this idea, and I respect them. I just hope they will respect me as well during this time. I am going to continue to cover, and nothing can stop that. This is my religion."

Women who adopted the headscarf after 9/11 often attributed their decision to the fact that they had become "more religious." As Muslims started reading the Qur'an more carefully, spending more time with other Muslims, and affiliating more closely with Islamic institutions, some individuals were persuaded that wearing the hijab was required and would fulfill a religious commitment to God.[28] "If people would ask me why I started covering [four months] after 9/11," a woman from New York City said, "I would tell them that it was because I started learning about Islam, getting more religious. I was already praying five times a day, but the next step was to wear the hijab. It allowed me to see that you do things for God, not to please those around you."

Muslims feared for their safety in the aftermath of the terrorist attacks, but they also felt a strong need to stand in solidarity with other Muslims who were being harassed. Shaheen pointed out that her sister began wearing the headscarf after 9/11 because she wanted to better represent the Muslim community:

> I have two sisters. The older one is twenty. I'm eighteen. She didn't wear the scarf. When this happened, she said, "You know, I'm going to start wearing a scarf now." I was like, "Of all the times, you're going to start now?!" She says, "I'm not Muslim enough. I can't support Muslims, because I don't seem like them to other people." Regardless of what the consequences of that were, she was like, "I want to start now, just for this reason."

Wahiba, who had never worn the scarf, also started covering after 9/11:

> I witnessed my friends being flipped off and glared at, and it made me want to wear a veil, just to show that they shouldn't have to change how they are because this happened. It's really horrible that people would relate what happened to the Twin Towers to women who wear veils in this country, as if they have anything to do with it. . . . They don't, but people think they do and mistreat them because of it.

Massoud, a Pakistani American male, said that he would "only occasionally" wear ethnic attire before 9/11. But for several weeks after the attacks, he wore traditional clothing to support his sister and in an effort to deflect attention away from potentially more "vulnerable" targets:

> I wasn't as concerned about my safety. I acknowledge that, being a man, I have a lot of privilege and a lot of security that a lot of people don't have. My concern was more for my sister. She can very easily be noticed as a person who's a Muslim because of the head covering, her scarf. So I personally dressed up in my traditional attire after 9/11.

> I wore a green Pakistani outfit. I wanted to detract attention from other people who would be put in a situation where they would be victims of hate crimes. This is again masculinity when I assume that I'm more able to bear a violent attack than my sister. In actuality, she's probably better prepared, because she knows tae kwon do, and I've never done that. [*Laughs.*] But I decided that I wanted to be as supportive of her and the other Muslim sisters as I could.

As has been noted elsewhere, people often react to perceived threats upon their identity by amplifying the most noticeable elements.[29] These elements then become symbols of their independence and chosen identity. Hafeez observed this pattern among the Muslim students who began attending Friday prayers after 9/11. After indicating that "attendance doubled" in the months following the attacks, he said, "It's like, if you're Muslim you're feeling the heat. When people have pressure put on them, they identify with what that pressure is directed towards. So if a lot of kids are getting crap because they're Muslim, they have a tendency to identify themselves more strongly with that."

Targeted group members may also use symbols to "defend" their religious or ethnic identity. Kaori, who did not wear the headscarf before 9/11, explained why she started covering after the terrorist attacks: "I came back to New York City [from Japan] one week after the towers collapsed. At that time, I wasn't covering myself. But after 9/11 happened, I realized that people are attacking Islam and attacking Muslims. I wanted to defend Islam, so I started to cover myself."

Muslims also tried to use their visibility to dispel widely held harmful stereotypes. For instance, many of the young women who wore the hijab wanted to show non-Muslims that they were not oppressed. Thus, they began to emphasize their personal and scholarly achievements to demonstrate that they could be Muslim women who cover and successful and productive members of society. Some of the women who were students said that they felt pressure to raise their hands and speak out in class so their professors and peers would know that they were intelligent and not afraid to express their own opinions. Badia, who attended college in Colorado, said:

> There are so many things that people believe, like we're not allowed to be educated or to live on our own. So by being visibly Muslim, people can see that at least in my situation this isn't true. That was something about being on campus. I was really proud to wear the hijab, because I wanted people to know that I was Muslim and I was educated. The biggest good consequence of covering is that I person-

> ally can break stereotypes in people's minds just by doing my daily routine. I don't even have to say much—just by seeing me and what I have done, people can get a new image.

Other interviewees participated in various activities to try to demonstrate to non-Muslims that they were indeed liberated, self-determined, self-confident, and happy. Leila, who was a vibrant and outgoing young woman, described her experience riding on a jet ski while wearing a headscarf:

> I always have to prove myself. With me, that's the reason I go on a jet ski with a headscarf, just to do crazy things. My friend did bungee jumps with a headscarf on. Crazy girl. I want people to see me and know, okay, that's a Muslim girl, but she's not oppressed. We know how to enjoy our life. I can wear this, my headscarf, and I can move on with my life. I go on a jet ski and do crazy things, although I'm horrible at it. I wear my headscarf because I want people to look at me and be like, wow, that's a Muslim girl. She can have fun with her life.

Because of their heightened visibility, Muslims also became much more aware of how even mundane interactions might be (mis)perceived in public. Madheeha, who had been married for just over a year when 9/11 happened, described how attentive she had become while walking outside with her husband:

> The media always makes women look oppressed. They completely misrepresent it. If you walk behind your husband, non-Muslims will say, "Oh, that's how it is." That's why sometimes when I'm walking outside with my husband, I'm careful where I'm walking. If he's walking in front of me, I'll say, "Wait, wait, let me go in front." I make sure that I'm always smiling. I hope that the way I portray myself might help others to see Islam in a different light.

Muslims faced an uphill battle in their quest for acceptance before 9/11. After the terrorist attacks, the climb steepened considerably. A young woman from New York described the magnitude of the situation: "You know how before 9/11, how much work we did to put up a good image? To educate people about our religion? It all, with the whole 9/11, all of it went to waste. It is going to take a very long time to put up a good image and to make people over here feel comfortable around us again."

The events of 9/11 precipitated a major assault on Muslim Americans' autonomy and dignity. In the weeks following the terrorist attacks, Muslims recoiled in fear and frustration. As time passed, the participants in this research began to take deliberate actions to alter their perceived future. Muslims forged a heightened sense of group solidarity, which involved crossing ethnic boundaries and developing new alliances. They strengthened their religious identification, increased their religious participation, and fostered meaningful relationships with other Muslims. Many felt they were becoming more spiritual and better Muslims, as they found comfort in Islam. And, rather than abandoning the most important symbols of their faith, Muslims attempted to use these visible markers to counter negative perceptions. The wave of hostility that was unleashed after the 9/11 attacks may have *victimized* Muslims, but they did not become passive *victims*. Instead, they actively struggled to reclaim their faith and to assert their positions in the American social landscape.

7

Conclusion

In the aftermath of the deadliest terror attacks in United States history, Muslims became the public and political scapegoats of 9/11. Some terrified and traumatized citizens, struggling to come to terms with the incalculable suffering caused by the attacks, directed their outrage at minorities who share—or were mistakenly assumed to share—a common religious or ethnic identity with those individuals actually responsible for the calamities. Key elected officials, desperate to demonstrate progress in the post-9/11 "War on Terror," encouraged Americans to accept harsh and discriminatory tactics ostensibly designed to keep the nation safe from so-called threatening outsiders.[1] As a result, Muslim Americans—who had nothing to do with the assaults on the World Trade Center or the Pentagon—have become the victims of an unrelenting backlash.

This final chapter addresses two general themes that have appeared throughout this book. The first part of the conclusion considers why Muslim Americans were so readily vilified and then so easily victimized by some of their fellow citizens and their government. Specifically, the discussion below is designed to help shed light on the social forces associated with postdisaster blame assignment and backlash.[2] The second part of the conclusion reflects upon the human impacts of the stereotyping, harassment, and exclusion that Muslim Americans have experienced since 9/11.

Blame and Backlash

Anny Bakalian and Mehdi Bozorgmehr were the first to introduce a theoretically grounded conceptualization of the widely used, but seldom defined, term "backlash." They characterize backlash as "an excessive and adverse societal and governmental reaction to a political/ideological crisis against a group or groups."[3] Further, they argue that during times of war or catastrophe, populations that share the same racial, ethnic, or religious background as the "enemy" of the state may be subject to backlash violence. Bakalian and Bozorgmehr explain that individuals and the government may perpetrate backlash, and it may take several forms, including stereotyping, harassment, hate crimes, and state-sanctioned repression of minority groups.

Bakalian and Bozorgmehr's insightful work contributes significantly to our understanding of backlash. But important questions remain. Why does backlash occur after certain crises, but not after others? Why are some individuals and groups singled out for blame and mistreatment, while others are left alone? After Timothy McVeigh and Terry Nichols detonated a massive bomb in the heart of Oklahoma City, killing 168 people and wounding hundreds of others, no public outrage against white American men erupted. No government roundups, no unlawful interrogations, and no detentions occurred. In fact, and as I have already described in previous passages of this book, Muslims and Arabs, yet again, became the victims of a surge of hate crimes after the media wrongfully associated "Middle Easterners" with the destruction of the Alfred P. Murrah Federal Building. The 9/11 attacks, which were perpetrated by foreign terrorists linked to Islam and the Arab world, precipitated the largest-ever spike in bias attacks against Muslims and Arabs. What, then, can the response to 9/11 teach us about the processes that set blame assignment and backlash into motion?

In the first place, the *intentional and malicious nature* of the 9/11 attacks prompted an extraordinary search for those who should be held accountable. Students of disaster have long recognized that what causes a crisis (the disaster agent, if you will) shapes the feelings and reactions that follow. Certain undeniable similarities exist between the ways that human communities respond to natural disasters, technological catastrophes, and acts of terrorism. But these distinct types of emergencies unfold in a variety of ways, and many of the differences can be attributed directly to the source of the disaster.[4]

Thomas Drabek and Enrico Quarantelli were among the first social scientists to write about the human need to assign blame after catastrophic events. Drawing on years of postdisaster fieldwork, they observe, "Disasters often bring out the best in individuals. Ability to endure suffering, desire to help others, and acts of courage and generosity come forth in time of crisis."[5] Drabek and Quarantelli caution, though, that "disasters can also evoke the worst in persons—a relentless search for scapegoats to blame for destruction and loss of life."[6] They add, "This tendency to seek the cause in a *who*—rather than a *what*—is most common after catastrophes not caused naturally."[7]

The 9/11 attacks fall into a broad category of events that specialists often refer to as "human-induced catastrophes." In contrast to natural disasters, human-induced catastrophes are unmistakably brought about by human actions.[8] Disasters that people have clearly caused can be further divided between acts of omission and acts of commission.[9] Acts of omission are unintentional and accidental. They occur when bridges collapse, when warning systems fail, and when trains carrying toxic substances derail. Acts of commission, on the other hand, involve premeditated acts of violence and terror. The perpetrators of such malevolent attacks willfully attempt to inflict pain, suffering, and death on their targets.

It is rare for individuals or groups to be assigned direct responsibility for the destruction that tornadoes, floods, hurricanes, or earthquakes cause. Even though the damage from such events can usually be traced back to the choices that human beings make about where and how they live, the media and affected populations tend to describe the losses in "non-personal and naturalistic" terms.[10] One scholar puts it this way: "Natural disasters are almost always experienced as acts of God or caprices of nature. They happen *to* us. They *visit* us, as if from afar."[11]

Human-induced catastrophes, however, unquestionably occur *because of* us. Human beings, rather than Mother Nature, represent the "agents of destruction." Human-caused disasters, whether unintentional or intentional, set off a hunt for those responsible for the devastation. Some sense of outrage, the desire to assign some degree of blame, and a feeling that the guilty should be punished for their actions always develop.[12] In technological disasters, blame is often fixed on public officials, business owners, or large corporations. Assigning blame in these instances is viewed as rational, even necessary, as it may force those responsible to take action to remedy the crisis situation.[13] However, and as has been well documented elsewhere, persons in power typically do not accept responsibility for technological mishaps and instead may engage in what sociologists Stephen Kroll-Smith and Stephen Couch refer to as "reciprocal blame attribution."[14] This process, which involves the victims blaming the powerful, the powerful blaming the victims, and the victims blaming one another, regularly escalates into conflict. In the end, the cycle of blame may become more debilitating than the hazard agent itself.[15]

Even considering all the dread and anger that technological disasters may engender, research suggests that intentional human-induced catastrophes are far more difficult for victims to comprehend or to assimilate.[16] Acts of apparently indiscriminate mass violence create acute feelings of helplessness and high rates of anxiety that endure for long periods of time.[17] Moreover, disasters that are caused by malicious human intent shatter individuals' views of the world as a just and meaningful place,[18] and, therefore, these events are especially likely to ignite resentments and to provoke blame.[19]

Almost immediately after the planes crashed into the World Trade Center, Muslims and Arabs were implicated as the prime suspects. By the time the U.S. government officially confirmed that the 9/11 hijackers were all Muslims from Arab nations (including Saudi Arabia, the United Arab Emirates, Lebanon, and Egypt), the media had already charged that the attacks were carried out "all in the name of Islam."[20] The link between 9/11 and Islam left all Muslims—no matter how different in terms of background or ideology—vulnerable to scapegoating based on their shared religious affiliation with the perpetrators of the attacks.

In the second place, the *magnitude of the losses* endured on 9/11 amplified the calls to avenge the victims and to bring the perpetrators to justice. The United States, of course, is not unfamiliar with the incredible damage that terrorism can do. Over the past two centuries, the citizens, corporations, military, and government of this nation have been subject to various forms of terrorist violence. The "American left" (e.g., labor activists, people's rights organizations), the "American right" (e.g., the Ku Klux Klan, neo-Nazis, antiabortion activists, antiestablishment militias), and international terrorist groups from around the globe have carried out numerous attacks.[21]

Furthermore, 9/11 was not the first time that Islamist militants had committed a terrorist act on U.S. soil. On February 26, 1993, a group of al Qaeda operatives detonated a truck bomb in a parking garage beneath the World Trade Center. The ensuing explosion opened a gaping hole seven stories up.[22] The terrorists failed in their attempt to topple the north tower onto the south tower "like a pair of dominoes," but they did kill six people, injure more than a thousand others, and shut down the two tallest buildings in New York City for weeks.[23]

After the arrest of one of the suspected conspirators in the 1993 World Trade Center bombing, Muslim Americans expressed concern that that their community would be collectively demonized in a "frenzy of stereotyping."[24] Their fears were justified, as just days after the bombing, vandals targeted a mosque in New Jersey where one of the terror suspects had worshipped.[25] Angry citizens heckled mosque congregants, and unknown callers left threatening voicemail messages at Islamic centers across the United States.[26] Law enforcement officials indicated, however, that they had received no formal complaints of hate crimes against Arab Americans or Muslims after the 1993 attack.[27]

The reaction to 9/11 was on an entirely different scale. In the three-month period following the terrorist attacks, the FBI documented more than four hundred anti-Islamic hate crimes. In the subsequent years, Arab and Muslim civil-rights groups confirmed thousands of additional allegations of bias and discrimination in the workplace, at schools and universities, and in airports and other public settings. The number of anti-Islamic and anti-Arab hate-related murders, which may have involved as many as nineteen victims, was also unprecedented.

The enormity of the catastrophe and its immense domestic and international impact explain, in part, the severity and duration of the post-9/11 backlash. The terrorist attacks led to the deaths of nearly three thousand people, caused tens of billions of dollars in economic losses, and sparked an open-ended U.S.-led War on Terror. The ruthlessness of the coordinated assaults, combined with the sheer terror that they evoked, led many lawmakers and journalists to refer to 9/11 as a "turning point" in the history of political violence.[28] Paul Bremer, former head of the U.S. National Commission on Terrorism, declared that 9/11 "is a different order of magnitude. . . . This is not only the worst terrorist attack in American history, it is the worst terrorist attack in history, period."[29]

In the third place, the *pre-9/11 social and political context* was characterized by excessive levels of hostility, prejudice, and mistrust directed toward Muslims and Islam. Several factors fueled these feelings of antipathy, including, but probably not limited to, the following: (1) an actual global increase in terrorist violence perpetrated in the name of Islam, (2) persistently negative Western media representations of the Islamic faith and its followers, (3) a general lack of familiarity with Muslims and Islamic beliefs among the American populace, and (4) the heightened visibility of the growing Muslim population in the United States.

Political scientist Kerem Ozan Kalkan and his colleagues have convincingly argued that negative attitudes toward Muslims emerged from a much larger syndrome that predated the 9/11 attacks.[30] Muslims' religious beliefs, cultural orientations, and ethnicities have long made them stand out in crucial ways from the dominant white, Judeo-Christian majority in the United States. The sense of "difference" associated with the Islamic faith made many Americans wary of Islam years before 9/11.[31] As such, the attacks on New York and Washington, D.C., served as a match that allowed these preexisting prejudices to flare.

During the latter half of the twentieth century, Christians, Jews, Hindus, Sikhs, Buddhists, Muslims, and members of many other religious sects carried out an alarming number of violent acts against government and civilian targets in countries around the world.[32] These acts sadly and repeatedly demonstrated that all religions have the potential to be used to provoke destruction. Yet in the American public imagination, the words "Arab," "Muslim," and "terrorist" have become virtually synonymous.

As Edward Said acknowledges in *Covering Islam,* a great many violent offenses, organized or not, have indeed been committed against Western and Israeli targets in the name of Islam. Yet, as Said maintains, "Islam" defines a relatively small proportion of what actually takes place in the Islamic world. Nevertheless, references to "Muslim terrorists" appear so regularly in the Western media that the relationship between the religion of Islam and violence is often accepted without question. Said's writing on the subject is worth quoting at length:

> Instead of scholarship [on Islam and Muslims], we often find only journalists making extravagant statements, which are instantly picked up and further dramatized by the media. Looming over their work is the slippery concept, to which they constantly allude, of "fundamentalism," a word that has come to be associated almost automatically with Islam, although it has a flourishing, usually elided, relationship with Christianity, Judaism, and Hinduism. The deliberately created associations between Islam and fundamentalism ensure that the average reader comes to see Islam and fundamentalism as essentially the same thing. Given the tendency to reduce Islam to a handful of rules, stereotypes, and generalizations about the faith, its founder, and all of its people, then the reinforcement of every negative fact associated with Islam—its violence, primitiveness, atavism, threatening qualities—is perpetuated.[33]

In the fourth place, the 9/11 attacks solidified the preexisting image of Muslims as *dangerous and threatening outsiders.* The coordinated hijackings and the assaults on the World Trade Center and the Pentagon dramatically escalated Americans' sense of threat from a foreign "enemy" arising from the Muslim and Arab worlds. This perception translated into extreme hostility against these groups, inciting discrimination and hate crimes across the United States.

The media had so thoroughly maligned Muslims and their faith that when the post-9/11 backlash began, many Americans were unsure whether they should be sympathetic toward or suspicious of the Muslims who were being harassed and discriminated against. What's more, most Americans lack direct contact with Muslims, and even fewer hold a deep understanding of the Islamic faith.[34] These interrelated issues have undoubtedly made it more difficult to challenge the monolithic view of Muslims as terrorists.

To be certain, some people in positions of power condemned the backlash violence. President George W. Bush, on several occasions, used his speeches to emphasize that America's quarrel was not with Islam. In an address to the nation on September 20, 2001, Bush said, "I also want to speak tonight directly to Muslims throughout the world. We respect your faith. It's practiced freely by many millions of Americans and by millions more in countries that America counts as friends. Its teachings are good and peaceful, and those who commit evil in the name of Allah blaspheme the name of Allah." After a period of applause from Congress, he continued: "The enemy of America is not our many Muslim friends; it is not our many Arab friends. Our enemy is a radical network of terrorists, and every government that supports them."[35]

Jeffrey Kaplan, a religious studies scholar, maintains that the leadership President Bush showed was one of the most important factors in turning the tide of anger away from individual Muslims after 9/11.[36] Although it is true that the most egregious acts of backlash violence largely subsided in the first three months after the terrorist attacks, reports of anti-Muslim bias and discrimination have continued to rise in the years since 9/11. This disturbing trend is in part a result of actions of the U.S. government, which continues to implement policies that target Muslims, Arabs, and South Asians (this is an argument that Michael Welch meticulously details in his book *Scapegoats of September 11th*).[37] In the minds of some bigoted individuals, these official government actions—the profiling, interrogations, raids, detentions, and deportations—appear to justify, and perhaps even sanction, acts of intolerance.

Although reported levels of prejudice toward minority groups in the United States have declined in recent decades, attitudes toward Muslims are an exception: Americans view Muslims less favorably than they do most other religious and racial minorities.[38] A 2006 national survey found that more than one-fourth (26.3 percent) of Americans said that Muslims "do not at all agree with my vision of American society."[39] Much lower percentages of respondents agreed with the same statement when asked about Hispanics (7.6 percent), Jews (7.4 percent), Asian Americans (7 percent), African Americans (4.6 percent), and whites (2.2 percent).[40]

Yet, contrary to this perspective, research has unequivocally demonstrated that Muslim Americans are "mostly mainstream" in terms of their attitudes and values. Muslims express positive views of American society: They see their communities as good places to live, they believe in the American dream, and, as a group, their income and education levels mirror those of the general public.[41] Nevertheless, Muslims are *perceived* as strange and potentially threatening religious and cultural "Others." In the aftermath of 9/11, these perceptions, and associated levels of fear and anger, played a central role in mobilizing considerable hostility toward Muslim Americans.

In the fifth place, the *visibility* and *identifiability* of the Muslim population also influenced their selection as scapegoats. Identifiability matters, because, for a group to be targeted for discrimination, its members must be detectable in some way.[42] (It is worth pausing for a moment to note that when stigmatized people are not easily recognized, hostile governments or regimes may take steps to ensure that the out-group is made visible. The Jews in Nazi Germany who were forced to sew colored patches on their garments to mark themselves as Jews in public serve as a tragic case in point.)

Emigration from Muslim-majority countries to the United States has increased dramatically since the passage of the 1965 Immigration Act. Subsequently, the number of mosques and Islamic schools and businesses in communities across the nation has grown steadily over the past several decades. Most Muslim Americans choose not to wear traditional Islamic dress. However, the practice is rapidly increasing in popularity, especially among second-generation Muslim youth and young adults, and it is now common to see Muslim women wearing headscarves in college classrooms and the workplace.

These and many other visible signifiers of the growth of the Muslim population have led some commentators to lament the loss of "American values" and to warn Americans of the "threat" of an Islamic takeover from within. In 2006, Republican Congressional Representative Virgil Goode issued a letter to his constituents in which he declares, "I fear that in the next century we will have many more Muslims in the United States. . . . To preserve the values and beliefs traditional to the United States of America [we must] adopt strict immigration policies." Like Goode, many other right-wing politicians used 9/11 as a window of opportunity to advance an anti-Muslim and anti-immigrant agenda.[43]

The Muslim American community is composed of a dizzying array of people from across the globe. But since 9/11, the considerable racial and ethnic diversity of the population has been largely obscured as Muslim Americans have been lumped together and racialized "brown."[44] Consequently, dark-skinned and dark-haired Muslims, as well as other dark-complexioned people mistakenly identified as Muslims, have been subject to violent threats, physical attack, and profiling. Again, although most Muslims choose not to wear traditional Islamic dress, those who do—such as Muslim women with headscarves or Muslim men who don the kufi—have been especially at risk for discrimination. In addition, other minorities who wear distinctive religious or ethnic clothing, including Indian women who dress in saris and turbaned Sikhs, have been confused for Muslims and consequently harmed. Immigrants from Muslim countries, those with Islamic-sounding names, persons with foreign accents, and community leaders associated with Islamic organizations have been excluded and mistreated as well.[45]

After 9/11, these various *markers of difference* led to heightened levels of vulnerability within the Muslim community. In 2003, the New York City Commission on Human Rights issued a report revealing that Muslims, as well as Arabs and South Asians, were regularly singled out and harassed after the attacks on the World Trade Center.[46] The study found that 69 percent of the 956 respondents were discriminated against in the disaster aftermath. Almost 80 percent of those surveyed indicated that the fallout from 9/11 had negatively affected their lives, regardless of whether they had been directly mistreated. National polls of Muslims yielded similar results. For example, Georgetown University's Muslims in the American Public Square project conducted a survey in 2001 that found that 52 percent of Muslims knew of individuals, businesses, or religious organizations in their community that had been targeted for attack after 9/11.[47]

Interestingly, most non-Muslim Americans also see Muslims living in the United States as facing more discrimination than other religious groups. The Pew Research Center conducted a survey in 2009 that found that nearly six in ten American adults (58 percent) believed that Muslims are subject to "a lot" of discrimination, far more than say the same about Jews (35 percent), evangelical Christians (27 percent), atheists (26 percent), or Mormons (24 percent).[48]

In the sixth place, the *relative powerlessness* of Muslims, especially when compared to other more enfranchised minority groups, contributed to their post-9/11 victimization. This final point is not meant to imply that Muslim Americans are entirely powerless as a people, nor is it intended to suggest that Muslims have not tried to respond to the issues affecting their community since 9/11. To the contrary, Muslim Americans have been quite active in working to correct misperceptions about their faith. They have engaged in extensive outreach efforts, formally and informally, aimed at educating non-Muslim Americans about Islamic beliefs and practices. National Islamic organizations have lobbied elected leaders to protect civil rights and have demanded an end to religious and ethnic profiling among law enforcement officials. Nevertheless, Muslims have confronted significant barriers in responding to the enormous challenges that they face in the post-9/11 era.

For one thing, Muslims represent just a fraction of the overall American population. Although estimates vary widely, most observers agree that Muslims make up only about 0.6 percent to 2 percent of the total population. With that said, and as mentioned above, the Muslim American community is growing rapidly (according to one study, the number of Muslims in the United States doubled between 1990 and 2001).[49] Nonetheless, for the immediate future, their numbers will remain comparatively small, and, therefore, Muslims will likely continue to struggle to have their voices heard.

Muslims are also vastly underrepresented in influential social institutions:

most notably, in the mass media and the political system. Because Muslims lack access to channels of power within these institutions, they have had an exceedingly difficult time in their quest to challenge derogatory representations and discriminatory policies that have seriously disadvantaged their community.

Malevolent stereotypes equating Islam with violence have endured for more than a century.[50] Following the 9/11 attacks, which spawned intense public fear of future terrorist strikes and two wars against two predominantly Islamic countries, an unending barrage of vicious and hateful slurs have been directed at Muslims. In the post-9/11 era, evangelical Christians label Islam "evil" and "wicked" on prime-time television without triggering widespread condemnation. Syndicated talk radio hosts openly advocate for the global "eradication" of Muslims. Newspaper columnists inform their readers that Muslims "breed like rats." Military generals proclaim that Americans should battle Islam "in the name of Jesus" and assert that Allah is "not a real God." And without raising much opposition, conservative politicians threaten to "take out" Islam's holiest cities, Medina and Mecca, through preemptive nuclear warfare.

These statements are so startling not just because of their maliciousness but also because we live in a time when racial or religious misrepresentations of every other cultural group are no longer circulated with such impunity.[51] Imagine if political leaders, pastors, or media pundits had said the same thing about African Americans, Jews, or Catholics. These sorts of sweeping mischaracterizations and violent intonations would be publicly decried, and the person responsible for the hate speech would likely be summarily dismissed.[52]

Why has the mass media basically gone unchecked in its transmission of this post-9/11 discourse of fear and hatred? First, it is well established that during times of armed conflict and national crisis, stereotyping meets the least resistance.[53] From this perspective, as long as the United States remains at war with Iraq and Afghanistan, the Muslim community will in all likelihood continue to be the subject of bigoted and slanderous representations in the media. Second, non-Muslims write and report much of the Western news that is produced about "Islam" and "Muslims." The virtual absence of a "Muslim voice" in American newsrooms contributes to uninformed, and at times wholly inaccurate, depictions of the Islamic faith and its followers.[54] Third, editors and news commentators have found a dearth of experts on Islam and Muslims who can communicate effectively to larger audiences. National Islamic organizations have been overwhelmed by requests for media interviews and thus have had a difficult time keeping up with the ever-increasing demand for a "Muslim perspective" on various events.[55]

Muslim Americans are even more underrepresented on the national political stage. During the 1990s, Islamic organizations in the United States began the painstaking process of mobilizing Muslim American voters. Their progress was slow and uneven, and prejudice from outsiders and conflicts from within the Muslim community over political priorities in domestic and international contexts often impeded it. As a result of their limited integration, the Muslim community has been described as a "nonfactor" in terms of the political power structure in the United States.[56]

After 9/11, which led to the passage of sweeping antiterrorism legislation, Muslims recognized the vulnerability associated with their insufficiently developed political clout. Without adequate political representation, Muslims found themselves dependent on the good will of others for the protection of their fundamental constitutional and human rights.[57] Muslims also felt betrayed by a president that they helped elect. (In the year 2000, national Muslim groups endorsed Bush for president. Given the close vote count in Florida that year, Muslim Americans, among other groups, took credit for putting Bush in the White House.[58] This endorsement was a choice that Muslims clearly came to regret, as evidenced by the "massive migration away from the Republican party by Muslim voters."[59] According to two separate polls Zogby International conducted, more than half of registered Arab and Pakistani Muslim voters cast their ballots for the Republican Bush/Cheney ticket in the 2000 presidential election. In 2004, only 7 percent of all Muslims said they voted for Bush/Cheney, while 76 percent voted for the Democratic Kerry/Edwards ticket.[60])

The Muslim American community has experienced a significant transformation in terms of its political activism since 9/11. CAIR, the Muslim Public Affairs Council, and several other national organizations have coordinated political rallies, held press conferences, established letter-writing campaigns to elected officials, and filed lawsuits on behalf of their constituents. As a result of these and many other efforts, Muslims have made some important inroads into the American political system. Most notably, in 2006, the state of Minnesota elected the nation's first Muslim congressional representative, Keith Ellison. In 2008, Indiana voters selected Andre Carson, the nation's second Muslim congressional representative, to serve in the U.S. House of Representatives. Even though gains have clearly been made, Muslim Americans recognize that they still have a long road ahead in their pursuit of equal political representation in a nation that remains deeply skeptical of their faith.

In summary, this research suggests that six interrelated factors contributed to the post-9/11 backlash against Muslim Americans (see Figure 7.1). Two of those factors—the intentional and malicious nature of the catastrophe and the magnitude of the losses endured—speak to the character of the events

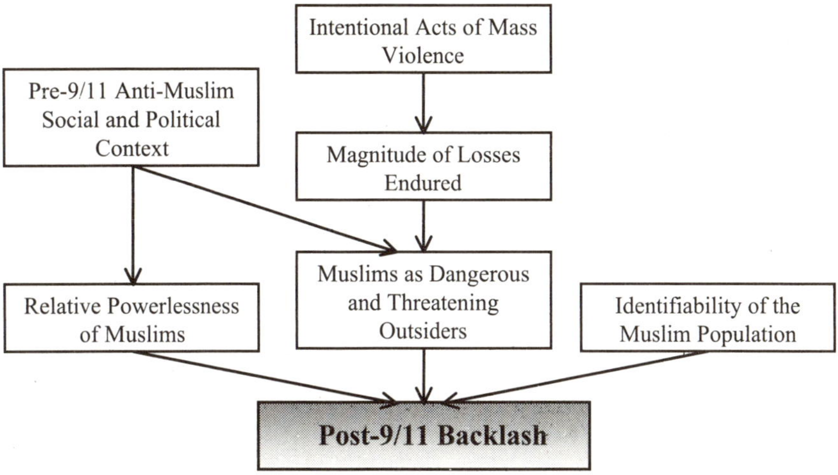

Figure 7.1. *Post-9/11 backlash: Contributing factors.*

of 9/11. The third factor—the pre-9/11 anti-Muslim social and political context—emphasizes the role that a highly negative cultural atmosphere can play in shaping postdisaster reactions toward minority groups. The final three factors—the heightened sense of threat associated with Islam, the identifiability of Muslims, and the relative powerlessness of the Muslim American community—all help explain why the backlash escalated so quickly and endured for such a long period of time. Any one of these factors alone is not likely to induce collective blame and backlash. It is the *cumulative force* of these factors that generates hostile reactions in the aftermath of catastrophe.

More could be said, of course, about the dynamics that shaped the response to 9/11. For now, I hope that this discussion can help us think more systematically about the social forces that contributed to the post-9/11 mistreatment of Muslim Americans. In turn, we may be better equipped to anticipate and to respond to backlash violence in the wake of future crises.

Exclusion and Invalidated Collective Grief

In the aftermath of 9/11, powerful voices joined together to tell *the* story of the terrorist attacks. Although the verses differed, the refrain almost always went something like this: "On the morning of September 11, 2001, Americans were shocked into collective solidarity. The airliners, turned into cruise missiles that crashed into the World Trade Center in New York City; into the Pentagon in Washington, D.C.; and into a field in Pennsylvania, brought to life a collective sense of humanity, vulnerability, and national connectedness. Through the televised repetition of images of physical devastation, human misery, and heroic acts by civil servants and civilians, Americans were drawn together in shared grief and pride."[61]

The quote above exemplifies what sociologist Monisha Das Gupta refers to as "the dominant interpretation" of 9/11.[62] This particular narrative, which privileges social solidarity and civic renewal above all else, is not *untrue* (at least in the sense that it does indeed capture how many Americans experienced 9/11), but the narrative is *incomplete.* The accounts of the Muslim American women and men represented in *Behind the Backlash* challenge the singular image of a "nation united." Their stories also remind us that although some Americans were "drawn together in shared grief and pride," others were discriminated against and denied membership in the community of sufferers.

Author Rebecca Solnit writes eloquently of the "series of emotional bonds" that 9/11 survivors formed as they attempted to make sense of the calamity, and she vividly describes the "concentric circles of support" that ringed the disaster site and rippled outward across the nation.[63] Muslims found themselves on the outermost edges of those concentric rings, looking inward, longing to be a part of the temporary community that arose after the towers fell. One young Muslim woman, whom we heard from earlier, captured the feeling perfectly: "I wanted to join those people who were volunteering downtown. . . . To me, that was the American community coming together and trying to do what they can. But I didn't feel like I could, for my own safety. I wear a headscarf. I wanted to be a part of that community, but I'm not really."

In the wake of disaster, most people experience a newfound sense of urgency, purpose, and solidarity. Indeed, the earliest disaster researchers were so struck by the high levels of empathy and mutual helpfulness that they observed following catastrophic acts of nature, they used such terms as "altruistic community" and "therapeutic social system" to depict the heightened sense of camaraderie.[64] These communities of compassion and care play an important role after disaster: They can lead to improved psychological functioning among traumatized victims and may even impel the entire disaster-stricken population toward a state of recovery.

Research conducted in the short- and longer-term aftermath of 9/11 has shown that joining together and taking action opened up significant pathways to personal healing.[65] Spontaneous volunteerism, in particular, provided an important outlet for 9/11 survivors to transform their feelings of grief and victimization into what sociologists Seana Lowe Steffen and Alice Fothergill refer to as "meaningful therapeutic recovery."[66] Steffen and

Fothergill also found that the opportunity to volunteer impacted community sentiment among volunteers by fostering new levels of identification with and affinity for members of their community.

The exclusion and compounded fear that Muslim Americans experienced after 9/11 rendered them incapable of fully participating in the postdisaster response—from taking part in the memorial services, to visiting the sites of the attacks, to volunteering—which represented an additional form of loss for Muslims. In the end, they were denied an important opportunity to resolve the traumatic impacts of the event, to bring closure, and to begin the process of individual and communal recovery.

Decades of research has demonstrated that disasters do more than cause death and physical destruction. Disasters can also do a great deal of damage to the human mind and to the body. "Individual trauma" is the term that is most often used to describe the pain, shock, and helplessness that disaster survivors experience. But as sociologist Kai Erikson has documented, the most severe events can also cause "collective trauma," a particular form of trauma that follows disaster and emerges as a result of the loss of the network of relationships that make up the general human milieu.[67] When people are wrenched out of their communities, torn from the landscapes and socialscapes in which they have been deeply enmeshed, collective trauma will likely ensue.

Erikson speaks of traumatized communities as something distinct from assemblies of traumatized persons. In his words, "Sometimes the tissues of community can be damaged in much the same way as the tissues of mind and body. . . . Traumatic wounds inflicted on individuals can combine to create a mood, an ethos—a group culture, almost—that is different from (and more than) the sum of the private wounds that make it up."[68] If collective trauma is the outcome, I would like to propose that *collective grief* represents the collective emotional response elicited by the losses caused by large-scale traumatic events.[69] Collective grief, like collective trauma, must be understood as something more than any given number of individual grief reactions.

It is not the emotions, per se, that separate individual and collective grief. In either case, affected persons are likely to report feeling sad, fearful, angry, and so forth. It should be noted, however, that the emotions may be more intense following disasters, given that extreme events result in widespread social disruption and a sense of shared danger and loss among hundreds, thousands, or even millions of people all at once. Thus, the *number of affected persons who simultaneously share the experience* distinguishes collective grief, as does the *collective expression* of grief-related emotions. With individual grief, suffering is most likely to occur in solitude or in intimate encounters between family members and close friends at visitations or funerals. Collective grief, on the other hand, entails the sharing of grief reactions with loved ones but also with strangers. Anyone who has survived a disaster would understand this phenomenon and could likely call to mind moments where persons completely unfamiliar with one another suddenly find themselves embracing, sharing their deepest feelings, and assisting with the most personal of matters. Therese Rando, a clinical psychologist, has noted that observing the grieving behaviors of other survivors (for example, seeing others overwhelmed, crying, leaving flowers in reaction to death or disaster), can catalyze grief responses in witnesses. This may, among other potential responses, invite imitation, disinhibit one's grief, and provide legitimization and permission to openly engage in grieving behaviors.[70] In moments of collective grief, people tend to join together, to develop organized and spontaneous public grieving rituals, and to talk about the event over and over and thereby find a forum for the expression of pain.[71] It is through participating in these processes that individuals, as well as the communities that they are a part of, begin to heal.

After the 9/11 attacks, bold lines were drawn between "us" and "them" that marked the beginning of a new sense of national connectedness for many Americans. Those who fell within the boundaries of the sharp dividing lines were thought of, by themselves and by others, as part of a community of sufferers. The collective grief that Americans experienced was widely viewed as legitimate, normal, expected, and something to be taken seriously.

Muslim Americans found themselves outside that bounded territory that separated the "legitimate sufferers" from others after 9/11. Of course, Muslims were not immune from the waves of sorrow that swept over the nation after the attacks. To the contrary, Muslims were genuinely distraught by the extraordinary devastation that will forever be associated with that day. Yet, in most cases, the grief that they experienced was left unexpressed, unshared, and unacknowledged beyond their own faith community, and at times, it was even actively contested by outsiders. In short, their grief was dismissed as illegitimate; one could say it was *invalidated.* As a consequence, their suffering remained largely invisible to the rest of America.

The fact that Muslims felt unwelcome to join together with their fellow Americans after 9/11 is significant, because recovery *requires* remembrance and mourning. As Judith Herman argues in *Trauma and Recovery,* "Restoring a sense of social community requires a public forum where victims can speak their truth and their suffering can be formally acknowledged."[72] Collective rituals of grief bind communities together. They provide an opportunity for disaster-affected populations to share their sadness with others, and they impose a sense of unity and order on communities struck low by collective tragedy.[73]

Scholars and civil-rights advocates have attempted to quantify the most visible injuries that Muslims sustained after 9/11—the harassment, hate crimes, and government detentions—while the more invisible forms of grief and suffering have remained mostly unacknowledged. What happened to Muslim Americans after 9/11, then, should serve as a reminder that altruistic communities have their limits. Until the boundaries of those communities are extended to encompass the most marginalized among us, those on the outside will be condemned to experience a second disaster, one that springs from the exclusionary practices of human beings.

Notes

CHAPTER 1

1. Pew Research Center, "Post-9/11 Attitudes: Religion More Prominent, Muslim Americans More Accepted" (report, Pew Research Center, Washington, DC, 2001).

2. Central Intelligence Agency, "The World Factbook," 2007, available at https://www.cia.gov/library/publications/the-world-factbook/index.html (accessed January 22, 2010).

3. Lori Peek, "Becoming Muslim: The Development of a Religious Identity," *Sociology of Religion* 66, no. 3 (2005): 215–242.

4. Edward W. Said, *Covering Islam: How the Media and the Experts Determine How We See the Rest of the World,* rev. ed. (New York: Vintage Books, 1997).

5. After 9/11, American evangelical leaders emerged as some of the most outspoken critics of Islam. In an effort to better understand the anti-Islamic discourse, Richard Cimino analyzed eighteen books written on Islam by evangelical authors. Five of the books were published before 9/11, and thirteen were written or reissued after the terrorist attacks. Cimino found that the two principal themes that distinguished the post-9/11 books were their emphasis on Islam's "inherently violent nature" and the assertion that Muslims worship a false god distinctly different than the God of Christianity and Judaism. See Richard Cimino, "'No God in Common': American Evangelical Discourse on Islam after 9/11," *Review of Religious Research* 47, no. 2 (2005): 162–174.

6. Although some condemned Franklin Graham's hateful rhetoric, others celebrated it. The evangelical news weekly *World* gave its annual "Daniel of the Year Award" (named after the Old Testament prophet who braved a lions' den) to Graham for "telling the hard truths about Islam" as well as for standing up for "Christian convictions"

in the face of a religiously and culturally relativistic society. See Cimino, "'No God in Common,'" 170.

7. Council on American-Islamic Relations, "American Muslims: One Year after 9/11" (report, Council on American-Islamic Relations Research Center, Washington, DC, 2002), 23.

8. Hal Lindsey, *The Everlasting Hatred: The Roots of Jihad* (Murrieta, CA: Oracle House Publishing, 2002), 10.

9. Jason Vest, "Exit Jesse, Enter Saxby," *The Nation*, November 12, 2002, available at www.thenation.com/doc/20021125/vest20021110 (accessed May 2, 2010).

10. Ibid.

11. "Students Discuss Koran Book after Battle," *ABC News*, August 25, 2002, available at http://abcnews.go.com/Nightline/story?id=128548&page=1 (accessed May 2, 2010).

12. Media Matters for America, "Savage: To 'Save the United States,' Lawmakers Should Institute 'Outright Ban on Muslim Immigration' and on 'The Construction of Mosques,'" *Media Matters for America*, November 29, 2006, available at http://mediamatters.org/mmtv/200611290005 (accessed May 2, 2010).

13. Teresa Watanabe, "Frustrated U.S. Muslims Feel Marginalized Again," *Los Angeles Times*, September 27, 2002, available at http://articles.latimes.com/2002/sep/27/local/me-muslim27(accessed June 30, 2010).

14. Cal Thomas, "It's Not Over," *Townhall.com*, October 29, 2002, available at http://townhall.com/columnists/CalThomas/2002/10/29/its_not_over (accessed May 2, 2010).

15. Robert K. Merton, "Foreword," in A. H. Barton, *Communities in Disaster: A Sociological Analysis of Collective Stress Situations* (Garden City, NY: Doubleday, 1969), vii–xxxvii.

16. Charles E. Fritz, "Disaster," in *Contemporary Social Problems*, ed. R. K. Merton and R. A. Nisbet (New York: Harcourt, Brace, and World, 1961), 651–694.

17. The interviews that I conducted during the initial phases of this project were with college students. As the study developed, I expanded the sample to include college students and young professionals. This expansion allowed me to understand the issues that Muslims faced in higher education and employment (see Chapter 4). In addition, many of the interviewees graduated from college during the two-year period of this study, so I was able to track their experiences as they applied for jobs and graduate school or married and started families.

18. Some researchers include in the second generation those children born abroad who came to the United States before age twelve. However, most scholars now make a distinction between the second and 1.5 generation to differentiate American-born children of immigrants (second generation) from those children who migrated to the United States before reaching adulthood (1.5 generation).

19. Standard racial and ethnic categories do not depict the true diversity of the sample population, as the interviewees identified with more than thirty different nationalities and a variety of cultures. The following are some of those backgrounds as reported by the participants in this study: Afghanistan, Albania, Bangladesh, Cambodia, Canada, Egypt, Germany, Great Britain, Greece, Guinea, Guyana, India, Indonesia, Iran, Iraq, Japan, Kuwait, Lebanon, Malaysia, Morocco, Pakistan, Palestine, Puerto Rico, Saudi Arabia, Syria, Trinidad, Turkey, United States, Uzbekistan, Yemen, and Zimbabwe.

20. Lori Peek and Alice Fothergill, "Using Focus Groups: Lessons from Studying Day-care Centers, 9/11, and Hurricane Katrina," *Qualitative Research* 9, no. 1 (2009): 31–59.

21. The following two volumes offer excellent overviews of methodological techniques and the special challenges of disaster research: Fran H. Norris, Sandro Galea, Matthew J. Friedman, and Patricia J. Watson, eds., *Methods for Disaster Mental Health Research* (New York: Guilford Press, 2006); Robert A. Stallings, ed., *Methods of Disaster Research* (Philadelphia: Xlibris, 2002).

22. Brenda Phillips, "Qualitative Methods and Disaster Research," in *Methods of Disaster Research,* ed. R. A. Stallings (Philadelphia: Xlibris, 2002), 194–211.

23. Sarah Michaels, "Perishable Information, Enduring Insights? Understanding Quick Response Research," in *Beyond September 11: An Account of Post-Disaster Research,* ed. J. L. Monday (Boulder: Institute of Behavioral Science, University of Colorado, 2003), 15–48.

24. The question of whether it is more effective to conduct fieldwork as an "insider" or an "outsider" has been the subject of substantial scholarly debate. Indeed, many writings on fieldwork have, with increasing attention and sensitivity, documented the myriad contexts and situations in which the ascribed statuses—such as race, gender, sexuality, age, or ethnicity—of the interviewer and interviewees can hinder or facilitate the acquisition of rich data. For example, feminist theorists contend that the researcher's identity and social location affect all aspects of the research process—from the articulation of a research question to the analysis and presentation of data—and therefore they encourage "strong reflexivity" and argue that researchers should subject themselves to the same level of scrutiny they direct toward the subjects of their inquiry.

Most significant to this study, I was a religious outsider; I identify as a nondenominational Christian, and all the interviewees were Muslim. In most cases, I was also a racial/ethnic outsider; I am white, and the majority of the participants were not. At the same time, I shared many values and characteristics with the participants. I, like many of my interviewees, was a student when I started this project. I was of a similar age, and I came from the same region as some of the respondents. Also, I am female, as were the majority of the participants. The point here is not to demonstrate that I did or did not share certain characteristics with the participants; rather, it is to emphasize that the notions of "insider" and "outsider" are fluid and depend on situational contexts and social settings. Indeed, in the field, differences and similarities are evaluated by the observer and the observed in many ways. Sharing certain characteristics does not guarantee that a researcher will become an "insider," nor does having differences mean that the researcher will always be an "outsider."

For thoughtful examinations of the insider versus outsider debate, see John Lofland, David Snow, Leon Anderson, and Lyn H. Lofland, *Analyzing Social Settings: A Guide to Qualitative Observation and Analysis,* 4th ed. (Belmont, CA: Wadsworth/Thompson Learning, 2006); Jill A. McCorkel and Kristen Myers, "What Difference Does Difference Make? Position and Privilege in the Field," *Qualitative Sociology* 26, no. 2 (2003): 199–231; Nancy A. Naples, "The Outsider Phenomenon," in *Feminist Perspectives on Social Research,* ed. S. N. Hesse-Biber and M. L. Yaiser (New York: Oxford University Press, 2004), 373–381.

25. Other disaster researchers have documented that respondents may actually receive emotional benefits from participating in interviews following catastrophic events.

This seemed to be particularly true in this study, as several of the participants commented that they genuinely appreciated having the opportunity to talk to someone about their experiences.

26. Katherine Pratt Ewing, "Introduction," in *Being and Belonging: Muslims in the United States Since 9/11*, ed. K. P. Ewing (New York: Russell Sage Foundation, 2008), 1–11.

27. Pew Research Center, "Muslim Americans: Middle Class and Mostly Mainstream" (report, Pew Research Center, Washington, DC, 2007).

28. Tom W. Smith, "The Muslim Population of the United States: The Methodology of Estimates," *Public Opinion Quarterly* 66 (2002): 404–417.

29. Ihsan Bagby, Paul M. Perl, and Bryan T. Froehle, "The Mosque in America: A National Portrait" (report, Council on American-Islamic Relations, Washington, DC, 2001).

30. Karen Armstrong, *Islam: A Short History* (New York: Random House, 2000); Jane I. Smith, *Islam in America* (New York: Columbia University Press, 1999).

31. Sharon McIrvin Abu-Laban, "Family and Religion among Muslim Immigrants and Their Descendants," in *Muslim Families in North America*, ed. E. H. Waugh, S. M. Abu-Laban, and R. B. Qureshi (Edmonton: University of Alberta Press, 1991), 6–31.

32. M. Arif Ghayur, "Muslims in the United States: Settlers and Visitors," *Annals of the American Academy of Political and Social Science* 454 (1981): 150–163.

33. Abu-Laban, "Family and Religion among Muslim Immigrants and Their Descendants."

34. Geneive Abdo, *Mecca and Main Street: Muslim Life in America after 9/11* (New York: Oxford University Press, 2006).

35. Ghayur, "Muslims in the United States: Settlers and Visitors."

36. The Muslim population in the United States has been growing at a rate of 6 percent per year, compared to .9 percent for the U.S. population overall. See Louise Cainkar, "Assessing the Need, Addressing the Problem: Working with Disadvantaged Muslim Immigrant Families and Communities" (report, Leadership Center at Morehouse College, Atlanta, GA, 2003).

37. Helen Rose Ebaugh, "Introduction," in *Religion and the New Immigrants: Continuities and Adaptations in Immigrant Congregations*, ed. H. R. Ebaugh and J. S. Chafetz (Walnut Creek, CA: AltaMira Press, 2000), 13–28; R. Stephen Warner, "Immigration and Religious Communities in the United States," in *Gatherings in Diaspora: Religious Communities and the New Immigration*, ed. R. S. Warner and J. G. Wittner (Philadelphia: Temple University Press, 1998), 3–34.

38. Diana L. Eck, *A New Religious America: How a "Christian Country" Has Become the World's Most Religiously Diverse Nation* (New York: HarperCollins Publishers, 2001); Gordon J. Melton, *The Encyclopedia of American Religions*, 7th ed. (Detroit: Gale Research, 2003).

39. A random sample survey of one thousand American households found that half of all respondents incorrectly believed that "almost all Muslims are Arab." See Council on American-Islamic Relations, "Islam and Muslims: A Poll of American Public Opinion" (report, Council on American-Islamic Relations Research Center, Washington, DC, 2004).

40. Pew Forum on Religion and Public Life, "Mapping the Global Muslim Population:

A Report on the Size and Distribution of the World's Muslim Population" (report, Pew Forum on Religion and Public Life, Washington, DC, 2009).

41. Ibid.

42. Since 1945, twenty-two nations where the primary language is Arabic have combined to form the League of Arab States. These Arab nations include Algeria, Bahrain, Comoros, Djibouti, Egypt, Iraq, Jordan, Kuwait, Lebanon, Libya, Mauritania, Morocco, Oman, Palestine, Qatar, Saudi Arabia, Somalia, Sudan, Syria, Tunisia, the United Arab Emirates, and Yemen.

43. Marvin Wingfield, "Arab Americans: Into the Multicultural Mainstream," *Equity and Excellence in Education* 39 (2006): 253–266.

44. Jen'nan Ghazal Read, "Discrimination and Identity Formation in a Post-9/11 Era: A Comparison of Muslim and Christian Arab Americans," in *Race and Arab Americans before and after 9/11: From Invisible Citizens to Visible Subjects,* ed. Amaney Jamal and Nadine Naber (Syracuse, NY: Syracuse University Press, 2008), 305–317.

45. Pew Research Center, "Muslim Americans: Middle Class and Mostly Mainstream."

46. Ibid.

47. John R. Logan and Glenn Deane, "The Muslim World in Metropolitan America" (report, Lewis Mumford Center for Comparative Urban and Regional Research, University of Albany, Albany, NY, 2002).

48. Ibid.

49. Abdo, *Mecca and Main Street.*

50. Gallup Poll, "Muslim Americans: A National Portrait" (report, Gallup, Washington, DC, 2009).

51. Ibid.

52. Logan and Deane, "The Muslim World in Metropolitan America."

53. Hillel Fradkin, "America in Islam," *Public Interest* 55 (2004): 37–55.

54. Abdo, *Mecca and Main Street.*

55. Gallup Poll, "Muslim Americans: A National Portrait."

56. Pew Research Center, "Muslim Americans: Middle Class and Mostly Mainstream."

57. Gallup Poll, "Muslim Americans: A National Portrait."

58. Pew Research Center, "Muslim Americans: Middle Class and Mostly Mainstream."

59. Gallup Poll, "Muslim Americans: A National Portrait."

60. Ibid.

61. Jack G. Shaheen, *Reel Bad Arabs: How Hollywood Vilifies a People* (Brooklyn, NY: Olive Branch Press, 2001).

62. Edward W. Said, *Orientalism* (New York: Vintage Books, 1978); Said, *Covering Islam.*

63. David Morris, "Unease over Islam: Poll: Critical Views of Muslim Faith Growing among Americans," *ABC News,* 2003, available at http://abcnews.go.com/sections/us/World/sept11_islampoll_030911.html (accessed January 22, 2010).

64. Council on American-Islamic Relations, "Islam and Muslims: A Poll of American Public Opinion."

65. Council on American-Islamic Relations, "American Public Opinion about Islam

and Muslims" (report, Council on American-Islamic Relations Research Center, Washington, DC, 2006).

66. Jon Cohen, "Poll: Americans Skeptical of Islam and Arabs: 9/11 Hardened Americans' Views of Muslims," *ABC News,* 2006, available at http://abcnews.go.com/US/story?id=1700599 (accessed January 22, 2010).

67. Lydia Saad, "Anti-Muslim Sentiments Fairly Commonplace: Four in Ten Americans Admit Feeling Prejudice against Muslims" (report, Gallup, Washington, DC, 2006).

68. Gallup Center for Muslim Studies, "In U.S., Religious Prejudice Stronger against Muslims" (report, Gallup, Washington, DC, 2010).

69. Ibid.

70. Council on American-Islamic Relations, "American Public Opinion about Islam and Muslims."

71. Ibid.

72. Cohen, "Poll: Americans Skeptical of Islam and Arabs"; Council on American-Islamic Relations, "Islam and Muslims: A Poll of American Public Opinion"; Council on American-Islamic Relations, "American Public Opinion about Islam and Muslims."

73. Kathleen Moore, "A Part of US or Apart from US? Post-September 11 Attitudes toward Muslims and Civil Liberties," *Middle East Report* 32, no. 3 (2002): 32–35.

74. Jörg Nagler, "Internment of German Enemy Aliens in the United States during the First and Second World Wars," in *Alien Justice: Wartime Internment in Australia and North America,* ed. Kay Saunders and Roger Daniels (St. Lucia, Queensland: University of Queensland Press, 2000), 66–77.

75. Ibid., 68–71.

76. George E. Pozzetta, "Alien Enemies or Loyal Americans? The Internment of Italian Americans," in *Alien Justice: Wartime Internment in Australia and North America,* 80–92.

77. Roger Daniels, "Incarcerating Japanese-Americans: An Atrocity Revisited," in *Alien Justice: Wartime Internment in Australia and North America,* 168–184.

78. Ibid., 182.

79. Yvonne Yazback Haddad, *Not Quite American? The Shaping of Arab and Muslim Identity in the United States* (Waco, TX: Baylor University Press, 2004).

80. Daniels, "Incarcerating Japanese-Americans."

81. Amir Marvasti and Karyn McKinney, *Middle Eastern Lives in America* (New York: Rowman and Littlefield, 2004).

82. Lewis Seiler and Dan Hamburg, "Rule by Fear or Rule by Law?" *San Francisco Chronicle,* February 4, 2008, B-7.

83. Aladdin Elaasar, *Silent Victims: The Plight of Arab and Muslim Americans in Post 9/11 America* (Bloomington, IN: AuthorHouse, 2004).

CHAPTER 2

1. According to *The 9/11 Commission Report,* top government officials also initially believed that an accident had occurred at the World Trade Center. Less than 10 minutes after the first plane struck the north tower, Senior Advisor to the President Karl Rove informed President George W. Bush and his staff that a small, twin-engine plane had

crashed into the World Trade Center. The president believed, as indicated in the report, that the incident "must have been caused by a pilot error." See National Commission on Terrorist Attacks upon the United States, *The 9/11 Commission Report: Final Report of the National Commission on Terrorist Attacks upon the United States* (Washington, DC: U.S. Government Printing Office, 2004), 35.

2. Ibid.

3. White House, "Remarks by the President after Two Planes Crash into World Trade Center," 2001, available at http://georgewbush-whitehouse.archives.gov/news/releases/2001/09/20010911.html (accessed January 23, 2010).

4. Before the 9/11 terrorist attacks, the October 23, 1983, truck bombings of U.S. and French military barracks in Beirut, Lebanon, stood as the most deadly act of terrorism in U.S. history. The 1983 attacks claimed a total of 295 lives. The deadliest pre-9/11 act of terrorism on U.S. soil was the 1995 Oklahoma City bombing, which resulted in 168 deaths.

5. National Commission on Terrorist Attacks upon the United States, *The 9/11 Commission Report.*

6. Centers for Disease Control and Prevention, "Rapid Assessment of Injuries among Survivors of the Terrorist Attack on the World Trade Center—New York City, September 2001," *Mortality and Morbidity Weekly Report* 51, no. 1 (2002): 1–5.

7. U.S. Government Accountability Office, "September 11: Health Effects in the Aftermath of the World Trade Center Attack," GAO-04–1068T, 2004, available at www.gao.gov/new.items/d041068t.pdf (accessed January 23, 2010).

8. Irwin Garfinkel, Neeraj Kaushal, Julien Teitler, and Sandra Garcia, "Vulnerability and Resilience: New Yorkers Response to 9/11," in *Wounded City: The Social Impact of 9/11,* ed. Nancy Foner (New York: Russell Sage Foundation, 2005), 28–75.

9. Centers for Disease Control and Prevention, "Mental Health Status of World Trade Center Rescue and Recovery Workers and Volunteers—New York City, July 2002—August 2004." *Mortality and Morbidity Weekly Report* 53, no. 35 (2004): 812–815.

10. Karen Seeley, "The Psychological Treatment of Trauma and the Trauma of Psychological Treatment: Talking to Psychotherapists about 9/11," in *Wounded City: The Social Impact of 9/11,* 263–289.

11. Mark A. Schuster, Bradley D. Stein, Lisa H. Jaycox, Rebecca L. Collins, Grant N. Marshall, Marc N. Elliott, Annie J. Zhou, David E. Kanouse, Janina L. Morrison, and Sandra H. Berry, "A National Survey of Stress Reactions after the September 11, 2001, Terrorist Attacks," *New England Journal of Medicine* 345, no. 20 (2001): 1507–1512.

12. Garfinkel et al., "Vulnerability and Resilience"; William E. Schlenger, Juesta M. Caddell, Lori Ebert, B. Kathleen Jordan, Kathryn M. Rourke, David Wilson, Lisa Thalji, J. Michael Dennis, John A. Fairbank, and Richard A. Kulka, "Psychological Reactions to Terrorist Attacks: Findings from the National Study of Americans' Reactions to September 11," *Journal of the American Medical Association* 288, no. 5 (2002): 581–588.

13. Alan Elsner, "An Anxious Nation," in *After September 11: New York and the World,* ed. Reuters Staff (Upper Saddle River, NJ: Pearson Education, 2003), 76–145.

14. U.S. Government Accountability Office, "Review of Studies of the Economic Impact of the September 11, 2001, Terrorist Attacks on the World Trade Center," GAO-02–700R, 2002, available at www.gao.gov/new.items/d02700r.pdf (accessed January 23, 2010).

15. Howard Chernick, ed., "Introduction," in *Resilient City: The Economic Impact of 9/11* (New York: Russell Sage Foundation, 2005), 1–20.

16. Brenda D. Phillips, *Disaster Recovery* (Boca Raton, FL: CRC Press, 2009).

17. Ibid., 292.

18. Seana Lowe and Alice Fothergill, "A Need to Help: Emergent Volunteer Behavior after September 11," in *Beyond September 11: An Account of Post-Disaster Research,* ed. J. L. Monday (Boulder: Institute of Behavioral Science, University of Colorado, 2003), 293–314; Monica Schoch-Spana, "Educating, Informing, and Mobilizing the Public," in *Terrorism and Public Health: A Balanced Approach to Strengthening Systems and Protecting People,* ed. B. S. Levy and V. W. Sidel (New York: Oxford University Press, 2003), 118–135; Gerald Turkel, "Sudden Solidarity and the Rush to Normalization: Toward an Alternative Approach," *Sociological Focus* 35, no. 1 (2002): 73–79.

19. Arthur Spiegelman and Patrick Rizzo, "New York: An End to Innocence," in *After September 11: New York and the World,* 2–75.

20. Richard T. Weber, David A. McEntire, and Robie J. Robinson, "Public/Private Collaboration in Disaster: Implications for the World Trade Center Terrorist Attacks," Quick Response Report #155, 2002, Boulder: Natural Hazards Research and Applications Information Center, University of Colorado, available at www.colorado.edu/hazards/research/qr/qr155/qr155.html (accessed January 23, 2010).

21. Samuel Henry Prince, *Catastrophe and Social Change* (New York: Columbia University Press, 1920).

22. Robert I. Kutak, "The Sociology of Crises: The Louisville Flood of 1937," *Social Forces* 17 (1938): 66–72.

23. Anthony F. C. Wallace, *Tornado in Worcester* (Washington, DC: Committee on Disaster Studies, National Academy of Sciences, National Research Council, 1956).

24. Martha Wolfenstein, *Disaster: A Psychological Essay* (Glencoe, IL: Free Press, 1957).

25. Allen H. Barton, *Communities in Disaster: A Sociological Analysis of Collective Stress Situations* (Garden City, NY: Doubleday, 1969).

26. Charles E. Fritz, "Disaster," in *Contemporary Social Problems,* ed. R. K. Merton and R. A. Nisbet (New York: Harcourt, Brace, and World, 1961), 651–694.

27. David Alexander, "Nature's Impartiality, Man's Inhumanity: Reflections on Terrorism and World Crisis in a Context of Historical Disaster," *Disasters* 26, no. 1 (2002): 1–9; Dennis S. Mileti, "Rising from the Ashes: In Disasters, We Are All the Same," *Denver Post,* September 16, 2001, E-1; Gary R. Webb, "Sociology, Disasters, and Terrorism: Understanding Threats of the New Millennium," *Sociological Focus* 35, no. 1 (2002): 87–95.

28. Kai T. Erikson, *A New Species of Trouble: The Human Experience of Modern Disasters* (New York: W. W. Norton, 1994).

29. Mohamed Nimer, "Muslims in America after 9/11," *Journal of Islamic Law and Culture* 7, no. 2 (2002): 1–35.

30. Yvonne Yazbeck Haddad, *Not Quite American? The Shaping of Arab and Muslim Identity in the United States* (Waco, TX: Baylor University Press, 2004).

31. American-Arab Anti-Discrimination Committee, "1991 Report on Anti-Arab Hate Crimes" (report, American-Arab Anti-Discrimination Committee Research Institute, Washington, DC, 1992).

32. Ibid.

33. Ibid.

34. Amardeep Singh, "'We Are Not the Enemy': Hate Crimes against Arabs, Muslims, and Those Perceived to Be Arab or Muslim after September 11," *Human Rights Watch Report* 14, no. 6 (2002): 1–42.

35. Council on American-Islamic Relations, "The Price of Ignorance" (report, American-Muslim Research Center, Washington, DC, 1996).

36. Mark Juergensmeyer, *Terror in the Mind of God: The Global Rise of Religious Violence* (Berkeley: University of California Press, 2000).

37. Haddad, *Not Quite American?* 42–43.

38. Chrystie Flournoy Swiney, "Racial Profiling of Arabs and Muslims in the U.S.: Historical, Empirical, and Legal Analysis Applied to the War on Terrorism," *Muslim World Journal of Human Rights* 3, no. 1 (2006): 1–36.

39. Council on American-Islamic Relations, "American Muslims: One Year after 9/11" (report, Council on American-Islamic Relations Research Center, Washington, DC, 2002), 3.

40. Despite the many statements of grief and condemnations of terrorism that Muslim American groups and leaders issued, numerous unsubstantiated and inflammatory references appeared in newspapers, on television, and on talk radio about Muslims' alleged "silence" after the 9/11 attacks. See Riad Z. Abdelkarim and Jason Erb, "How American Muslims *Really* Responded to the Events of September 11," *CounterPunch*, September 7, 2002, available at www.counterpunch.org/riad0907.html (accessed May 3, 2010).

41. Nada O. El Sawy, "Islam and Violence: The American Media Link" (Master's thesis, Columbia University, 2002).

42. Geneive Abdo, *Mecca and Main Street: Muslim Life in America after 9/11* (New York: Oxford University Press, 2006).

43. Jacques Steinberg, "The Koran: Experts Say bin Laden Is Distorting Sacred Text," *New York Times*, October 8, 2001, B-8.

44. Alexa Capeloto, "Hijab Campaign: Women Don Scarves in Solidarity with Female Muslims," *Detroit Free Press*, October 18, 2001, 1.

45. Qamar-ul Huda, "The Diversity of Muslims in the United States: Views as Americans" (report, United States Institute of Peace, Washington, DC, 2006).

46. Southern Poverty Law Center, "Raging against the Other: September's Terrorist Strikes Trigger a Violent Outbreak of American Xenophobia," *Intelligence Report*, 2001, available at www.splcenter.org/intel/intelreport/article.jsp?aid=159 (accessed January 23, 2010).

47. Alana Semuels, "Workplace Bias against Muslims, Arabs on Rise, Advocates Say," *Los Angeles Times*, October 3, 2006, available at http://articles.latimes.com/2006/oct/03/business/fi-eeoc3 (accessed May 3, 2010).

48. U.S. Department of Justice, Civil Rights Division, "Initiative to Combat Post-9/11 Discriminatory Backlash," 2008, available at www.usdoj.gov/crt/legalinfo/nordwg_mission.php (accessed January 23, 2010).

49. U.S. Department of Justice, Civil Rights Division, "Remarks of President George W. Bush at the Islamic Center, September 17, 2001," available at www.usdoj.gov/crt/legalinfo/bushremarks.html (accessed January 23, 2010).

50. Federal Bureau of Investigation Uniform Crime Reporting Program, "Hate Crime Statistics 2001," available at www.fbi.gov/ucr/01hate.pdf (accessed January 23, 2010).

51. The United States was not the only place where anti-Islamic incidents increased. The European Monitoring Center on Racism and Xenophobia reported that Muslims across Western Europe experienced growing hostility and physical attacks after 9/11. In Britain alone, more than three hundred assaults on Muslims were reported after the terrorist attacks. A post-9/11 survey of more than five thousand Australians revealed strong anti-Muslim sentiment among the population. More than half of those surveyed said they would be concerned if a relative married a Muslim, about 45 percent said that some cultural groups do not belong in Australia, and almost half believed Australia was weakened by people of different ethnic groups. See Joel S. Fetzer and J. Christopher Soper, "The Roots of Public Attitudes toward State Accommodation of European Muslims' Religious Practices before and after September 11," *Journal for the Scientific Study of Religion* 42, no. 2 (2003): 247–258; Dominic Hughes, "Anti-Muslim Shift in Australia," *BBC News,* February 19, 2003, available at http://news.bbc.co.uk/2/hi/asia-pacific/2778821.stm (accessed May 3, 2010).

52. Federal Bureau of Investigation Uniform Crime Reporting Program, "Hate Crime Statistics 2001."

53. Council on American-Islamic Relations, "American Muslims."

54. Singh, "'We Are Not the Enemy,'" 18.

55. Kevin Anderson, "U.S. Muslims Suffer Backlash," *BBC News World Edition,* November 19, 2002, available at http://news.bbc.co.uk/2/hi/americas/2488829.stm (accessed May 3, 2010).

56. After Waqar Hasan's murder, Democratic Congressional Representative Rush Holt ushered a private relief bill through Congress to gain legal residency for the Hasan family. Hasan's wife and four daughters were faced with deportation, because their visas and green card applications were dependent upon his pending American citizenship. In 2004, the U.S. House of Representatives passed HR 867, granting the family permanent residency.

57. "Jury Convicts Texan in Killing Tied to 9/11," *New York Times,* April 3, 2002, available at www.nytimes.com/2002/04/03/us/jury-convicts-texan-in-killing-tied-to-9-11.html?pagewanted=1 (accessed May 3, 2010).

58. Robert E. Pierre, "Victims of Hate, Now Feeling Forgotten," *Washington Post,* September 14, 2002, A-1.

59. Robert F. Worth, "Police Arrest Brooklyn Man in Slayings of Four Shopkeepers," *New York Times,* March 31, 2003, F-1.

60. Singh, "'We Are Not the Enemy.'"

61. Louise Cainkar, "The Impact of the September 11 Attacks on Arab and Muslim Communities in the United States," in *The Maze of Fear: Security and Migration after 9/11,* ed. John Tirman (New York: New Press, 2004), 215–239.

62. Derek Thomson, "Arab-Americans Feel Backlash: Firebombs, Name-Calling, Threats Reported," *ABC News,* September 14, 2001, available at http://abcnews.go.com/US/story?id=92461&page=1 (accessed May 3, 2010).

63. In his analysis of anti-Islamic hate crime, Jeffrey Kaplan asserts that the number of violent acts perpetrated against Muslim Americans dropped off rapidly after

September 11 for four primary reasons: (1) leadership in the form of effective intervention by President Bush; (2) decisive law enforcement intervention on the federal and local levels; (3) grassroots outreach to Muslims by religious, civic, and educational groups; and (4) moral ambiguity in the rapid dissolution of American consensus over the War on Terror following the invasion of Iraq. Kaplan's argument is persuasive, but I would also contend that Muslims themselves played a key role in stemming the tide of violence. Islamic advocacy groups, Muslim religious leaders, and ordinary Muslim Americans worked tirelessly after September 11 to dispel stereotypes about their faith and to demonstrate their loyalty to the United States. See Jeffrey Kaplan, "Islamophobia in America? September 11 and Islamophobic Hate Crime," *Terrorism and Political Violence* 18, no. 1 (2006): 1–33.

64. Caroline Wolf Harlow, "Hate Crime Reported by Victims and Police" (report, U.S. Department of Justice, Bureau of Justice Statistics, Washington, DC, 2005).

65. Equal Employment Opportunity Commission Fact Sheet, "Muslim/Arab Employment Discrimination Charges since 9/11" (report, U.S. Equal Employment Opportunity Commission, Washington, DC, 2002).

66. Singh, "'We Are Not the Enemy,'" 16.

67. South Asian American Leaders of Tomorrow, "American Backlash: Terrorists Bring War Home in More Ways than One" (report, South Asian American Leaders of Tomorrow, Washington, DC, 2001).

68. Hussein Ibish, ed., "Report on Hate Crimes and Discrimination against Arab Americans: The Post September 11 Backlash" (report, American-Arab Anti-Discrimination Committee Research Institute, Washington, DC, 2003).

69. Sikh American Legal Defense and Educational Fund, "Victims of Hate," 2008, available at www.saldef.org (accessed January 23, 2010).

70. Kush Bambrah, Rosaline Chan, June Han, Sin Yen Ling, Cezar B. Lopez, and Dennis Ming Wu, "Backlash Final Report: 2001 Audit of Violence against Asian Pacific Americans" (report, National Asian Pacific American Legal Consortium, Washington, DC, 2001).

71. Singh, "'We Are Not the Enemy,'" 15.

72. Council on American-Islamic Relations, "American Muslims: One Year after 9/11."

73. For an excellent overview of the policy response in the aftermath of 9/11, see Michael Welch, *Scapegoats of September 11th: Hate Crimes and State Crimes in the War on Terror* (New Brunswick, NJ: Rutgers University Press, 2006).

74. Aladdin Elaasar, *Silent Victims: The Plight of Arab and Muslim Americans in Post 9/11 America* (Bloomington, IN: AuthorHouse, 2004).

75. Elsner, "An Anxious Nation."

76. Lewis Seiler and Dan Hamburg, "Rule by Fear or Rule by Law?" *San Francisco Chronicle,* February 4, 2008, B-7.

77. American-Arab Anti-Discrimination Committee, "2003–2007 Report on Hate Crimes and Discrimination against Arab Americans" (report, American-Arab Anti-Discrimination Committee Research Institute, Washington, DC, 2008).

78. Council on American-Islamic Relations, "The Status of Muslim Civil Rights in the United States: Unequal Protection" (report, Council on American-Islamic Relations Research Center, Washington, DC, 2005).

79. U.S. Department of Justice, Office of the Inspector General, "The September 11 Detainees: A Review of the Treatment of Aliens Held on Immigration Charges in Connection with the Investigation of the September 11 Attacks" (report, U.S. Department of Justice, Washington, DC, 2003).

80. Cainkar, "The Impact of the September 11 Attacks on Arab and Muslim Communities in the United States."

81. Council on American-Islamic Relations, "The Status of Muslim Civil Rights in the United States: Guilt by Association" (report, Council on American-Islamic Relations Research Center, Washington, DC, 2003).

82. Swiney, "Racial Profiling of Arabs and Muslims in the U.S."

83. Ibid.

84. Arab American Institute, "Healing the Nation: The Arab American Experience after September 11" (report, Arab American Institute Foundation, Washington, DC, 2002).

85. NSEERS requires that all men age sixteen or older who hold temporary visas from twenty-five select countries report to Immigration and Naturalization Service offices to be fingerprinted, photographed, and interviewed by federal agents. The special registration countries include Afghanistan, Algeria, Bahrain, Bangladesh, Egypt, Eritrea, Indonesia, Iran, Iraq, Jordan, Kuwait, Lebanon, Libya, Morocco, North Korea, Oman, Pakistan, Qatar, Saudi Arabia, Somalia, Sudan, Syria, Tunisia, United Arab Emirates, and Yemen. All the countries, with the exception of North Korea, have predominantly Muslim and/or Arab populations.

86. Anastasia Hendrix, "Protests Today at INS Office: Strong Objections to Immigrant Registration," *San Francisco Chronicle,* January 10, 2003, A-23.

87. For an explanation of the usefulness of qualitative methods in social science research, see Herbert J. Rubin and Irene S. Rubin, *Qualitative Interviewing: The Art of Hearing Data,* 2nd ed. (Thousand Oaks, CA: Sage Publications, 2005).

CHAPTER 3

1. Edward W. Said, *Covering Islam: How the Media and the Experts Determine How We See the Rest of the World,* rev. ed. (New York: Vintage Books, 1997).

2. John L. Esposito, *The Islamic Threat: Myth or Reality?* (New York: Oxford University Press, 1995).

3. Yvonne Yazbeck Haddad, "The Dynamics of Islamic Identity in North America," in *Muslims on the Americanization Path?* ed. Y. Y. Haddad and J. L. Esposito (New York: Oxford University Press, 1998), 19–46.

4. Kathleen Moore, "The Hijab and Religious Liberty: Anti-Discrimination Law and Muslim Women in the United States," in *Muslims on the Americanization Path?* 105–127.

5. Runnymede Trust, "Islamophobia: A Challenge for Us All" (report, Runnymede Trust, London, 1997).

6. Lorraine P. Sheridan, "Islamophobia Pre- and Post-September 11, 2001," *Journal of Interpersonal Violence* 21, no. 3 (2006): 317–336.

7. Jane I. Smith, *Islam in America* (New York: Columbia University Press, 1999), 176.

8. Ihsan Bagby, Paul M. Perl, and Bryan T. Froehle, "The Mosque in America: A National Portrait" (report, Council on American-Islamic Relations, Washington, DC, 2001).

9. Geneive Abdo, *Mecca and Main Street: Muslim Life in America after 9/11* (New York: Oxford University Press, 2006).

10. Lori Peek, "Becoming Muslim: The Development of a Religious Identity," *Sociology of Religion* 66, no. 3 (2005): 215–242.

11. Spencer E. Cahill, "Language Practices and Self Definition: The Case of Gender Identity Acquisition," *Sociological Quarterly* 27, no. 3 (1986): 295–311; Debra Van Ausdale and Joe R. Feagin, *The First R: How Children Learn Race and Racism* (Lanham, MD: Rowman and Littlefield, 2001).

12. Marvin Wingfield, "Arab Americans: Into the Multicultural Mainstream," *Equity and Excellence in Education* 39 (2006): 253–266; Jasmin Zine, "Unveiled Sentiments: Gendered Islamophobia and Experiences of Veiling among Muslim Girls in a Canadian Islamic School," *Equity and Excellence in Education* 39 (2006): 239–252.

13. Gordon W. Allport, *The Nature of Prejudice*, 25th ann. ed. (Cambridge, MA: Perseus Books, 1979).

14. Elizabeth Barlow, ed., *Evaluation of Secondary-Level Textbooks for Coverage of the Middle East and North Africa*, 3rd ed. (Ann Arbor: Center for Middle Eastern and North African Studies, University of Michigan, 1994); William J. Griswold, *The Image of the Middle East in Secondary School Textbooks* (New York: Middle East Studies Association of North America, 1975); Glenn Perry, "Treatment of the Middle East in American High School Textbooks," *Journal of Palestine Studies* 4, no. 3 (1975): 46–58.

15. Jack G. Shaheen, *Guilty: Hollywood's Verdict on Arabs after 9/11* (Northampton, MA: Olive Branch Press, 2008).

16. Council on American-Islamic Relations, "American Public Opinion about Islam and Muslims" (report, Council on American-Islamic Relations, Washington, DC, 2006).

17. Khyati Y. Joshi, "The Racialization of Hinduism, Islam, and Sikhism in the United States," *Equity and Excellence in Education* 39 (2006): 211–226.

18. For an interesting discussion of "unmeltability" among immigrants, see Joshi, "The Racialization of Hinduism, Islam, and Sikhism in the United States," 214.

19. See, for example, Jen'nan Ghazal Read, "Challenging Myths of Muslim Women: The Influence of Islam on Arab-American Women's Labor Force Activity," *Muslim World* 96 (2002): 19–38; Jen'nan Ghazal Read and John P. Bartkowski, "To Veil or Not to Veil? A Case Study of Identity Negotiation among Muslim Women in Austin, Texas," *Gender and Society* 14 (2000): 395–417.

20. Yvonne Yazbeck Haddad, Jane I. Smith, and Kathleen M. Moore, *Muslim Women in America: The Challenge of Islamic Identity Today* (New York: Oxford University Press, 2006).

21. Said, *Covering Islam*.

22. Peter Gottschalk and Gabriel Greenberg, *Islamophobia: Making Muslims the Enemy* (Lanham, MD: Rowman and Littlefield, 2008).

23. Ibid.

24. Jack G. Shaheen, *Reel Bad Arabs: How Hollywood Vilifies a People* (Brooklyn, NY: Olive Branch Press, 2001).

25. Said, *Covering Islam.*

26. Jeffrey M. Jones, "Americans Felt Uneasy toward Arabs Even before September 11," Gallup, 2001, available at www.gallup.com/poll/4939/Americans-Felt-Uneasy-Toward-Arabs-Even-Before-September.aspx (accessed January 24, 2010).

CHAPTER 4

1. Gordon W. Allport, *The Nature of Prejudice,* 25th ann. ed. (Cambridge, MA: Perseus Books, 1979).

2. Adalberto Aguirre, Jr., and Jonathan H. Turner, *American Ethnicity: The Dynamics and Consequences of Discrimination,* 6th ed. (Boston: McGraw Hill Higher Education, 2009).

3. Khyati Y. Joshi, "The Racialization of Hinduism, Islam, and Sikhism in the United States," *Equity and Excellence in Education* 39 (2006): 211–226.

4. Such derogatory names have made their way into popular culture, as evidenced by the 2006 Academy Award–winning film *Crash.* In one of the movie's opening scenes, a Persian man and his daughter attempt to purchase a gun. The gun store owner, a white, middle-aged man, incorrectly assumes that the father and daughter are Arab after they speak to one another in Farsi. He proceeds to yell at the man, "Yo, Osama! Plan the jihad on your own time. What do you want?"

5. Joe R. Feagin and Melvin P. Sikes, *Living with Racism: The Black Middle-Class Experience* (Boston: Beacon Press, 1994).

6. Council on American-Islamic Relations, "American Muslims: One Year after 9/11" (report, Council on American-Islamic Relations Research Center, Washington, DC, 2002), 25.

7. Stanley Crouch, "Drawing the Line on Racial Profiling," *Daily News,* October 4, 2001, 41.

8. Council on American-Islamic Relations, "The Status of Muslim Civil Rights in the United States: Stereotypes and Civil Liberties" (report, Council on American-Islamic Relations Research Center, Washington, DC, 2002), 22.

9. Hussein Ibish, ed., "Report on Hate Crimes and Discrimination against Arab Americans: The Post-September 11 Backlash" (report, American-Arab Anti-Discrimination Committee, Washington, DC, 2003), 130.

10. Louise Cainkar, "No Longer Invisible: Arab and Muslim Exclusion after September 11," *Middle East Report* 32, no. 3 (2002): 22–29.

11. Ibid., 23.

12. Jeffrey M. Jones, "The Impact of the Attacks on America," Gallup, 2001, available at www.gallup.com/poll/4894/Impact-Attacks-America.aspx (accessed January 25, 2010).

13. Survey research conducted after 9/11 confirmed that high levels of patriotism were associated with negative evaluations of Muslims and Arabs. See Darren W. Davis, *Negative Liberty: Public Opinion and the Terrorist Attacks on America* (New York: Russell Sage Foundation, 2007), 210.

14. Feagin and Sikes, *Living with Racism.*

15. John Howard Griffin, *Black Like Me* (New York: Signet, 1961).

16. Elaine S. Povich, "King's Remarks Outrage Muslims," *Newsday,* February 12, 2004, A-18.

17. Noah Shachtman, "Bush's Year of U.S. Surveillance," *Wired,* January 2, 2003, available at www.wired.com/politics/security/news/2003/01/57005 (accessed May 6, 2010).

18. Jason Leopold, "Did Bush Continue to Secretly Operate Total Information Awareness?" *Truthout,* September 18, 2009, available at www.truthout.org/091909A (accessed May 6, 2010).

19. Shachtman, "Bush's Year of U.S. Surveillance."

20. Leopold, "Did Bush Continue to Secretly Operate Total Information Awareness?"

21. For a classic statement on the gap between the American ideal of equality for all persons and actual conduct, see Robert K. Merton, "Discrimination and the American Creed," in *Discrimination and National Welfare: A Series of Addresses and Discussions,* ed. R. M. MacIver (Port Washington, NY: Kennikat Press, 1949), 99–126.

22. Alana Semuels, "Workplace Bias against Muslims, Arabs on the Rise, Advocates Say," *Los Angeles Times,* October 3, 2006, C-1.

23. European Monitoring Centre on Racism and Xenophobia, "Muslims in the European Union: Discrimination and Islamophobia" (report, European Monitoring Centre on Racism and Xenophobia, Vienna, Austria, 2006); Judy Vashti Persad and Salome Lukas, "'No Hijab Is Permitted Here': A Study on the Experiences of Muslim Women Wearing Hijab Applying for Work in the Manufacturing, Sales, and Service Sectors" (report, Women Working with Immigrant Women, Toronto, Canada, 2002).

24. Amardeep Singh, "'We Are Not the Enemy': Hate Crimes against Arabs, Muslims, and Those Perceived to Be Arab or Muslim after September 11," *Human Rights Watch Report* 14, no. 6 (2002): 1–42.

25. Monisha Das Gupta, "On Hardship and Hostility: The Impact of 9/11 on New York City Taxi Drivers," in *Wounded City: The Social Impact of 9/11,* ed. Nancy Foner (New York: Russell Sage Foundation, 2005), 208–241.

26. Arab American Institute, "Healing the Nation: the Arab American Experience after September 11" (report, Arab American Institute Foundation, Washington, DC, 2002).

27. Ruth Sidell, *Battling Bias: The Struggle for Identity and Community on College Campuses* (New York: Penguin, 1995).

28. Jack Levin and Jack McDevitt, *Hate Crimes Revisited: America's War on Those Who Are Different* (Boulder, CO: Westview Press, 2002).

29. Ibish, "Report on Hate Crimes and Discrimination against Arab Americans."

30. Frederick Mathewson Denny, *An Introduction to Islam,* 2nd ed. (New York: Macmillan, 1994).

31. Diana Jean Schemo, "Electronic Tracking System Monitors Foreign Students," *New York Times,* February 17, 2003, A-11.

32. Dan Eggen, "FBI Taps Campus Police in Anti-Terror Operations," *Washington Post,* January 25, 2003, A-1.

33. Ibid.

34. Diane Carroll, "U.S. Colleges See Fewer Students from Islamic Countries," *Kansas City Star,* November 3, 2003, A-2.

35. Ellen Sorokin, "Drop in Middle Easterners at U.S. Schools Tied to Visas," *Washington Times,* November 29, 2002, A-4.

36. Louise Cainkar, "The Impact of the September 11 Attacks on Arab and Muslim Communities in the United States," in *The Maze of Fear: Security and Migration after 9/11*, ed. John Tirman (New York: New Press, 2004), 215–239.

37. Chrystie Flournoy Swiney, "Racial Profiling of Arabs and Muslims in the U.S.: Historical, Empirical, and Legal Analysis Applied to the War on Terrorism," *Muslim World Journal of Human Rights* 3, no. 1 (2006): 1–36.

38. U.S. Department of Justice, Civil Rights Division, "Guidance Regarding the Use of Race by Federal Law Enforcement Agencies," 2003, available at www.usdoj.gov/crt/split/documents/guidance_on_race.php (accessed January 25, 2010).

39. Swiney, "Racial Profiling of Arabs and Muslims in the U.S."

40. Sam Howe Verhovek, "Civil Liberties: Americans Give in to Race Profiling," *New York Times*, September 23, 2001, A-1.

41. Erik C. Nisbet and James Shanahan, "The Media and Society Research Group Special Report: Restrictions on Civil Liberties, Views of Islam, and Muslim Americans" (report, Cornell University, Ithaca, NY, 2004).

42. Lynette Clemetson, "Traces of Terror: Arab Americans; Civil Rights Commissioner under Fire for Comments on Arabs," *New York Times*, July 22, 2002, A-14.

43. Swiney, "Racial Profiling of Arabs and Muslims in the U.S."

44. Michael Welch, *Scapegoats of September 11th: Hate Crimes and State Crimes in the War on Terror* (New Brunswick, NJ: Rutgers University Press, 2006).

45. Ibish, "Report on Hate Crimes and Discrimination against Arab Americans."

46. Ibid.

47. For an account of hate crimes against Sikhs, Hindus, Hispanics, and others who were wrongly perceived to be Arab or Muslim and were subsequently targeted after 9/11, see Ibish, "Report on Hate Crimes and Discrimination against Arab Americans"; Singh, "'We Are Not the Enemy.'"

CHAPTER 5

1. Serge Schmemann, "Hijacked Jets Destroy Twin Towers and Hit Pentagon," *New York Times*, September 12, 2001, A-1.

2. Allen H. Barton, *Communities in Disaster: A Sociological Analysis of Collective Stress Situations* (Garden City, NY: Doubleday, 1969); Charles E. Fritz, "Disaster," in *Contemporary Social Problems*, ed. R. K. Merton and R. A. Nisbet (New York: Harcourt, Brace, and World, 1961), 651–694.

3. Charles E. Fritz, "Disasters and Mental Health: Therapeutic Principles Drawn from Disaster Studies" (Disaster Research Center Historical and Comparative Series, #10, Disaster Research Center, University of Delaware, Newark, 1996).

4. Barton, *Communities in Disaster*, 207.

5. Fritz argues that the persistence of the therapeutic community in time and its total effect in changing the pre-existing social system are variables determined in large part by (1) the scope and destructive power of the disaster, (2) the possibility of continuing or recurrent danger, and (3) the power of the remaining societal components to superimpose either the preexisting system or a variant system on the emergent community. Fritz, "Disasters and Mental Health," 30.

6. Ibid., 63.

7. Kathleen J. Tierney, "From the Margins to the Mainstream? Disaster Research at the Crossroads," *Annual Review of Sociology* 33 (2007): 503–525.

8. Samuel Henry Prince, *Catastrophe and Social Change* (New York: Columbia University Press, 1920).

9. Edward W. Said, *Covering Islam: How the Media and the Experts Determine How We See the Rest of the World,* rev. ed. (New York: Vintage Books, 1997).

10. Susan B. Glasser, "U.S. Figures Show Sharp Global Rise in Terrorism," *Washington Post,* April 27, 2005, A-1.

11. Dexter Ingram, "Facts and Figures about Terrorism" (report, Heritage Foundation, Washington, DC, 2001).

12. Ibid.

13. Jean Baudrillard describes the terrorism of the late twentieth century as a "peculiarly modern form" because of the impact that it has had on public consciousness through electronic media. See Jean Baudrillard, *The Transparency of Evil: Essays on Extreme Phenomena* (New York: Verso, 1993), 76.

14. Tracy Wilkinson, "Anti-U.S. Displays Worry Palestinians," *Los Angeles Times,* September 16, 2001, A-1.

15. Nicola Webber, "Extremists Deny Role in Carnage," *Herald Sun,* September 12, 2001, 8.

16. John F. Burns, "A Day of Terror: The Militant; America the Vulnerable Meets a Ruthless Enemy," *New York Times,* September 12, 2001, A-1.

17. It was not until October 2004 that Osama bin Laden admitted that he ordered the airline hijackings that hit the World Trade Center and the Pentagon. In claiming responsibility for the attacks, the al Qaeda leader said he did so because of injustices against Lebanese and Palestinian people by Israel and the United States.

18. The general tendency in postdisaster media reporting, especially in the immediate aftermath of an event, is to overestimate deaths, injuries, and economic damages. Overestimates may occur as a result of the disruptive impact of disaster and the special pressures these events introduce regarding the production of news, conflicting estimates from different sources, and the absence of authoritative sources of information. Reliance on unofficial sources and eyewitness accounts may lead to the inflation of disaster-loss estimates. A political advantage also may emerge from issuing high property-damage estimates, as the disaster-stricken area is more likely to be declared a federal disaster area, resulting in federal aid and/or low-cost loans for rebuilding. See Henry W. Fischer, III, *Response to Disaster: Fact versus Fiction and Its Perpetuation: The Sociology of Disaster,* 3rd ed. (Lanham, MD: University Press of America, 2008); Kathleen J. Tierney, Michael K. Lindell, and Ronald W. Perry, *Facing the Unexpected: Disaster Preparedness and Response in the United States* (Washington, DC: Joseph Henry Press, 2001).

19. The National Institutes of Standards and Technology has estimated that between 16,400 and 18,800 civilians were in the World Trade Center complex at the time of the first plane collision on the morning of September 11, 2001. The death toll on September 11 would have almost certainly been much higher had the hijackers struck later in the day, when more employees and visitors would have been inside the Twin Towers. For more information, see National Commission on Terrorist Attacks upon the United States, *The 9/11 Commission Report: Final Report of the National Commission on Terrorist Attacks upon the United States* (Washington, DC: U.S. Government Printing Office, 2004), 316.

20. Irwin Garfinkel, Neeraj Kaushal, Julien Teitler, and Sandra Garcia, "Vulnerability and Resilience: New Yorkers Response to 9/11," in *Wounded City: The Social Impact of 9/11,* ed. Nancy Foner (New York: Russell Sage Foundation, 2005), 28–75; Louis Uchitelle, "A Nation Challenged: The Consumer; Sales Drop and Spending Waits as Uncertainty Grips Economy," *New York Times,* September 30, 2001, A-1.

21. Randall Collins, "Rituals of Solidarity and Security in the Wake of Terrorist Attack," *Sociological Theory* 22, no. 1 (2004): 53–87.

22. Wahiba Abu-Ras and Soleman H. Abu-Bader, "The Impact of the September 11, 2001, Attacks on the Well-Being of Arab Americans in New York City," *Journal of Muslim Mental Health* 3 (2008): 217–239; Anny Bakalian and Mehdi Bozorgmehr, *Backlash 9/11: Middle Eastern and Muslim Americans Respond* (Berkeley: University of California Press, 2009).

23. Council on American-Islamic Relations, "American Muslims: One Year after 9/11" (report, Council on American-Islamic Relations Research Center, Washington, DC, 2002).

24. American-Arab Anti-Discrimination Committee, "1991 Report on Anti-Arab Hate Crimes" (report, American-Arab Anti-Discrimination Committee, Washington, DC, 1992).

25. Council on American-Islamic Relations, "The Price of Ignorance" (report, American-Muslim Research Center, Washington, DC, 1996).

26. Council on American-Islamic Relations, "American Muslims."

27. Joe R. Feagin and Karyn D. McKinney, *The Many Costs of Racism* (Lanham, MD: Rowman and Littlefield, 2003).

28. South Asian American Leaders of Tomorrow, "American Backlash: Terrorists Bring War Home in More Ways than One" (report, South Asian American Leaders of Tomorrow, Washington, DC, 2001).

29. Ibid.

30. Hussein Ibish, ed., "Report on Hate Crimes and Discrimination against Arab Americans: The Post September 11 Backlash" (report, American-Arab Anti-Discrimination Committee, Washington, DC, 2003).

31. Ann Coulter, "This Is War: We Should Invade Their Countries," *National Review Online,* September 13, 2001, available at www.nationalreview.com/coulter/coulter.shtml (accessed January 30, 2010).

32. "The Wisdom of Ann Coulter," *Washington Monthly,* October 2001, available at www.washingtonmonthly.com/features/2001/0111.coulterwisdom.html (accessed January 30, 2010).

33. Bakalian and Bozorgmehr, *Backlash 9/11.*

34. Joe R. Feagin and Melvin P. Sikes, *Living with Racism: The Black Middle-Class Experience* (Boston: Beacon Press, 1994), 224.

35. Robert N. Bellah, Richard Madsen, William M. Sullivan, Ann Swidler, and Steen M. Tipton, *Habits of the Heart: Individualism and Commitment in American Life,* updated ed. (Berkeley: University of California Press, 1996); Joe R. Feagin, "The Continuing Significance of Race: Antiblack Discrimination in Public Places," *American Sociological Review* 56, no. 1 (1991): 101–116; Alice Fothergill, *Heads above Water: Gender, Class, and Family in the Grand Forks Flood* (Albany: State University of New York Press, 2004).

36. Michael Welch, *Scapegoats of September 11th: Hate Crimes and State Crimes in the War on Terror* (New Brunswick, NJ: Rutgers University Press, 2006).

37. Council on American-Islamic Relations, "American Muslims."

38. Eliott C. McLaughlin, "FBI Planting Spies in U.S. Mosques, Muslim Groups Say," *CNN,* March 20, 2009, available at www.cnn.com/2009/US/03/20/fbi.muslim.groups/index.html (accessed May 6, 2010).

39. Bakalian and Bozorgmehr, *Backlash 9/11.*

40. Council on American-Islamic Relations, "American Muslims"; Ibish, "Report on Hate Crimes and Discrimination against Arab Americans."

41. Ibish, "Report on Hate Crimes and Discrimination against Arab Americans."

42. Council on American-Islamic Relations, "The Status of Muslim Civil Rights in the United States: Unpatriotic Acts" (report, Council on American-Islamic Relations Research Center, Washington, DC, 2004).

43. Hussein Ibish, ed., "Report on Hate Crimes and Discrimination against Arab Americans 2003–2007" (report, American-Arab Anti-Discrimination Committee, Washington, DC, 2008).

CHAPTER 6

1. Lewis A. Coser, *The Functions of Social Conflict,* 2nd ed. (Glencoe, IL: Free Press, 1964); Emile Durkheim, *The Division of Labor in Society,* trans. W. D. Halls (New York: Free Press, [1893] 1984); Georg Simmel, *Conflict and the Web of Group Affiliations* (Glencoe, IL: Free Press, 1955).

2. Henri Tajfel, *The Social Psychology of Minorities* (New York: Minority Rights Group, 1978).

3. For a discussion of master status-determining traits, see Everett C. Hughes, *The Sociological Eye: Selected Papers* (New Brunswick, NJ: Transaction Books, 1984).

4. Jane I. Smith, *Islam in America* (New York: Columbia University Press, 1999), 181.

5. Ibid., 181–182.

6. Earle H. Waugh, "North America and the Adaptation of the Muslim Tradition: Religion, Ethnicity, and the Family," in *Muslim Families in North America,* ed. E. H. Waugh, S. M. Abu-Laban, and R. B. Qureshi (Edmonton: University of Alberta Press, 1991), 68–95.

7. Anny Bakalian and Mehdi Bozorgmehr, *Backlash 9/11: Middle Eastern and Muslim Americans Respond* (Berkeley: University of California Press, 2009).

8. Peter Skerry, "America's Muslims Never Had to Unite—Until Now," *Washington Post,* January 5, 2003, B-2.

9. Council on American-Islamic Relations, "American Muslims: One Year after 9/11" (report, Council on American-Islamic Relations Research Center, Washington, DC, 2002).

10. Ibid.

11. In their book *Backlash 9/11,* Bakalian and Bozorgmehr observe that "despite the painful outcomes of the terrorist attacks, new opportunities opened up for Middle Easterners and Muslims, allowing them to emerge as a distinct, visible category in American society." Bakalian and Bozorgmehr convincingly argue that Muslim American community-based organizations used the post-September 11 "window of opportunity" to mobilize their constituents and to encourage greater integration into U.S. society. Muslim Americans were invited to participate in meaningful ways in groups that had previously been closed off to them, they fought for and won reasonable religious accom-

modations in the workplace and in schools, and they asserted their political voice as an influential voting bloc. For a complete discussion of the organizational response to 9/11, see Bakalian and Bozorgmehr, *Backlash 9/11.*

12. Yvonne Yazbeck Haddad, *Not Quite American? The Shaping of Arab and Muslim Identity in the United States* (Waco, TX: Baylor University Press, 2004), 1.

13. According to a national survey conducted soon after 9/11, approximately 90 percent of Americans turned to religion as a coping response to the trauma caused by the attacks. In particular, increased religious practice and rising church attendance rates across the nation marked the post-9/11 period. The spike in religious attendance was relatively short-lived, however. By November 2001, polls indicated that church attendance had retreated back to normal levels. See Janice Bell Meisenhelder and John P. Marcum, "Responses of Clergy to 9/11: Posttraumatic Stress, Coping, and Religious Outcomes," *Journal for the Scientific Study of Religion* 43, no. 4 (2004): 547–554; Mark A. Schuster, Bradley D. Stein, Lisa H. Jaycox, Rebecca L. Collins, Grant N. Marshall, Marc N. Elliott, Annie J. Zhou, David E. Kanouse, Janina L. Morrison, and Sandra H. Berry, "A National Survey of Stress Reactions after the September 11, 2001, Terrorist Attacks," *New England Journal of Medicine* 345, no. 20 (2001): 1507–1512; Jeremy E. Uecker, "Religious and Spiritual Responses to 9/11: Evidence from the Add Health Study," *Sociological Spectrum* 28 (2008): 477–509.

14. Uecker analyzed the influence of September 11 on the religious and spiritual lives of young Protestant and Catholic adults in the United States. He found that the attacks exerted only modest and short-lived effects on various aspects of young adults' religiosity and spirituality. Based on this nationally representative study, Uecker concluded that no remarkable "religious revival" occurred after September 11. Because of small sample sizes, Muslims—among other religious groups—were not included in the analysis. See Uecker, "Religious and Spiritual Responses to 9/11."

15. "Transcript of President Bush's Address." *CNN.com,* September 21, 2001, available at http://archives.cnn.com/2001/US/09/20/gen.bush.transcript/ (accessed January 31, 2010).

16. Darren W. Davis, *Negative Liberty: Public Opinion and the Terrorist Attacks on America* (New York: Russell Sage Foundation, 2007), 201.

17. Bakalian and Bozorgmehr, *Backlash 9/11.*

18. Wahiba Abu-Ras, Ali Gheith, and Francine Cournos, "The Imam's Role in Mental Health Promotion: A Study at 22 Mosques in New York City's Muslim Community," *Journal of Muslim Mental Health* 3 (2008): 155–176.

19. Arwa Gunja, "Give Religion a Home at NYU," *Washington Square News,* February 8, 2005, 4.

20. Wahiba Abu-Ras and Soleman H. Abu-Bader, "The Impact of the September 11, 2001, Attacks on the Well-Being of Arab Americans in New York City," *Journal of Muslim Mental Health* 3 (2008): 217–239.

21. Louise A. Cainkar, *Homeland Insecurity: The Arab American and Muslim American Experience after 9/11* (New York: Russell Sage Foundation, 2009).

22. Geneive Abdo, *Mecca and Main Street: Muslim Life in America after 9/11* (New York: Oxford University Press, 2006), 2–3.

23. Kristin Hanley, "Panel Examines Islam in Media," *Washington Report on Middle East Affairs* (November 2002): 84–90.

24. Lori Peek, "Becoming Muslim: The Development of a Religious Identity," *Sociology of Religion* 66, no. 3 (2005): 215–242.

25. Jennifer L. Bryan, "Constructing 'the True Islam' in Hostile Times: The Impact of 9/11 on Arab Muslims in Jersey City," in *Wounded City: The Social Impact of 9/11,* ed. Nancy Foner (New York: Russell Sage Foundation, 2005), 133–159.

26. Cainkar, *Homeland Insecurity.*

27. Bryan, "Constructing 'the True Islam' in Hostile Times"; Haddad, *Not Quite American?*

28. It is important to note that the contention that God commands wearing the hijab is by no means universally accepted by all Muslims or all Islamic scholars. Jane Smith argues that "the Qur'an, despite what some Muslim women [and men] seem to think, does not actually specify exactly how much of the body has to be covered." See Smith, *Islam in America,* 108.

29. Muslim Public Affairs Council, "The Impact of 9/11 on Muslim American Young People: Forming National and Religious Identity in the Age of Terrorism and Islamophobia" (report, Muslim Public Affairs Council, Washington, DC, 2007).

CHAPTER 7

1. Michael Welch, *Scapegoats of September 11th: Hate Crimes and State Crimes in the War on Terror* (New Brunswick, NJ: Rutgers University Press, 2006).

2. For discussions regarding the need for more systematic investigations of blame and scapegoating, see David M. Neal, "Blame Assignment in a Diffuse Disaster Situation: A Case Example of the Role of an Emergent Citizen Group," *International Journal of Mass Emergencies and Disasters* 2 (1984): 251–266; Brenda Phillips with Mindy Ephraim, "Living in the Aftermath: Blaming Processes in the Loma Prieta Earthquake" (Working Paper #80, Natural Hazards Research and Applications Information Center, University of Colorado, Boulder, 1992).

3. Anny Bakalian and Mehdi Bozorgmehr, *Backlash 9/11: Middle Eastern and Muslim Americans Respond* (Berkeley: University of California Press, 2009), 13.

4. For an excellent comparison of communal response to natural disasters, technological accidents, and terrorist attacks, see Krzysztof Kaniasty and Fran H. Norris, "Social Support in the Aftermath of Disasters, Catastrophes, and Acts of Terrorism: Altruistic, Overwhelmed, Uncertain, Antagonistic, and Patriotic Communities," in *Bioterrorism: Psychological and Public Health Interventions,* ed. R. J. Ursano, A. E. Norwood, and C. S. Fullerton (Cambridge: Cambridge University Press, 2004), 200–229.

5. Thomas E. Drabek and Enrico L. Quarantelli, "Scapegoats, Villains, and Disasters," *Trans-action* 4 (1967): 12–17.

6. Ibid., 12.

7. Ibid., 12.

8. This statement is not meant to imply that "natural disasters" are wholly "natural" events. In fact, consensus within the scientific community is that all disasters are in large measure a consequence of human action or, all too often, inaction. Yet, regardless of how scientists conceptualize disaster, the pervasive view of natural disasters is that they are inevitable. To wit, the general public continues to see natural disasters as random, tragic acts of God or nature.

9. Kaniasty and Norris, "Social Support in the Aftermath of Disasters, Catastrophes, and Acts of Terrorism."

10. Drabek and Quarantelli, "Scapegoats, Villains, and Disasters," 13.

11. Kai T. Erikson, *A New Species of Trouble: The Human Experience of Modern Disasters* (New York: W. W. Norton, 1994), 142.

12. Ibid.

13. Rue Bucher, "Blame and Hostility in Disaster," *American Journal of Sociology* 62, no. 5 (1957): 467–475.

14. J. Stephen Kroll-Smith and Stephen Robert Couch, *The Real Disaster Is Above Ground: A Mine Fire and Social Conflict* (Lexington: University Press of Kentucky, 1990), 170.

15. Ibid., 170.

16. In their meta-analysis of disaster mental health research, Fran Norris and colleagues found that survivors of mass violence were far more likely to experience severe psychological impairment than other disaster-affected populations. Specifically, they report that 67 percent of samples that experienced mass violence were severely or very severely impaired, compared to 39 percent of those assessed after technological disasters and 34 percent of those assessed after natural disasters. See Fran H. Norris, Matthew J. Friedman, and Patricia J. Watson, "60,000 Disaster Victims Speak: Part II. Summary and Implications of the Disaster Mental Health Research," *Psychiatry* 65, no. 3 (2002): 240–260.

17. Fran H. Norris, Matthew J. Friedman, Patricia J. Watson, Christopher M. Byrne, Eolia Diaz, and Krzysztof Kaniasty, "60,000 Disaster Victims Speak: Part I. An Empirical Review of the Empirical Literature, 1981–2001," *Psychiatry* 65, no. 3 (2002): 207–239.

18. Ibid.

19. Kaniasty and Norris, "Social Support in the Aftermath of Disasters, Catastrophes, and Acts of Terrorism."

20. The White House, "Press Briefing by Ari Fleisher," September 12, 2001, available at http://georgewbush-whitehouse.archives.gov/news/releases/2001/09/20010912-8.html (accessed May 7, 2010).

21. Gus Martin, *Understanding Terrorism: Challenges, Perspectives, and Issues* (Thousand Oaks, CA: Sage Publications, 2003).

22. National Commission on Terrorist Attacks upon the United States, *The 9/11 Commission Report: Final Report of the National Commission on Terrorist Attacks upon the United States* (Washington, DC: U.S. Government Printing Office, 2004), 71.

23. Martin, *Understanding Terrorism,* 13.

24. Deborah Sontag, "The Twin Towers: Backlash; Muslims in the United States Fear an Upsurge in Hostility," *New York Times,* March 7, 1993, A-1.

25. Andrea Stone, "Anger, Fear of Backlash Follow Arrest," *USA Today,* March 5, 1993, A-3.

26. Ibid.

27. Sontag, "The Twin Towers."

28. Martin, *Understanding Terrorism,* 2.

29. "A Different Order of Magnitude," *Security Management,* October 2001, available at www.securitymanagement.com/library/001128.html (accessed February 6, 2010).

30. Kerem Ozan Kalkan, Geoffrey C. Layman, and Eric M. Uslaner, "'Bands of

Others?' Attitudes toward Muslims in Contemporary American Society," *Journal of Politics* 71, no. 3 (2009): 847–862.

31. Pew Research Center, "Muslim Americans: Middle Class and Mostly Mainstream" (report, Pew Research Center, Washington, DC, 2007).

32. Mark Juergensmeyer, *Terror in the Mind of God: The Global Rise of Religious Violence* (Berkeley: University of California Press, 2000).

33. Edward W. Said, *Covering Islam: How the Media and the Experts Determine How We See the Rest of the World,* rev. ed. (New York: Vintage Books, 1997), xvi.

34. Council on American-Islamic Relations, "American Public Opinion about Islam and Muslims" (report, Council on American-Islamic Relations, Washington, DC, 2006).

35. The White House, "President Bush's Address to a Joint Session of Congress and the American People," September 20, 2001, available at http://georgewbush-whitehouse.archives.gov/news/releases/2001/09/20010920-8.html (accessed May 7, 2010).

36. Jeffrey Kaplan, "Islamophobia in America? September 11 and Islamophobic Hate Crime," *Terrorism and Political Violence* 18 (2006): 1–33.

37. Welch, *Scapegoats of September 11th.*

38. Kalkan, Layman, and Uslaner, "'Bands of Others?'"

39. Penny Edgell, Douglas Hartmann, and Joseph Gerteis, "Atheists as 'Other': Moral Boundaries and Cultural Membership in American Society," *American Sociological Review* 71 (2006): 211–234.

40. Ibid., 218.

41. Pew Research Center, "Muslim Americans."

42. Adalberto Aguirre, Jr., and Jonathan H. Turner, *American Ethnicity: The Dynamics and Consequences of Discrimination,* 6th ed. (Boston: McGraw Hill, 2009).

43. Richard Cimino, "'No God in Common': American Evangelical Discourse on Islam after 9/11," *Review of Religious Research* 47, no. 2 (2005): 162–174.

44. Nadine Naber, "Introduction," in *Race and Arab Americans before and after 9/11: From Invisible Citizens to Visible Subjects,* ed. Amaney Jamal and Nadine Naber (Syracuse, NY: Syracuse University Press, 2007), 1–45.

45. In its annual civil-rights reports, the Council on American-Islamic Relations (CAIR) tracks the specific religious practices and symbols most likely to trigger anti-Muslim discrimination. CAIR has documented, year after year, that Muslims are most likely to be singled out for mistreatment when they are physically visible (due to their skin complexion or attire), when they have a "Muslim-sounding" name, or when they actively associate with the Muslim community as activists, community leaders, or through membership in religious organizations.

46. New York City Commission on Civil Rights, "Discrimination against Muslims, Arabs, and South Asians in New York City since 9/11" (report, New York City Commission on Civil Rights, New York, 2003).

47. Geneive Abdo, *Mecca and Main Street: Muslim Life in America after 9/11* (New York: Oxford University Press, 2006).

48. Pew Forum on Religion and Public Life, "Views of Religious Similarities and Differences: Muslims Widely Seen as Facing Discrimination" (report, Pew Forum on Religion and Public Life and Pew Research Center for People and the Press, Washington, DC, 2009).

49. Katherine Pratt Ewing, ed., "Introduction," in *Being and Belonging: Muslims in the United States Since 9/11* (New York: Russell Sage Foundation, 2008), 1–11.

50. Jack G. Shaheen, *Guilty: Hollywood's Verdict on Arabs after 9/11* (Northampton, MA: Olive Branch Press, 2008).

51. Said, *Covering Islam.*

52. Shaheen, *Guilty.*

53. Ibid.

54. Alan Blank, "Media to Blame for Islamic Misconceptions," *Daily Pilot,* March 3, 2008, available at www.dailypilot.com/articles/2008/03/04/religion/dpt-bennett 03042008.txt (accessed May 7, 2010).

55. Bakalian and Bozorgmehr, *Backlash 9/11.*

56. "First Muslim Elected to Congress," *MSNBC News,* November 7, 2006, available at www.msnbc.msn.com/id/15613050/ (accessed May 7, 2010).

57. American-Arab Anti-Discrimination Committee, "2003–2007 Report on Hate Crimes and Discrimination against Arab Americans" (report, American-Arab Anti-Discrimination Committee Research Institute, Washington, DC, 2008).

58. Bakalian and Bozorgmehr, *Backlash 9/11.*

59. Ibid., 234.

60. Ibid.

61. Gerald Turkel, "Sudden Solidarity and the Rush to Normalization: Toward an Alternative Approach," *Sociological Focus* 35, no. 1 (2002): 73–79.

62. Monisha Das Gupta, "On Hardship and Hostility: The Impact of 9/11 on New York City Taxi Drivers," in *Wounded City: The Social Impact of 9/11,* ed. Nancy Foner (New York: Russell Sage Foundation, 2005), 234.

63. Rebecca Solnit, *A Paradise Built in Hell: The Extraordinary Communities that Arise in Disaster* (New York: Viking, 2009).

64. Allen H. Barton, *Communities in Disaster: A Sociological Analysis of Collective Stress Situations* (Garden City, NY: Doubleday, 1969); Charles E. Fritz, "Disaster," in *Contemporary Social Problems,* ed. R. K. Merton and R. A. Nisbet (New York: Harcourt, Brace, and World, 1961), 651–694.

65. Seana Lowe and Alice Fothergill, "A Need to Help: Emergent Volunteer Behavior after September 11," in *Beyond September 11: An Account of Post-Disaster Research,* ed. J. L. Monday (Boulder: Natural Hazards Center, University of Colorado, 2003), 293–314; Seana Lowe Steffen and Alice Fothergill, "9/11 Volunteerism: A Pathway to Personal Healing and Community Engagement," *Social Science Journal* 46 (2009): 29–46.

66. Steffen and Fothergill, "9/11 Volunteerism."

67. Kai T. Erikson, *Everything in Its Path: Destruction of Community in the Buffalo Creek Flood* (New York: Simon and Schuster, 1976).

68. Erikson, *A New Species of Trouble,* 230–231.

69. Ellen Zinner and Mary Beth Williams use the concept of "group survivorship" to describe the behavioral and emotional reactions of a community that has experienced the loss of one or more group members due to a traumatic event. I use the term "collective grief" to refer to the specific emotional reaction that is commonly observed in the aftermath of disaster. See Ellen S. Zinner and Mary Beth Williams, eds., *When a Community Weeps: Case Studies in Group Survivorship* (Philadelphia, PA: Brunner/Mazel, 1999).

70. Therese A. Rando, "Foreword," in *When a Community Weeps: Case Studies in Group Survivorship*, xix.

71. Mary Beth Williams, Ellen S. Zinner, and Richard R. Ellis, "The Connection between Grief and Trauma," in *When a Community Weeps: Case Studies in Group Survivorship*, 3–17.

72. Judith Herman, *Trauma and Recovery: The Aftermath of Violence—from Domestic Abuse to Political Terror* (New York: Basic Books, 1997), 242.

73. Anne Eyre, "Remembering: Community Commemoration after Disaster," in *Handbook of Disaster Research*, ed. H. Rodríguez, E. L. Quarantelli, and R. R. Dynes (New York: Springer, 2006), 441–455.

Index

Page numbers followed by the letter t *refer to the table. Page numbers followed by the letter* f *refer to figures.*

Lori Peek is Assistant Professor of Sociology and Co-director of the Center for Disaster and Risk Analysis at Colorado State University. She also serves as Associate Chair for the Social Science Research Council Task Force on Hurricane Katrina and Rebuilding the Gulf Coast. She has published widely on vulnerable populations in disaster and is co-editor of *Displaced: Life in the Katrina Diaspora*. She earned her Ph.D. in Sociology from the University of Colorado–Boulder in 2005. In 2009 the American Sociological Association Section on Children and Youth honored her with the Early Career Award for outstanding scholarship. In addition, she was named the 2010 Professor of the Year, and she has been the recipient of the Best Teacher Award and the Excellence in Teaching Award at Colorado State University.